MW01040530

# BETWEEN SACRED MOUNTAINS

*Navajo Stories and Lessons from the Land*

Volume 11

SUN TRACKS
An American Indian Literary Series

*Series Editor*
Larry Evers

*Editorial Committee*
Vine Deloria, Jr.
N. Scott Momaday
Emory Sekaquaptewa
Leslie Marmon Silko
Ofelia Zepeda

*Other Sun Tracks volumes*

# BETWEEN SACRED MOUNTAINS

*Navajo Stories and Lessons from the Land*

## STORYTELLERS AND TEACHERS

Claudeen Arthur (*Tsé Níjíkiní*)
John Barbone (*Tł'ógí*)
Fanny D. Begay (*Ta'neeszahnii*)
Leo Beno (*Tł'ízí Łání*)
Robert W. Billie (*Táchii'nii*)
George Blueeyes (*Tábąąhí*)
Amos Coggeshall (*Kin Łichíi'nii*)
Tom Dodge (*Kin Łitsonii*)
Ken Foster (*Kin Yaa'áanii*)
Frank Harvey (*Naakaii Dine'é*)
Hashk'aan Ts'ósí (*Hashk'ąą Hadzohó*)
Al Henderson (*Áshįįhí*)
Byron Huskon (*Tsé Deeshgiizhnii*)
Emma Jim (*Kin Łichíi'nii*)
Rex Lee Jim (*Kin Łichíi'nii*)
K'ai Bii' Tóonii (*Tł'ízí Łání*)

Mina Lansa (Hopi Parrot Clan)
Eugene Leonard (*Tł'ízí Łání*)
Thomas Littleben, Jr. (*Ma'ii Deeshgiizhnii*)
Alice Luna (*Tł'ízí Łání*)
Avery Luna (*Tó Dich'íi'nii*)
Florence Luna (*Tł'ízí Łání*)
Many Mules' Granddaughter (*Tó'áhaní*)
Charles Yazzie Morgan (*Kin Yaa'áanii*)
Grandma Pahe (*Tł'ááshchí'í*)
Elsie Peshlakai (*Áshįįhí*)
Bill Skeet (*Honágháahnii*)
Son of Old Man Hat (*Bit'ahnii*)
Tł'ááshchí'í Sání (*Tł'ááshchí'í*)
Hastiin Tó Diłhił Biye' (*Áshįįhí*)
Charlie Yellow (*Tł'ízí Łání*)
Ned Yazzie (*Tó'áhaní*)

## SEEKERS WHO ASKED AND UNDERSTOOD

Judy Apachee (*Táchii'nii*)
Rex Lee Jim (*Kin Łichíi'nii*)

## ARTISTS WHO LOOKED AND DREW

Rudy Begay (*Kin Łichíi'nii*)
Wayne Charlie (*Naaneesht'ézhí*)
Hank Willie (*Tsi'naajinii*)

## LISTENERS, LEARNERS, AND SCRIBES

Sam and Janet Bingham

**Sun Tracks and the University of Arizona Press**
TUCSON, ARIZONA

## OTHERS WHO ASKED AND UNDERSTOOD

Bobby Begay (*Táchii'nii*); Rosie Begay (*Kin Łichíi'nii*); Thomas Benally (*Kin Łichíi'nii*); Frank Harvey (*Naakaii Dine'é*); Leroy Tsinajinnie (*Tł'ízí Łání*).

## FRIENDS WHO SHARED SPECIAL KNOWLEDGE

Wilson Aronilth Jr. (*Kin Łichíi'nii*), Navajo culture; David Brugge, Anasazi; J. Lee Correll, historical research; Maggie Dawes (*Tsi'naajinii*), plants; James Eychaner, ground water; Rosalie Fanale, range use; Ken Foster (*Kin Yaa'áanii*), wildlife; Bill Gillespie, Chaco Canyon; James Goodman, geography; Jerry Kammer, Navajo-Hopi Land Dispute; John L. Kessell, Spanish history; Vernon Mayes, plants; Barney Mitchell (*Táchii'nii*), Navajo culture; Philip Reno, economic development; Allan Savory, range management; Jack Seltzer, range management; John Shelton, geology; Mike Walker, wildlife; Daniel Wiener, reclamation; Yellowman's Brother (*Kin Yaa'áanii*), range use; Robert W. Young, historical research.

## PEOPLE OF THE ROCK POINT SCHOOL COMMUNITY WHO READ AND CRITICIZED THE WORK

Benjamin Barney (*Tó'aheedlíinii*); Agnes Holm (*Dibé Łizhiní*); Jean Mead.
Also: Bobby Begay (*Táchii'nii*); Rosie Begay (*Kin Łichíi'nii*); Clay Caldwell; Carol Curtis; Johnson Dennison (*Tábąąhí*); Mark Dressman; Peggy Kaveski; Della Singer (*Tó'aheedlíinii*); Stella Tsinajinnie (*Tó'aheedlíinii*); and Rock Point High School students.

## TYPESETTERS AND BOOKSMITHS

Stanley Stillion and Leslie Penick, text; Ginger Griffin, notes; Valerie Bernal and Louise Spencer-Casias (*Kin Yaa'áanii*), Navajo poems.

Thomas Benally (*Kin Łichíi'nii*) spelled the Navajo words.

Carolyn Kinsman designed the book.
Shandling Lithographing Company printed it.

This volume represents a four-year project of the Rock Point Community School, carried out under the Rock Point School Board, with advice from parent committees. It was completed with assistance from the National Endowment for the Humanities, a federal agency.

## ROCK POINT SCHOOL BOARD

Kim L. Nih, Chairman (*Kin Łichíi'nii*)
Kee Pahe, Vice Chairman (*Tł'ááshchí'í*)
Tapaha Begay, Treasurer (*Kin Łichíi'nii*)
Harry Tso Begay, member (*Kin Łichíi'nii*)
Frank W. Begay, member (*Kin Łichíi'nii*)
Paul Jones, member (*Ta'neeszahnii*)

## ROCK POINT PARENT COMMITTEE

Alice D. Begay (*Ta'neeszahnii*)
Peter Benally (*Bit'ahnii*)
Louise Gene (*Tó'aheedlíinii*)
Rita Nih (*Ta'neeszahnii*)
Susie Pahe (*Táchii'nii*)
Martha Paul (*Tábąąhí*)
Ray Yazzie (*Tábąąhí*)

*Royalties from the sale of this book benefit the children and young people at Rock Point Community School.*

*Sun Tracks* is an American Indian literary series sponsored by the American Indian Studies Program and the Department of English, University of Arizona, Tucson, Arizona. All correspondence concerning text should be sent to: *Sun Tracks*, Department of English, Modern Languages Building #67, University of Arizona, Tucson, Arizona 85721. All orders should be sent to: University of Arizona Press, 250 E. Valencia Rd., Tucson, Arizona 85706. Volumes 1–5 of *Sun Tracks* are out of print. They are available on microfiche from Clearwater Publishing Company, Inc., 1995 Broadway, New York, NY 10023.

SUN TRACKS AND
THE UNIVERSITY OF ARIZONA PRESS
First printing 1984
Manufactured in the U.S.A.

Library of Congress Cataloging in Publication Data
Main entry under title:

Between sacred mountains.

(Sun tracks, ISSN 0300-788X ; v. 11)
Reprint. Originally published: Chinle, Ariz.:
Rock Point Community School, c1982.
Bibliography: p.
Includes index.
1. Navajo Indians—Addresses, essays, lectures.
I. Arthur, Claudeen. II. Bingham, Sam. III.
Bingham, Janet. IV. Rock Point School. V. Series:
Sun tracks; 11.
[PS501.S85 vol. 11] [E99.N3] 810.8s [970.004'97]
84-121

ISBN 0-8165-0855-0
ISBN 0-8165-0856-9 (pbk.)

# TABLE OF CONTENTS

# Maps

# FOREWORD

Not long ago I had the good fortune of floating out over the earth in a great, multicolored hot-air balloon. It would have been an unforgettable personal experience in any case, but this particular excursion was very special indeed, for it enabled me to see, from an angle I had never seen before, one of the most powerful and beautiful and (to me) beloved landscapes that I know—*Diné bikéyah*, Navajo country. I had lived in that landscape as a child—at Chinle, at Tuba City, at Shiprock—and through the years of my life I have returned to it often and traveled widely over it. I have always been glad to be there, genuinely and deeply glad, glad in my heart.

The balloon rose slowly through the bars of early-morning light. Gradually the earth spread out to the whole circle of the sky. Directly below was a long sandstone spine, a succession of great red walls like vertebrae, curving out toward the sun. In every direction I could see distant mountains, sacred mountains. Here and there were hogans far below, flocks of sheep grazing, dogs barking faintly across the long vertical and diagonal distances. Innumerable facets of rock caught fire in the west. I inhaled the thin, cold air, and I was again glad in my heart. A line from Isak Dinesen came to mind. "In the highlands you woke up in the morning and thought: Here I am where I ought to be."

No words can better express the Navajo's spiritual comprehension of the world than his own. *Diné bizaad* and Navajo oral tradition embody some of the richest verbal formulae known to man. Consider, for example:

First Song of Dawn Boy
*Where my kindred dwell,*
*    There I wander.*
*The Red Rock house,*
*    There I wander.*
*Where dark* kethawns *[sacred sticks]*
*    are at the doorway,*
*    There I wander.*

*At the* yuni [*seat of honor*] *the striped*
*    cotton hangs with pollen.*
*    There I wander.*
*Going around with it.*
*    There I wander.*
*Taking another, I depart with it.*
*    With it I wander.*
*In the house of long life,*
*    There I wander.*
*In the house of happiness,*
*    There I wander.*
*Beauty before me,*
*    With it I wander.*
*Beauty behind me,*
*    With it I wander.*
*Beauty below me,*
*    With it I wander.*
*Beauty above me,*
*    With it I wander.*
*Beauty all around me,*
*    With it I wander.*
*In old age traveling,*
*    With it I wander.*
*On the beautiful trail I am,*
*    With it I wander.*

Such a song as this requires no more explication than does, say, the Twenty-third Psalm. It is wholly contained in itself, wholly self-evident, and it exists forever in beauty, for its own sake. And as the expression of a people's character and soul, it is all but inimitable. One would be hard put to find a poem or a prayer or a song that is equal to this in precision, lyricism, dignity, beauty and, in a special sense, belief. Here is great faith in the efficacy of language, in the fundamental power and beauty of words. Here is the clear reflection of a people possessed of self-knowledge and self-respect, a people safe and comfortable in the universe.

*Between Sacred Mountains* is a small encyclopaedia of Navajo country. One can learn a good deal about the Navajo people and their world by looking closely into the pages of this book, and that learning is very valuable, of course. But the book is more than a fund of practical information. It is preeminently an evocation of the spirit that informs *Diné* and *Diné bikéyah,* a spirit that has persisted through time, even as *Diné bizaad,* the Navajo language, has persisted through time and of which the People say, "it is endless."

And the book is physically handsome. The photographs and drawings are entirely appropriate (the Navajos have a very highly developed sense of the appropriate, a sense that supports the very center of their great dignity). Like the text, they indicate the ingredients of wonder, beauty, forebearance and wisdom, those qualities that are the hallmarks of the *Diné,* the People, the Navajo.

N. Scott Momaday

# ABOUT THIS BOOK

*A long time ago people used to say that if you remembered the stories that were passed down, they would make you strong. Even just a little portion of the stories—that part would keep you and your children strong so you could face whatever is in the future.*

—Ray Yazzie
Rock Point Parent Committee

*Between Sacred Mountains* was originally written for the young people of Rock Point Community School on the Navajo Reservation. It was commissioned by the Navajo parents and grandparents on the Rock Point School Board because they wanted their children to be aware of their own unique history and to understand its relevance to the problems and challenges of today. Both parents and teachers saw a need to help young people bridge the gap between their textbook and TV world and the thread of wisdom their grandparents carry on, unbroken, from the past.

Rock Point consists of a trading post, a mission, a meeting house, and the school, set in a valley of red sandstone rocks beneath a vast expanse of Arizona sky. Most of the community's 1,500 Navajos live in small frame houses or circular one-room hogans scattered over miles of harsh desert scrub. The nearest town is 100 miles away. Many families raise sheep and cattle for a living. Some bring in extra money by weaving or by flying out in forest service planes during the summers to fight fires throughout the West. Ninety-five percent of Rock Point children enter school knowing no English.

This book is only part of a community effort to provide Rock Point children with relevant high-quality education. Rock Point School is a community-controlled "contract" school—one of ten schools on the Navajo Reservation that are funded under contract with the Bureau of Indian Affairs (BIA). Contract schools differ from over 50 reservation BIA schools in that an elected school board

at each school has total control over curriculum, personnel, and budgeting.

Children at Rock Point learn to read and write in both Navajo and English. The school has about 450 students from kindergarten through twelfth grade. The three Rs are taught entirely in Navajo until third grade, although an intensive English as a Second Language program prepares students for transition to largely English instruction after that. Science and social studies, however, continue in Navajo through junior high school, and much of high school social studies is in Navajo as well. The traditional Navajo clan relationship system is taught in classrooms. Emphasis is placed on the training of local Rock Point teachers.

Production of this book involved community people of all ages, from 80-year-old George Blueeyes, who still plants an annual crop of corn and melons with a planting stick, to Rex Lee Jim, who was 15 years old and a Rock Point high school student when he began working on the book during the summers.

Ideas for chapters came in many ways. Members of a parent committee submitted suggestions, listened to tapes of stories already collected, and offered feedback at regular intervals.

Rex, remembering a story he had heard since childhood about the kidnapping of his great-great-grandmother by Mexican raiders, asked his mother to retell the story on tape. Using the bilingual skills he had learned in school, Rex wrote down his mother's Navajo words, edited them, and published his own book in Navajo. The English version appears in this book.

Rex also enjoyed a unique rapport with storyteller George Blueeyes, a relationship which itself echoed of time past. Rex's grandfather had been a teacher of George Blueeyes. The Navajo poems Rex edited from Mr. Blueeyes's spoken words appear in the book.

Mr. Blueeyes spent many hours, not just with Rex, but with numerous other students from the high school. He told stories and taught them how to make moccasins and plant in the old way. His wife showed them how to use corn to make kneel-down bread and other traditional foods.

Other grandparents showed similar interest in sharing with young people. The opening chapter of the book features interviews with three Rock Point grandparents, including Littleben, an 80-year-old herder. The book closes with a poem written by a Rock Point tenth grader—Littleben's grandson, Thomas Littleben, Jr.

Interviews are not limited to oral histories from Rock Point, and contributors to the book, both young and old, come from communities throughout the Navajo Reservation. They do not speak only of the past but of the problems of the present and of different approaches toward solving them. Their viewpoints are not always the same, but their focus is always on the land and the lessons to be learned from it.

History can be seen in many ways and from many different angles. Not everyone, not even all Navajos, share the viewpoints of all those who speak in this book. And that is as it should be. In the Navajo oral tradition, every individual carries with him a bit of history. Every individual has something to teach, something to share.

The purpose of this book is not to "fix one truth" but to encourage readers, no matter what their culture, to go out and actively seek many truths from the land and the people around them.

# INTRODUCTION

This book tells about a piece of land, *Diné Bikéyah*, Navajo Country. It tells of how this land has supported life, of the invasions and wars that have passed over it, and the economic, legal, and cultural questions touching Navajo land today.

From hunting and plant gathering, to Anasazi history, to coal mining and the legal battles of the Navajo-Hopi Land Dispute, stories of the land are told by people from all over Navajo Country, or are put together from historical records. In each chapter, notes giving technical and historical background follow the stories.

Although the stories cover many events and subjects rarely found in history books, one theme remains clear from beginning to end. As the forces of ecology, economics, and politics have changed this land down the centuries, the people of *Diné Bikéyah*, the *Diné* themselves, have met the challenge of every age, and still do.

The strength to survive so well against such odds has come from many sources, and so it seemed right that many kinds of people should help make this book—medicine men, sheep herders, university professors, hunters, teachers, and scientists. Each explains the life and history of the land in his own way. Each can begin his story at the beginning of the world, but the stories are not the same. They give different answers to questions like "Where do we come from?" or "Why do plants grow where they do?"

In the end, however, all the answers come from the land itself—sometimes by scientific experiment, sometimes by life experience, sometimes by tradition handed down from the roots of time. The land is the teacher, and the medicine man, the scientist, and we ourselves are students together. When we do not agree, perhaps it is because none of us sees far enough. People living on opposite sides of a mountain rarely see the land the same way until they meet at the top.

So the stories here cannot tell all of Navajo history. They only point out paths that you might climb in Navajo Country. They try to show how history is recorded for you to find. In the end a person must go beyond books and climb many paths to reach an understanding of life and history that belongs to him alone. He must look for wisdom everywhere—in the stones at his feet, in the life around him, and in the words of his elders. The higher a person goes on his own, the more he will see.

In Navajo Country one sees many miles of land that looks quite empty, but someone who has learned enough to recognize even one plant will see life right to the horizon. The lacy heads of Indian rice grass that have fed men and animals for thousands of years have stories for those who can read them. Here the rice grass grows tall, there short, there grazed out by sheep, there pushed out by tumbleweed. Rain and dryness, animals that came and went, people who live on the land, fight over it, and love it, all speak through the grass. Such are the lessons of *Diné Bikéyah*, and they may guide you up many mountains.

We call the land Navajo Country, but *Diné Bikéyah* is also Hopi Country, Zuni Country, Tewa Country, New Mexican Country, sheep country, antelope country, and many more. Yet all of these "countries" are only one land that is home for many. That is what one sees from the top of a mountain. A Hopi, Mina Lansa, of Old Oraibi, said it well:

> . . . Look on all land as our land. All things on it and all people that are on it are in our care. Our songs and ceremonies call us caretakers of this land for all people. We have been taught to take care of this land in this way so that all people will benefit and all living things.

So with those words we dedicate this book to the young people of *Diné Bikéyah*, who will decide its future.

Rock Point Community School, 1982

# LAND

*A piece of land is like a book. A wise person can look at stones and mountains and read stories older than the first living thing that crawled on the earth. Hidden in the land are the bones of giant animals and plants that died before the first people lived. And since the first people made homes on the land, many people and tribes have come and gone. The land still remembers them, however, and keeps their houses, tools and other things they left behind.*

*Today you can look at the land and the roads, towns, fences and other things that can be seen on it, and you can learn much about how people are living now. The land even holds secrets about how people might live in the future.*

*This book is about Diné Bikéyah, Navajo Country, where Navajos have lived for a long time, but it is not the whole story. The earth is old. No book can tell all that is written on the land.*

*Sis Naajiní`*

*Tsoodził*

*Dook'o'oosłííd*

Our Navajo Laws are represented by the
Sacred Mountains which surround us.

| | |
|---|---|
| Sis Naajiní | Blanca Peak |
| Tsoodził | Mount Taylor |
| Dook'o'oosłííd | San Francisco Peaks |
| Dibé Nitsaa | Hesperus Peak |
| Dził Ná'oodiłii | Huerfano Mountain |
| Ch'óol'į'í | Gobernador Knob |

They were placed here for us.
We think of them as our home.

Blanca Peak is adorned with white shell.
Mount Taylor is adorned with turquoise.
San Francisco Peaks are adorned with abalone.
Hesperus Peak is adorned with jet.

Huerfano Mountain is dressed in
    precious fabrics,
While Gobernador Knob is clothed in
    sacred jewels.

This is how they sit for us.
We adorn ourselves just as they do,

With bracelets of turquoise,
And precious jewels about our necks.

The Sacred Mountains have always been
    where they are now.
They have been like that from the beginning.
They were like that in worlds before this.
They were brought up from the Underworld
And were put back in their respective places.

When the mountains were replaced,
Earth was made.
Sky was made.
Dawn was made.

Earth is Our Mother.
Sky is Our Father.
Sun gives us light.
Moon does the same.
All of these were made for us to live by.

The Dawn People say to us,
    "Get up, my grandchildren!
    "Rise! Do your work!
    "Do all the things that you must do!"

At noon the Sun tells us,
    "It's time to eat!"
And in the evening, when the Sun sets,
Darkness says to us,
    "Rest! Sleep, my grandchildren!"
Then Darkness blankets us,
And we rest until dawn.
This is how they have regulated our lives
    since the beginning.

These mountains and the land between them
Are the only things that keep us strong.
From them, and because of them we prosper.
It is because of them that we eat plants and
    good meat.

We carry soil from the Sacred Mountains in a
    prayer bundle that we call dah nídiilyééh.
Because of this bundle we gain sheep, horses,
    and cattle.
We gain possessions and things of value,
    turquoise, necklaces, and bracelets.
With this we speak, with this we pray.
This is where the prayers begin.

—George Blueeyes

2

*Dibé Nitsaa*

*Dził Ná'oodiłii*

*Ch'óol'į́'í*

Díí Dził ahééníniligíí
Nihi Bee Haz'áanii át'é.

   Sis Naajiní
   Tsoodził
   Dook'o'oosłííd
   Dibé Nitsaa
   Dził Ná'oodiłii
   Ch'óol'į́'í

Kót'éego éí nihá ályaa.
Éí nihighan át'é.

Sis Naajiní yoołgaii yee hadít'é.
Tsoodził dootł'izhii yee hadít'é.
Dook'o'oosłííd diichiłí yee hadít'é.
Dibé Nitsaa bááshzhinii yee hadít'é.

Dził Ná'oodiłii yódí yee hadít'é.
Ch'óol'į́'í nitł'iz yee hadít'é.

Ákót'éego nihá naazdá.
T'áá éí bíni' bik'ehgo
Yoo' dóó látsíní bee hadíníit'é.

Níléídę́ę́' ni' bitł'ááhdę́ę́' háát'i'.
Dził sinil áadi t'áá kót'éego
Nídahidiijaa'ii áádę́ę́' bił ha'azná,
T'áá íídą́ą́' dziłígíí ninádaas'nil.

Kodi dził ninádaas'nil.
Nahasdzáán ánályaa.
Yádiłhił ánályaa.
Hayoołkááł ánályaa.

Nahasdzáán nihimá.
Yádiłhił nihitaa'.
Jíhonaa'éí nihik'éé' diiłdíín.
Tł'éhonaa'éí dó'.
Éí bik'ehgo kééhwiit'į.

Níláhdę́ę́' hayoołkááł.
Hayoołkááł dine'é ádaaní,
   "Nídoohjeeh, nídoohjeeh!
   "Shitsóóké nídoohjeeh!"

Jíhonaa'éí t'áá ákót'éego hanáánádzih,
   "Nídoohjeeh, nídoohjeeh!
   "T'áadoo le'é baa naahkai.

"Nidaałnish!
"Hat'íí shį́į́ ádaałééh, ádaałe'."

Ałné'é'aahgo ánáádí'niih,
   "K'ad nááda'ohdą́."

E'e'áahgo chahałheeł nihik'i náánéildoh,
   "Háádaałyį́įh, háádaałyį́įh, da'ołhosh."
Háada'ayį́įhgo yiłkááh.

Kót'éego éí bił hosiidlį́į'.
Kót'éego éí bii' kééhwiit'į́.

Dził t'éí bee nihidziil.
Dził t'éí bee hat'íí da neiilyé.
Dził t'éí bee iidą́, bee iilghał.

Dził bileezh nideiijaah, Dah Nídiilyééh bidii'ní.
Binahjį' dibé, béégashii, łį́į' da nidaakai.
Binahjį' naalyéhé, yódí da nidaajaah.
Bee yáti', bee tsohodizin.
Tsodizin bits'ą́ą́dóó deezt'i'.

                -Tábąąhí Ts'ósí

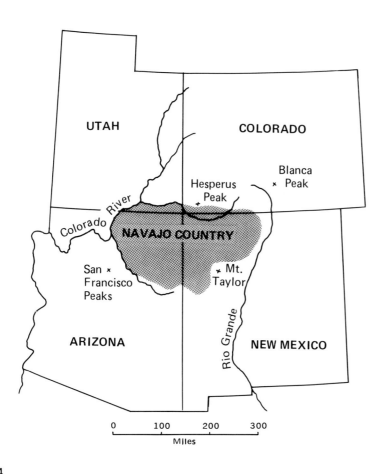

# DINÉ TAH

It is said that after the Navajos came into this world, they first lived east of the center of the land between the mountains. This part of Navajo Country is still known as *Diné Tah*, which means "Among the People." It is high country, covered with piñon and juniper trees, and in the canyons there is water for small farms. The hunting there is good.

In the stories of the early times, First Man and First Woman, Changing Woman, Monster Slayer, and his twin brother Child Born for Water all lived in the *Diné Tah*.

First Man and First Woman lived near *Dził Ná'oodiłii*, Huerfano Mountain. They found Changing Woman as a baby on top of *Ch'óol'į́'í*, Gobernador Knob. Changing Woman's children, Monster Slayer and Child Born for Water, came home to Huerfano Mountain after killing the monsters that troubled the world at that time. Some say they are there to this day.

From their beginnings in the *Diné Tah* the Navajos grew and became stronger. East of them lived the Pueblo tribes of the Rio Grande Valley. Later the Spaniards and the Comanches also became strong in the east. To the north lived the Utes. Acomas, Lagunas, and Zunis held the south. So the Navajos in time moved west, and there they became the largest of all the tribes in the land north of Mexico.

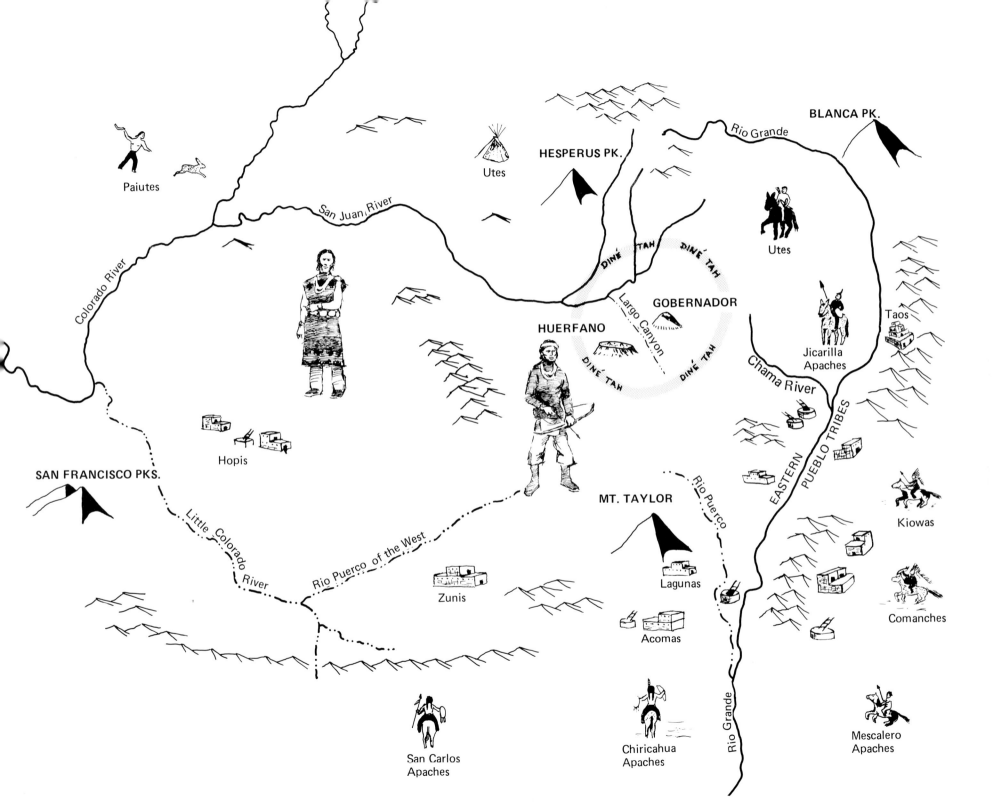

Paiutes

Utes

HESPERUS PK.

BLANCA PK.

Rio Grande

San Juan River

Colorado River

DINÉ TAH    DINÉ TAH

Utes

GOBERNADOR

Largo Canyon

DINÉ TAH    DINÉ TAH

HUERFANO

Taos

Jicarilla
Apaches

Chama River

Hopis

EASTERN    PUEBLO TRIBES

SAN FRANCISCO PKS.

MT. TAYLOR

Rio Puerco

Little Colorado River

Rio Puerco of the West

Kiowas

Zunis

Lagunas

Acomas

Comanches

Rio Grande

San Carlos
Apaches

Chiricahua
Apaches

Mescalero
Apaches

# HIGH COUNTRY FORESTS

In the mountains of Navajo Country air is cool, rain falls often, and forests grow of pine, spruce, fir, and aspen. The high country is summer pasture for livestock. It supplies firewood, wood for homes and corrals, and logs for the tribal sawmill. Three or four feet of snow often fall in winter. From east to west the names are:

## JEMEZ MOUNTAINS

In Navajo *Dził Łizhinii*, Black Mountains, they rise just west of the Rio Grande and south of the Chama River. Once a huge volcano, the center is now a round meadow twenty miles across. The volcano left there a natural black glass called obsidian that once made fine arrow heads. Navajos used to raid towns along the Rio Grande from hideouts in the Jemez Mountains.

## SAN MATEO OR CEBOLLETA MOUNTAINS

These run northeast from *Tsoodził*, Mount Taylor. They too were stopping places for Navajos going to the Rio Grande and were home to the Canyoncito Navajos who still live just to the east.

## ZUNI MOUNTAINS

These rise southwest of Mount Taylor and were once home to the Ramah Navajos who still hold land further south.

## MESA DE LOS LOBOS OR LOBO MESA

This high mesa northeast of Gallup has a wide valley through the center where there are lakes and springs. The highest point is *Ak'iih Nást'ání*, Hosta Butte, a holy place, said to be the home of *Hadahoniye' Ashkii* and *Hadahoniye' At'ééd*, Mirage Stone Boy and Girl.

## CHUSKA AND LUKACHUKAI MOUNTAINS

These follow the Arizona–New Mexico state line and have the reservation's best water, grass, and forest. Most maps label the whole range Chuska Mountains, but the north end is also called the Lukachukais. The highest places are: *Dził Dah Neeztínii*, Roof Butte; *Tsé Binááyołí*, Matthews Peak; *Tsézhin Dits'in*, Tsaile Peak; *Ch'óshgai*, Chuska Peak; and *Dziłk'i Hózhónii*, Beautiful Mountain.

## CARRIZO MOUNTAINS

This small group of peaks stands north of the Chuskas. Deep canyons of black rock cut into them on all sides. Grizzly bears and bighorn sheep survived there longer than almost anywhere else on the reservation. The Carrizos are called *Dził Náhooziłii*.

## BLACK MESA

The gray cliffs of *Dziłíjiin* can be seen across the Chinle Valley from the Chuska Mountains. The mesa slopes from there to the southwest, sending water from winter snow and summer showers down wide green valleys to the Little Colorado. Thick layers of coal lie under the ground.

## NAVAJO MOUNTAIN

*Naatsis'áán* is the highest place on the Navajo Reservation (10,388 feet). It stands by itself and looks the same from every side.

The Carrizo and Chuska Mountains together are often spoken of as a person. According to the late Frank Mitchell, a medicine man from Chinle, a male figure lies along them. His legs lie at the Carrizos, his neck at *Béésh Łichíi'ii Bigiizh*, Red Flint or Washington Pass, and his head at Chuska Peak. He is in charge of all plants and wildlife.

Across the valley a woman rests her head at Navajo Mountain, her body at Black Mesa, and her feet at Balakai Mesa. Her arms lie in Shonto Wash. Her cane is *Aghaałá*, a tall black rock near Kayenta. She rules all water and water creatures.

*Lake in the Lukachukai Mountains.*

*Eagle's view of Canyon del Muerto and Canyon de Chelly.*

8

# PINON AND JUNIPER

In Navajo Country few tall trees grow below 8,000 feet. In the warmer, drier land around the high places, pinon, juniper, and sagebrush take over from the pines and firs. On maps most of these areas are called "Plateaus" (say it plaTOE), which means a flat place that is higher than the land around it. From east to west the best-known plateaus in Navajo Country are:

> **The Chaco Plateau**
> **The Manuelito Plateau**
> **The Defiance Plateau**
> **The Shonto Plateau**
> **The Rainbow Plateau**
> **The Kaibito Plateau**

# CANYONS

Deep canyons cut through almost all the pinon and juniper country of Navajo land. In them people have found protection from their enemies and water for their crops since the beginning of time. Ancient ruins, old Navajo hogans, and stories of the past fill them all:

> **Largo Canyon in the *Diné Tah***
> **Chaco Canyon in Chaco Mesa**
> **Canyon de Chelly and Canyon del Muerto**
> **  in the Defiance Plateau**
> **Tsegi Canyon in the Shonto Plateau**
> **Navajo Canyon in the Rainbow Plateau**
> **Paiute Canyon in the Rainbow Plateau**

In the side of every mountain there are canyons that someone has called home.

*Defiance Plateau*

*Steppe country south of Rock Point, Arizona, toward Tsé Biná'ookahí.*

# STEPPE

Steppe (it sounds just like step) is a Russian word. It means a dry flat place that is not quite desert. Many languages use the Russian word because the Russian steppes are the largest in the world. Below the land of pinon and juniper is the Navajo steppe country. Sage, greasewood, yucca, and grass are plants of the steppe. Some years the plants grow well. In dry years they may not. Tumbleweed is also a plant of the steppes. It came from Russia (it is also called Russian Thistle). There were no tumbleweeds in North America before about 1870.

Good farm land is rare in steppe country, so the people of the steppes usually depend on livestock. This is true in Navajo Country, in Russia, China, South Africa or wherever steppes are found.

# DESERT

A true desert is so dry that few plants grow, and most of the animals are small. Only two areas in Navajo Country might be called deserts. Many places in the world are much drier.

### MONUMENT VALLEY
This piece of land between Black Mesa and the San Juan River has become world famous because of movies made along its towers of red sandstone. But the rocks are dry, even below the ground, so there are few wells and water is scarce. The Navajo name, *Tsé Bii' Nidzisgai*, means Plain in the Rocks.

### THE PAINTED DESERT
Bare rock and sand that seem to be painted many colors border the Navajo Reservation along the Colorado and Little Colorado Rivers. This is the driest part of Navajo Country. Even here, however, people irrigate farms along the Little Colorado and in places where springs flow out of the Echo Cliffs. In Navajo such land is called *Halchíítah*, Among the Colors.

*Thomas Littleben Jr. on dunes.*

*Wind-deposited sandstone near Rock Point.*

# EARTH, AIR, FIRE, AND WATER

Navajo Country is a land of rock. Its history cannot be told without naming the cliffs and towers where that history was made.

Wind and water made the rock. Water washed sand and clay down from distant mountains into ancient seas, spread them across beaches and forgotten plains. Wind raised up mighty dunes. And as the seas came and went again, the beaches and dunes became sandstone. The clay became mudstone and shale.

Plants that grew in lakes and swamps were pressed into coal, and from the sea life came limestone. Then the slow movement of the continents bent and twisted the land, and wind and water carved the face it has today.

Last came fire. Two of the sacred mountains, *Dook'o'oosłííd*, the San Francisco Peaks, and *Tsoodził*, Mount Taylor, rose as volcanoes. Hot lava, cinders, and ash poured from the roots of both of them less than a thousand years ago. *Tsé Bit'a'í*, Shiprock, was a volcano. So was *Aghaałá*, El Capitan near Kayenta. Hot rock pushing from below made Navajo Mountain and the Carrizos. Lava made many of the Hopi Buttes north of Holbrook and the black cliffs of the Chuskas. Southeast of Mount Taylor, red-hot lava foamed over 25 square miles of land like blood from a butchering. It is called *Yé'iitsoh Bidił*, Monster's blood. and is said to be the blood of a giant killed by the twin sons of Changing Woman.

By earth, air, fire and water, a home for the people was made.

*Tsé Bit'a'í, Shiprock, and volcanic dike.*

13

# DINÉ BIKÉYAH FROM SPACE

A satellite flying 567 miles over Navajo Country in October of 1975 made the picture on these pages. Along the eastern edge runs the dark line of the Rio Grande. On the west the waters of the Colorado River mark the black outline of Lake Powell and the sandstone walls that guide its way southwest toward Grand Canyon.

History has woven such fantastic patterns over this land that we seldom see the pattern of the land itself, its mountains, mesas, and canyons. But from space, as the rocket-launched camera shows, the works of people look small beside the works of nature. Irrigated farms along rivers, a few lakes (including Lake Powell), some coal mines, and the city of Albuquerque are the only man-made things easily seen. The rest is Mother Earth's own design.

Plant life shows dark, so higher places which are cooler, wetter and greener are darker in this picture. High country forests over 7,500 feet above sea level usually get more than 16 inches of rain yearly and look almost black here. Piñon, juniper, and sage brush areas down to 6,000 feet are gray. Rainfall there is 12–16 inches a year. Light gray to white land is steppe or desert 5,000 to 6,000 feet above sea level with less than twelve inches of rain. Washes, irrigated areas, lava flows, dunes and dark rock or soil have their own colors.

Important places mentioned in this book are listed below in alphabetical order and are numbered on the satellite picture from east to west.

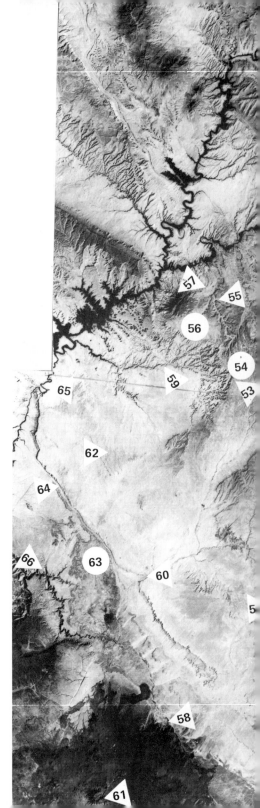

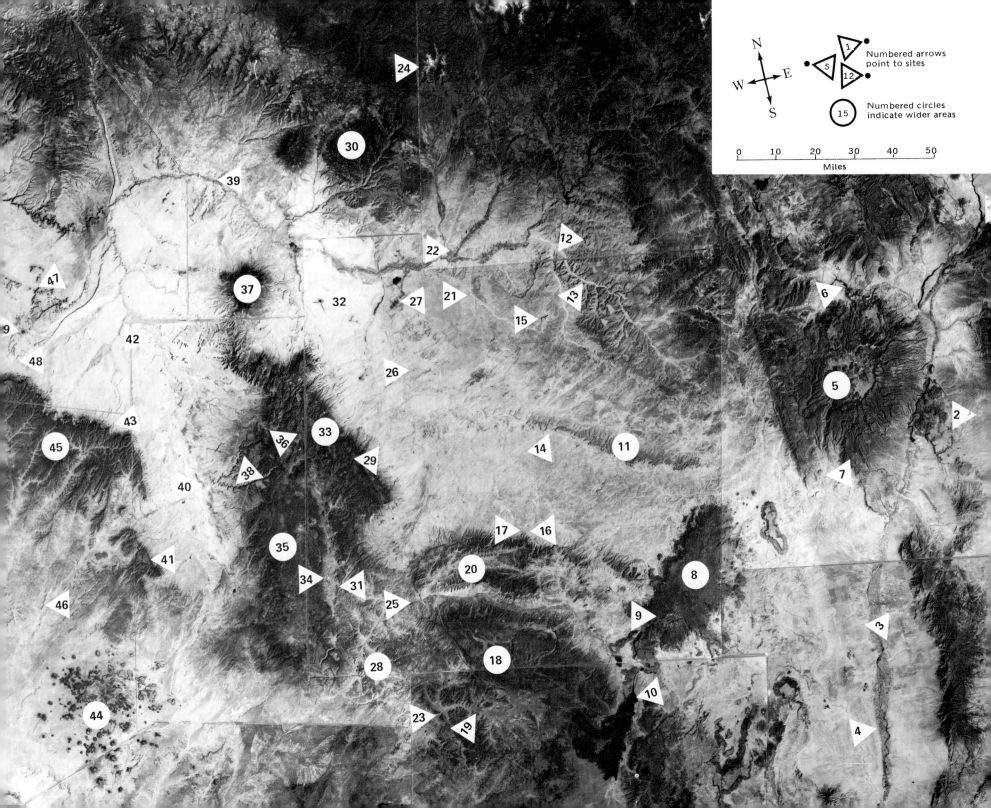

N

W E

S

1

5

12

Numbered arrows point to sites

15

Numbered circles indicate wider areas

0  10  20  30  40  50

Miles

24

30

39

47

37

32

22

12

9

48

42

27

21

13

26

15

6

43

45

33

36

29

5

2

38

40

14

11

7

41

35

34

31

25

17

16

20

9

8

46

28

18

3

44

23

19

10

4

# PLANT WATCHERS

*We say Nahasdzáán Shimá:*
*Earth, My Mother.*
*We are made from her.*
*Even though she takes us daily,*
*We will become part of her again.*
*For we ARE her.*

*The Earth is Our Mother.*
*The Sky is Our Father.*
*Just as a man gives his wife beautiful*
   *things to wear,*
*So Our Father Sky does the same.*
*He sends rain down on Mother Earth,*
*And because of the rain the plants grow,*
*And flowers appear of many different colors.*
*She in turn provides food for him.*

*He dresses her as a man would dress*
   *his woman.*
*He moves clouds and male rain.*
*He moves dark mists and female rain.*
*Dark mists cloak the ground,*
*And plants grow with many colored blossoms.*

*The plants with colored blossoms are her*
   *dress.*
*It wears out. Yes, the earth's cover wears out.*
*The plants ripen and fade away in the fall.*
*Then in the spring when the rains come*
   *again,*
*Mother Earth once again puts on her finery.*
*The plants are restored again in beauty.*
*This is what the stories of the Elders say.*

—George Blueeyes

18

Nahasdzáán shimá dii'ní.
Bits'ą́ą́dóó neidá.
T'áá ákwíí jį́ náánihiidlááh nidi
T'áá bí néidleeł.
T'áá éí ániit'é.

Nahasdzáán nihimá.
Yádiłhił nihitaa'.
Díí asdzání yá'át'éehgo bił naash'aash doo
    jinízin łeh.
Nihitaa' t'áá ákwíinízin, áájí háidiil'įįh.
Níłtsą́ áádę́ę́' kojį' kóyiił'įįh.
Ch'il bílátah hózhóón ałtah áát'eełii haajah.
Kodóó yidinínáádóó yitsą́ á'áł'įįh.

Yádiłhił díí asdzáníígíí háidiil'įįh.
Níłtsą́ bika' dóó k'osígíí nayiiłná.
Níłtsą́ bi'áád dóó ááh diłhił nayiiłná.
Ááh diłhił ni' nikééshígish.
Ch'il ałtah áát'eełii haajah, bílátah da'ałtso,
    da'alchíí'.

Ch'il bílátah hózhóón éí bi'éé'.
Nídidoot'ołígíí éí nídidoot'oł.
Nahasdzáán t'áá biki' ni'diit'ood.
Ch'iłígíí aak'eego nit'įįh.
Daango éí ninááháłtin.
Áko hanínáádiit'įįh, hanínáádidoo'níłł.
Aadę́ę́' náádínóoséeł.
Kót'éego hastói badahane'.

-Tábą̨ą́hí Ts'ósí

Clan: *Hashk'ąą Hadzohó*
Born for: *Tábąąhí*

# PLANT WATCHERS

*Winter dies hard in Navajo Country. Through all of March, April and May, heat and cold fight each other across the land, filling the air with dust and sending clouds racing down the sky. In these months of wild weather, Earth gives birth to her greatest gifts—the plants that every creature needs, from the smallest ant to the people and their livestock. In hope and fear those who live on the land must wait to see what each new spring will bring. Old people have seen springs that brought flowers and grass and springs that brought starvation. They measure their lives by the life of the land.*

## THE HERDER

*Hashk'aan Ts'ósí*, also known as Littleben, lives at *Halgai Tó*, Spring-on-the-Plain, southeast of Rock Point, Arizona. Further to the southeast the Lukachukai Mountains rise up out of the plain, and red cliffs stand around on all sides. *Halgai Tó* is a small world by itself. Members of the *Bit'ahnii* Clan have lived there for over 100 years. It is steppe country.

One hot June day we found *Hashk'aan Ts'ósí* on his horse, far away by the cliffs where his sheep find shelter from the noonday sun. His five panting dogs had crawled under the salt bushes and only moved to snap at flies. *Hashk'aan Ts'ósí* himself did not move, but under the shade of his white straw hat his eyes watched carefully. He saw the ground squirrel creep from its hole near the sleeping dogs and grab a rice grass seed. He saw the lamb nibble at the broom grass, then jump back from its sharp leaves. He saw the old billy goat stand on its hind legs to steal bits of green from the top of a salt bush.

He saw us coming through the tumbleweeds lower down and reached for the ancient leather whip that hung from his saddle horn. The horse raised its head and the five dogs jumped to attention and raced ahead of their master to greet us.

He pulled up beside us and nodded his head but said nothing. His large hands rested easily on the saddle horn, and his eyes looked past us at some bird or plant that we did not see. He listened to us say who we were and what we wanted. Our questions made the wrinkles of his face turn into a smile.

"You say you want to know about this land as far back as I can remember. I could say something about that." But for a long time he said nothing as his mind hunted back through 80 years of seasons, dust storms, snow clouds and thunderbolts like some people might hunt through the pages of an old book.

The land and the weather are more than a book to him. They are life and death. A lifetime on the plain will teach a person many things. *Hashk'aan Ts'ósí* can name a hundred different plants and more in every season. He knows the favorite food of every animal and which plants are poison. He knows things that university professors may never know.

21

*Hashk'aan Ts'ósí* swept his eyes across the land. "Back when I first began to understand, a grass grew here," he said. "*Tł'oh ts'ózí* it is called. There was a lot of it! And *nididlídii* (Indian rice grass) too! There was a lot of that. And *tł'ohdeii* (goosefoot) of different kinds. There was a lot. There were so many different kinds of plants that stretched across the land as far as you could see. But now there are none. Just too much tumbleweed.

"Another plant, *ch'il dilyésii* (snakeweed), grows now where those other plants used to grow. Those plants over there with the yellow flowers—that's them. Where once fields of *tł'oh dahakałii* (sacaton grass) grew so tall, today those other plants have taken over. The stock won't eat them. Sunflowers once covered the dunes that you see there all white in the sun. When I was young they grew high enough to give me shade at noon. Everywhere the grass was tall enough to hide a sheep. But that is finished. These days it seems that everything is going wrong."

*Hashk'aan Ts'ósí* got off his horse and walked with us across the sand. We saw nothing but snakeweed and tumbleweed, but he saw more. He pointed out three kinds of milkweed, one of them poisonous. He saw an evil-looking plant he said caused itching and sores. He picked a small purple-brown grass with hard black seeds—cheat grass. "I just call this 'horse grass'," he said. "The seeds hurt a sheep's lips. But they eat it, and we eat the sheep, so I guess we're made of that plant too."

We came to the top of a small hill where a few tall grasses leaned forward in the breeze as if they were listening to *Hashk'aan Ts'ósí*. They were hard to see because they grew so thin and far apart, but they reached above his waist. "These are the *tł'oh ts'ózí*," he said. "These are the ones that once could hide a sheep."

We gazed at the slender willowy grass, which in English is known as "needle-and-thread." He said nothing for a while, and we tried to imagine thick tall grass covering the land, and *Hashk'aan Ts'ósí* riding through it as a young man, his horse belly-deep in green, and rabbits and birds flying up in all directions.

Thunder clouds were piling up over the Lukachukais off to the southeast. *Hashk'aan Ts'ósí* looked at them hopefully. "There used to be more rain," he said. "In my youth it rained and rained. And in winter there was snow. It came up above our knees some-

times. People used to move up on the mesa when it snowed. There was water up there then. Then there came a year when no rain fell at all. Horses and other livestock died of starvation. People my age remember 'The-Year-the-Horses-Died-of-Starvation.' They say, 'My cousin was born two years after 'The-Year-the-Horses-Died-of-Starvation,' or, 'My uncle passed away just before 'The-Year-the-Horses-Died-of-Starvation.'

"The summer after that it rained and rained. Sunflowers grew everywhere, and maybe it repaid for the year before. But since that time, good years and bad years have taken turns.

"They used to have ceremonies to bring rain in times like this. I remember a man called *Ch'ah Ditł'oii* (Fur Cap). He did it once when there was no rain. They built a hogan for him on the mesa above *Tó Likan* (Sweetwater). Then they heard thunder far away on the horizon.

" 'It will rain a long time,' said *Ch'ah Ditł'oii*, 'because the thunder's roll is long.' That really happened. It rained and rained through the fall until the heads of the *bé'ézhóó'* (broom grass) turned from yellow to red.

"When it rains the sheep are happy about it and just eat. They probably don't think, 'We should have rain. We should have plants.' They just run around trying to find their favorite plants and biting them off, even though there are many things for them to eat around here. They just go wild and run all over. They're so happy about it."

*Hashk'aan Ts'ósí* picked one of the tall stalks of needle-and-thread grass, carefully pulled out one of the seeds on its long thread, and gave it to the wind. Would the rain come and give it life? Would tall grass again cover the plain? Perhaps he knew the answer, but he did not speak.

The land and the plants and the livestock have been his school, his college and his doctor's degree. His knowledge would make a scientist famous, but he learned it in the silence of the plain, and he is silent about it.

*Note:* The Navajo plant names are those used by the people in these stories. Other families or people in other parts of the reservation may use different names for the same plants. English names may also be different in different places.

Clan: *Tábąąhí*
Born for: *Tł'ízí Łání*

## THE *HATAALII*

In a canyon just north of *Halgai Tó* you will often hear singing. A cheerful Navajo song comes and goes on the wind among the echoing rocks. George Blueeyes is out gathering plants.

He walks lightly, although his back is bent a little by his years and a little more by his work. Sometimes only his hat shows among the hills and bushes. It is an old black cowboy hat he has worn so long his friends can recognize it at once. Turquoise beads swing from his neck. Silver shines at his wrists. He looks like someone going to greet important people.

If you ask him, he will say, yes, he is among important people, and they are his friends. He is a *Hataałii*—a singer and medicine man—and he calls plants "Plant People." They are his friends. He talks and sings to them and calls them by special names.

Back at his home George Blueeyes and his wife Elizabeth will sit together in the afternoon sun sorting the plants. Many small bundles will be tied with string and bits of cloth and stored away. Their house is full of Plant People. The little bundles are everywhere—in the roof beams, hanging from the wall, in jars tucked here and there.

"The Plant People were put here for us," says George Blueeyes. "The sky is the one who does the planting. He moves clouds over the plants. He moves clouds and male rain. He moves the female rain and dark mists over the plants, and they grow.

"We live by the plants. They are our food and our medicine and the medicine for our livestock. From the Plant People we have *Iináájí Azee'*—the medicines of the Life Way, and other medicines.

"There are medicines for lightning. There are medicines for bear wounds and the same for snakes. There are medicines for evil done by water. There are medicines against all those that do harm.

"With our Life Way medicines, people get well. A person who is broken all over, even he can survive with these medicines. We have songs for preparing the medicines. 'You will cure the person!' That's how we pray to the plants. Then we gather them and sing again, 'Let him be well! Let him be cured!' That's how people get well. That's how the plants were made for us."

Visitors come to the Blueeyes' camp from far away because of the plants—a young man afraid of an illness, a mother whose son has an insect bite the doctors can't recognize. Each time George Blueeyes calls on the Plant People for help.

Many come for knowledge as well. An older Navajo lady comes with her niece and nephew. The young people seem very modern. They drive a car and speak English easily. Their aunt seems shy and old fashioned. But when she speaks, her words have a special power. The young people obey at once.

She has come down from her home in the mountains behind the sawmill at Navajo and carries her own small bundles in the folds of her red Navajo skirt. She introduces herself quietly. By the way she speaks, the Blueeyes understand that she is a plant watcher like themselves.

Mountain plants are different from the plants of the canyon and steppe. So, when the coffee is boiling and the food is laid out, the experts sit down together and trade knowledge.

Mr. Blueeyes explains that for many medicines you must collect the female plants or female parts of a plant from the Female Mountain (Black Mesa), and the male plants or male parts of a plant from the Male Mountain (the Chuskas). "We pay each other to learn the names of plants and how to recognize them. Medicine men spend time and money to learn, and there is no end to this learning. There are plants that grow only between here and Mexican Water. People come hundreds of miles to see them."

But there is a bit of sadness in his voice as he speaks. "There were more plants long ago," he says. "It seemed as if there was no bare ground. Sunflowers covered the earth with yellow, and among them were flowers of red and blue. There were so many different plants. But the plant people move wherever they please. If they choose to go back to the land, they will. You cannot plant these

kinds of plants. If they choose to go back to the land, they will. If they choose to move somewhere else, it is up to them.

"When I go to Farmington, I see a lot of things growing beside the highway that used to grow everywhere. I could show you someday."

Wherever he goes, George Blueeyes looks out for his friends the Plant People. Even in the town of Farmington itself, where most of us know only cement, noise and exhaust smoke, you may find George Blueeyes singing softly, gathering pollen from cattails that grow behind a certain car wash he knows. That is his work.

## THE GRANDMOTHER

West of *Halgai Tó* the plain squeezes between two red sandstone mesas. There at *Tsé Giizhí* (Rock Gap), hogans, houses, corrals and roads cover the land like the roots of a small town. Nearly a hundred people live there, but all of them belong to the family of Grandma Pahe.

In Navajo she is *Asdzą́ą́ Tł'ááshchí'iłbáhí*, Gray Woman of the *Tł'ááshchí'í* Clan. She is the oldest of the people of *Tsé Giizhí*. She can remember coming there more than 60 years ago with only her husband and her sister. They built one hogan, and it became a town.

She leans on the cane and looks out over the land. "I feel so thankful," she says. "I look at the houses and I say to myself, 'Those are my children! They're from me! And their children—my grandchildren.' That's how I think when I look across this land."

The children are from the land too. When Grandma Pahe was a young mother, she got everything she needed to care for them from the land itself.

"The plants were our food," she says. "We ate *chiiłchin* (sumac berries) and *k'ostse'* (wild mustard) and *tł'ohdeii* (goosefoot). We ate *hashk'aan*—the fruit of the yucca. We ate *naazkaadii* (amaranth). We ate boxthorn berries mixed with white clay. We called them Food of the Holy People, *Haashch'éédą́ą́*. They used to be a mass of red when you looked over toward the cliffs. There were *nímasii* (wild potatoes) and *chąąsht'ezhii*, which is something like a wild carrot.

"In the hungry time before the corn was ripe, we went out with baskets to gather grass seeds. Where *nididlídii* (rice grass) or *tł'oh dahakałii* (sacaton grass) grows, you lean the plant over the basket and beat out the seed without cutting the plant. We call the early plants like rice grass *shị yináldzidí*—'summer-fearing'—because they dry up when hot weather comes.

Clan: *Tł'ááshchí'í*
Born for: *Tó'aheedlíinii*

25

"In those days we did not have the things we have now. We had no diapers! We did not even have flour sacks to use for diapers. But our babies had no problems, no diaper rash. That does not happen when you use the bark of *awééts'ááł* (cliff rose). The inside of the bark is like white feathers. We used that and very soft dirt right on the cradleboard.

"*Awééts'ááł* usually comes from higher country. It doesn't grow much around here. Women who brought down large bundles of it could trade it for sheep."

Grandma Pahe shakes with laughter as she looks around the room at her tall sons. Some of them are grandparents themselves, and she thinks of herself making diapers for them out of bark and collecting grass seed to feed them. Her great grandson is crawling along the floor. There are cans of beans and a box of Pampers on the shelf. She waves her hand at all that.

"You see, this is how we get along now. We buy groceries and live that way. The plants we used to eat are gone. If we had to live the old way, we would starve. Only the *k'ostse'* still seems to grow everywhere. A little *chiiłchin* is left where water runs out of the cliffs. And there is a tiny spot of *tł'ohdeii* as well. But the rest are hard to find now."

The old foods may be hard to find, but they are not forgotten. Under the bed is a sack of dried wild celery that took many hours of picking in the early spring. It will not keep the family from starvation, but it will flavor many pots of stew. Behind the door lies a pile of yucca roots. The soap made from them will not wash the diapers at the laundromat, but it will keep white hair or black shiny clean.

A sack of sumac hangs from a nail in the corner. It will not kill the hunger the herders feel after a long day, but when a medicine man comes to sing the Blessing Way over Grandma Pahe's granddaughter, it will be ground and cooked in the old way.

Then guests will pass a bowl of the thick, bitter-sweet sumac from hand to hand as they sit on the sheep skins by the fire. Grandma Pahe will watch with sparkling eyes to see the old taste make them smile. And when the bowl comes around to her, she will hold a spoonful on her tongue for a moment and let her thoughts go back to her youth. She will see herself walking lightly through tall green grass. And she will be thankful for all that the land has given her.

*IN MEMORIAM: Grandma Pahe passed away on September 11, 1981, as this book was going to press. She leaves behind 90 descendants, including five children, 25 grandchildren, 39 great-grandchildren, a great-great-grandchild, and numerous grandnieces and grandnephews. Most of them live at Tsé Giizhí.*

The Plant Watchers were in their late seventies or early eighties when they were interviewed during the summer of 1979 by Leroy Tsinajinnie, Rex Lee Jim, and Thomas Benally, all of Rock Point.

# THE CIRCLE OF LIFE

The herder, the medicine man and the grand-mother knew a great deal about plants and how to find and use them. But that does not explain why Littleben smiles when he looks at the grass and says, "We are made of that, too," or why George Blueeyes calls plants "Plant People" or why Grandma Pahe is proud to offer her guests sumac mush.

They do these things because they have seen that all life depends on plant life. In modern times we often forget that lesson, but they have learned it many times while herding, gathering food and medicine and suffering hunger when the plants did not grow.

They have all seen the plant life change in their own lifetimes. They know that has also changed their own lives. "If we had to live the old way, we would starve," says Grandma Pahe. "We buy groceries now...." Littleben says when he looks over his land, "Another plant, snakeweed, grows now where those other plants used to grow," and he knows that snakeweed has changed the way he herds and the size of his flock.

George Blueeyes prays to Plant People because he knows that nature has the power of life and death over him and his patients.

There is an English word for this kind of under-standing--*ecology*. It comes from Greek that means "house". Just as all things that happen in a house make up the life of that household, so, everything that happens in the world is part of one life.

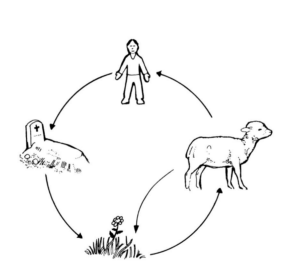

Life moves in circles that have no end. Sun and rain bring plant life from the earth. The plant life gives life to animals, to sheep and horses, prairie dogs and deer. They in turn give life to man and mountain lion, hawk and badger, flea and gnat. The buzzards and worms will also be fed, and in the end everything will go back to the ground to feed new plant life.

28

Nothing is wasted. Everything that is taken from the earth is given back, so that all life on earth is really part of one life. Even death brings new life.

But what happens if a circle is broken, if life no longer passes from one living thing to the next? Could that ever happen?

Traditional Navajo thinkers do not argue with the word *ecology*. They speak of the sacred mountains as posts of a hogan, and all life in this hogan as part of the same creation.

Life on Earth begins with plants and goes on and on. Plants die. They are eaten. They go back to the earth and become food for new life. "We are made from Mother Earth," says George Blueeyes. "Even though she takes us daily, we will become part of her again."

The Circle of Life can go on until the sun burns out and Earth falls into darkness. Again, the old ones are right. Without the sun, no plant would have power to grow.

But people have power to upset the Circle of Life. We have made weapons that kill more game than we need. We have farmed land that should have been left wild. We have dug ditches and built dams. All these things have changed the life around us, and in the end have changed us too.

Modern machines, roads, farms, factories and mines give us more terrible power than ever over life. But what has happened to the wisdom of herder, medicine man and grandmother? What are we doing to plant life around us? How will this change our own lives? Do we have power to save as well as destroy?

On the next few pages are some ideas from the science of ecology that help explain why the Plant People move and change the way they do. They are ideas about Plant People, but they explain much about any kind of people.

# SNAKEWEED

Littleben says snakeweed now grows where sacaton grass once did. Snakeweed helps cure ant bites and snake bites and is used in Navajo ceremonies, but it poisons livestock.

Snakeweed is a disaster for sheep raisers. It means fewer animals can live on the land. People grow poorer and must leave to make a living elsewhere.

There are several kinds of snakeweed, but it is very hard to tell them apart. The Navajo name is *ch'il dilyésii*.

On much Navajo steppe country more snakeweed grows now than any other plant. This has happened in the last 80 years. Why? Grasses should grow better on the steppe, and people like Littleben have seen them.

But snakeweed has a power that grass doesn't. It tastes bad. Livestock eat grass and leave snakeweed. Biting off the same grass many times before it can grow will kill it. Snakeweed can move in. And it does!

As the pictures on this page show, livestock seems to change the rules on the plants. Snakeweed was made to survive and grass to be eaten. Can that really be true?

If it is, then taking livestock away should let grass push out snakeweed. But we know huge wild herds of antelope, bison and elk ate grass too, and snakeweed didn't take over then. Why not?

Why do Plant People move? Maybe for the same reasons other living things move: to find work they like to do, to live among friends, to find a better home, and to escape crowds. Scientific names for these reasons are *specialization*, *interdependence*, *succession*, and *limitation*. Snakeweed, grass, and animals all have a place.

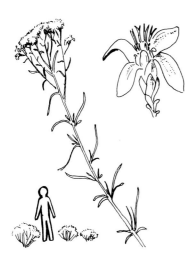

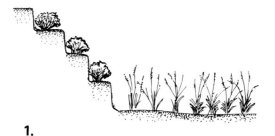

**1.**

The natural home of snakeweed is probably a rocky slope. Grasses grow better on the soils of the plain.

**2.**

Animals can kill off grasses by biting them off again and again before they have a chance to grow. This leaves space where new plants will start.

**3.**

If livestock keeps the grasses from growing, the snakeweed will take over the open ground.

**4.**

When the snakeweed takes over, the animals go hungry.

# SPECIALIZATION

Like humans, Plant People live in different "communities" because they, like humans, live in different ways. All need soil, water and sun, but they need different kinds and amounts. That is why steppe and mountain have different plant communities. George Blueeyes found a cattail community by a car wash in Farmington.

Plants are *specialized*. They grow where special talents make them stronger than other plants. Plant watchers know where to find the community they want.

Wherever different plants grow together in a community, they are specialized to use *that* soil, water and sun differently.

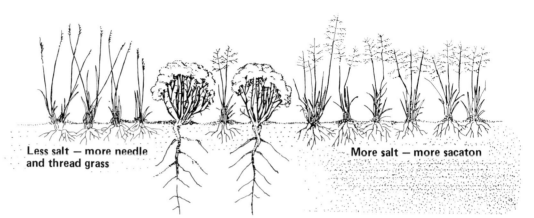

**Less salt — more needle and thread grass**

**More salt — more sacaton**

The roots of grasses are specialized to catch rain water quickly. Healthy steppe grass leaves only enough water for a few deep-rooted plants like snakeweed to grow.

Soil also makes a difference. Littleben's sacaton grass is specialized to use salty soil and will push out plants that don't like salt.

# INTERDEPENDENCE

Like people, plants in a community depend on each other. They are *interdependent*. They need each other the way human communities need different kinds of people -- doctors, mechanics, farmers, teachers, etc.

Plants and animals are also interdependent because they are all part of a Circle of Life. Exactly what each plant or animal does for its neighbors may be hard to see until it is killed off. Then the whole community may change.

Animals can help grasses as well as kill them. Deep-rooted plants that manage to survive among grasses also help and are helped by them.

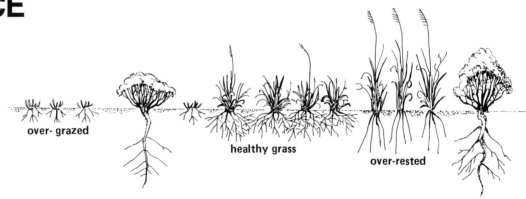

**over- grazed**

**healthy grass**

**over-rested**

To grow thick roots and healthy leaves, grass needs to be eaten. If eaten too often it dies of over-grazing, but if no animals eat it, it becomes old and weak and dies from over-resting. To grow thick roots and healthy leaves, it must be bitten from time to time.

31

# SUCCESSION

What will bring back the old flowers and grasses? "You cannot plant these kinds of plants," says George Blueeyes. "If they choose to come back, they will."

If you killed all plants in one place and tried to grow them again, you probably could not. People are the same. If you tore down a city, the people would not come back until homes were built for them.

The pictures show how one kind of plant follows another when steppe land is cleared. These changes are called a *succession*, which means "following". Snakeweed is in the middle of the succession, grasses at the end.

Quick-growers like tumbleweed come first. They prepare the soil and protect it from wind. Deep-rooted plants like snakeweed then move in. They bring plant food from deep underground and fertilize the topsoil with their leaves. Grasses take over as soon as the other plants have prepared the soil for them.

# LIMITATION

The rule of *limitation* says that the amount of plant life on a piece of land depends on the soil, water and sunlight there. These *limit* the growth of plants, and it will not increase without fertilizer, irrigation or better weather.

Farmers learn this quickly. Planting more seeds doesn't always mean more melons. More vines, maybe; but smaller ones.

Nature is the same. The soil, water and sunlight limit life on the land. Plant life is limited and that limits animal and human life.

Seeds in pots are also limited. An easy experiment shows this.

In three small pots plant 5, 10 and 15 bean, corn or lentil seeds. Give them the same soil, water and sunlight for six weeks.

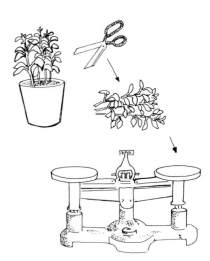

Cut all the plants off at the soil level and dry them completely in three bundles. Which weighs the most?

32

# ROADSIDES

George Blueeyes says plants still grow by high-ways that once grew everywhere. A roadside *is* a good place to look for plants.

The fence keeps stock out most of the time, and rain running off the road brings extra water. Often plant communities change clearly at the fence line.

You can measure this change by counting the number of different plants in a similar area on each side of the fence and measuring how much ground the plants cover.

With a rope 12 yards long lay out squares of 9 square yards on each side of a highway fence. For each square count the number of different kinds of plants. For each square yard, estimate what percent of the ground is covered by plant life. What percent of plant life is snakeweed? What makes the difference? The road? The fence? The shape of the ground? Nothing?

#1 ROADSIDE FENCE
PLANT TYPE 1B

| | %COVER | %SW |
|---|---|---|
| 1 | | |
| 2 | 10 | — |
| 3 | 20 | — |
| 4 | 10 | 10 |
| 5 | 50 | 25 |
| 6 | 25 | — |
| 7 | 30 | — |
| 8 | 10 | 10 |
| 9 | 90 | 30 |

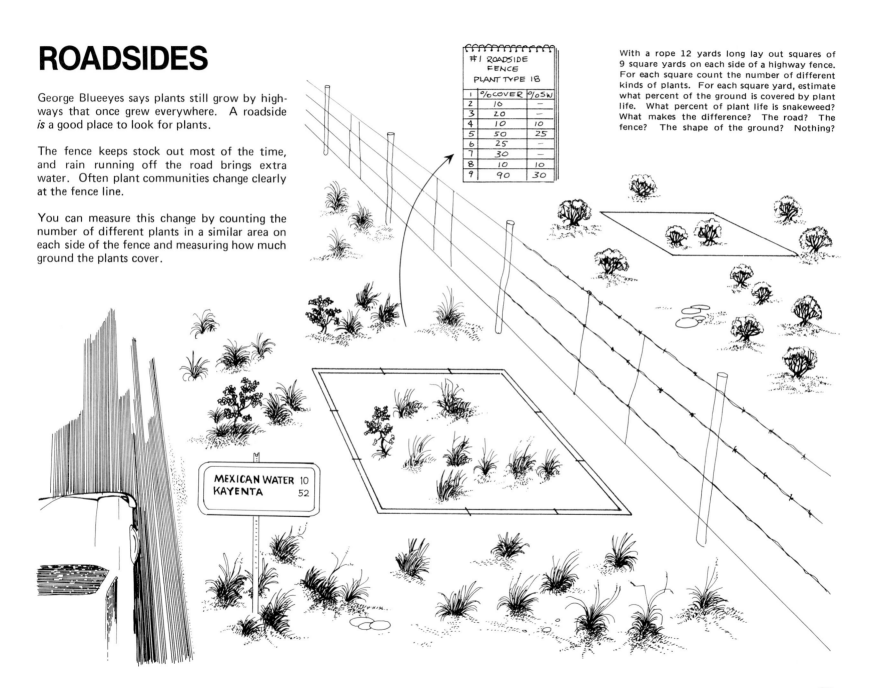

MEXICAN WATER 10
KAYENTA 52

# PLANT PEOPLE OF THE STEPPE

### NEEDLE AND THREAD GRASS

One of the only tall grasses in Navajo country with a feathery top. The feathers are the "threads". Each one leads to a sharp seed, the "needle". Livestock eat it most before the seed has grown and after it falls. Latin name: *stipa comata.* Navajo: *troh ts'ózi, troh adishishi.*

### INDIAN RICE GRASS

A "summer-fearing" grass that seldom grows more than two feet high. It looks like a tangle of thread. The seeds are big enough to eat in May and have been used for food since Anasazi times. Latin: *oryzopsis hymenoides.* Navajo: *nididlídii.*

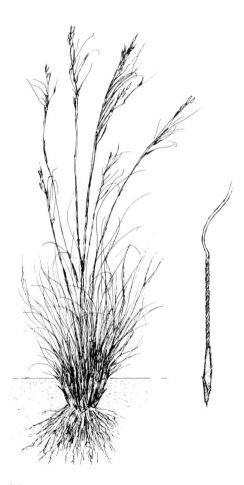

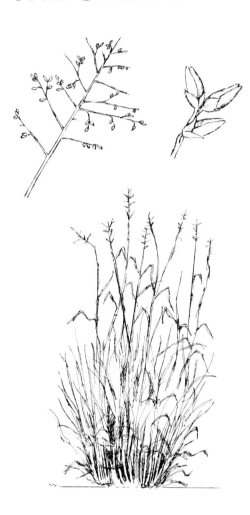

### ALKALI SACATON GRASS

One of the only tall grasses in Navajo country with a top shaped like a Christmas tree. It likes salty, clay soil. The small black seeds were food for Anasazis as well as Navajos. Latin: *sporobolus airoides.* Navajo: *troh dahakalii.*

## GALLETA GRASS

A short grass that often grows in a small circle. The leaves are quite sharp and tough. The seeds grow on a single spike that stands above the plant. When they fall, the spike and its zigzag top stays. It can stand drier weather than many grasses. Latin: *hilaria jamesii.* Navajo: *t'oh tsahii.*

## WINTER-FAT

A gray-colored bush, waist-high or less. The ends of the branches become woolly like lambs' tails when the seeds fall. Sheep eat it all winter. Latin: *eurotia lanata.* Navajo: *gahtsohdą́ą́'.*

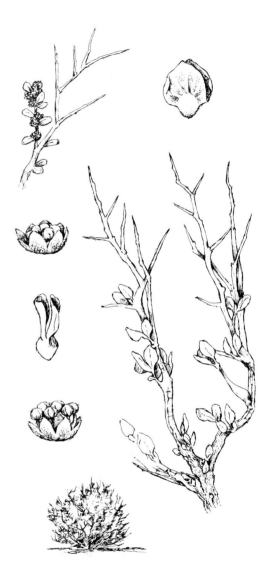

## SPINY SALTBUSH (SHADSCALE)

A gray bush, less than waist high. It has sharp thorns and round leaves that fall in winter. Seeds look like a double leaf. Latin: *atriplex confertifolia.* Navajo: *dá'ák̨ǫ́zh deeníní.*

## SUMAC

A tall bush that grows in shady canyons and alcoves. The red berries are eaten with sugar or cooked with cornmeal. Baskets are made from sumac branches (k' ii'), and dye is made from the leaves. Latin: *rhus trilobata*. Navajo: *chiilchin*.

## FOUR-WING SALTBUSH

Looks very much like spiny saltbush but its leaves are thin, it has no thorns, and its seeds have four "wings". Latin: *atriplex canescens*. Navajo: *díwózhiilbáí*.

## BOXTHORN

This relative of the tomato has small red berries, like tomatoes. Grandma Pahe mixed them with white clay. The berries may be eaten without the clay, but too many will cause stomach cramps. Latin: *lycium pallidum*. Navajo: *haashch'éédą́ą́'*.

## GOOSEFOOT

There are several kinds. The biggest, also called lambs' quarters, grows higher than a man and needs lots of water. Other kinds can stand drier places. The leaves and stems can be eaten early in the spring. Later the seeds can be harvested. Latin: *chenopodium album.* Navajo: *tł'ohdeii tsoh.*

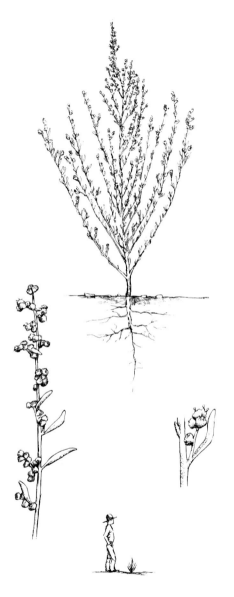

Also shown is another kind of goosefoot that seldom grows more than waist high and has narrow leaves. Latin: chenopodium fremonti Navajo: *tł'ohdeii.*

## WILD CELERY

A small plant that grows almost flat on the ground. For the best taste, it should be picked early in the spring before the flowers bloom. It is dried and used in soup and stew. Latin: *cymopterus glomeratus.* Navajo: *haza'aleeh.*

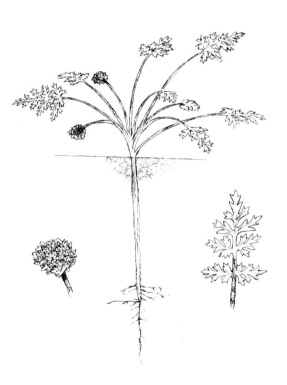

HUNTERS

# THE HUNTER

*In his cabin in the Lukachukai Mountains, our grandfather of the Tł'ááschí'í clan talked of hunting. Few men left now still know the ancient songs and ceremonies of the hunt. Few can talk of the Deer People as he can.*

*The hunting ceremonies go back very far, to a time before Navajos had livestock and were starving for meat. The Holy People taught them the hunting so that the Diné would not starve.*

*The hunter began his story beside his roaring stove. The snowy world outside where the Deer People live seemed far away. As he talked, however, we forgot the warm cabin and forgot the stove. By the end of the story, the fire had died, the mountain air had turned our breath to smoke and frozen our feet. Now the world of Nature seemed strong and close and our modern comforts were weak and far away.*

What I tell you now is not something I've created myself. It began long ago with the Holy People. You've heard their names before, *Haashch'éélti'í*, Talking God, and his relative *Haashch'ééshzhiní*, Black God. These two Holy People started this in their own home. Nobody has ever done anything like it!

The old men, including myself, make hunting plans in the sweathouse. First we build a big fire in front of the sweathouse and heat up the rocks. Then the rocks are placed inside. We go in and say, "Let us go hunting. Let Talking God and Black God give us the best meat, the most tasty meat from their supply. Let us swallow this good meat!" That's how it is.

In the sweathouse we wash off the dirt and odor from our bodies. The bathtub has become the sweathouse of the younger generation, while the sweathouse itself is almost forgotten. I wonder if a bathtub feels like going into a sweathouse early in the morning with a group of people.

Songs are sung in the sweathouse. Talking God and Black God taught them to the first hunters, saying, "We will not hide the deer from you, for they are your livestock, your food. We will place them in front of you. But you must keep these songs sacred. From the time you leave the sweathouse until the time you come home, keep to the holy way. Don't talk foolishly and don't make jokes."

The first hunters left the next day. Before they left, Talking God told them what weapons to take: the dark bow, *ałíí' diłhił*, and the tail-feathered arrow known as *atsee' beist'áán*.

Clan: *Tł'ááshchí'í*
Born for: *Tó'aheedlíinii*

41

Black God also taught those first hunters. "My grandchildren," he said. "Keep this holy. Take the feathered bow, *ałtįį́ʼ tsélkanii*, and the second tail-feathered arrow—the one that is going to kill the deer. This is called *tsékʼih dziitsoii.*"

Black God taught those first hunters well. Today we still do as he said. Before leaving to hunt, we stand single file on the north side of the hogan and sing the sacred songs that the Holy People taught. As we file out, we must hold our weapons properly (tucked under the left arm, pointing forward).

From then on a hunter must keep holy thoughts. He keeps them serious, keeps them sacred. Up in the mountains the hunter talks about the game in a special language. It is an ancient language for hunting only. It will harm you if you use it at home.

Never point with your finger or use words like "far away." The game hears well. Even if the Holy People are sending one toward you, he will hear you and laugh if you are coming jokingly, without being serious. He will say, "Here they come. I hear them." And you will see nothing. That's what is said.

Lots of things can harm you near the deer, so be careful. Black God warned us. The game might cry out or make a noise or rush at the place where you are hidden. Then if you don't remain calm, if you yell or cry out, you will fall into "deer fright," *bįįh honeeshił.* You will stand there with a blank face, tears rolling down and your nose running heavily, while the game just wanders away.

Do everything correctly in the holy way and the game will be waiting for you. But if you or any of your partners act wrongly you will find that the twelve-pointed buck has become a mountain mahogany bush. The big doe who might cross your path has become a cliff rose. The *deekʼáliitsoh*—the great buck with spreading antlers—has become a rock covered with moss. The old doe will appear only as a rotten stump. Sometimes you see such an old tree stump with the roots sticking out. Those were the legs and tail of the doe. That is all you will see.

There are rules also for skinning your kill, for treating the head, the antlers and bones. Talking God and Black God whispered this knowledge into the ears of the first hunters. From that time on, all people born into this land were to hunt this very way. If you do not do this, you will live in a land that is hard and flat like a rock, a desert area, a place where living is hard.

All those things you learn in the sweathouse. The hunting itself is learned out on the mountain. That is where you are told, "Do this. Do that," and where you learn to use your weapon.

Long ago, when game was very scarce, I began to use this knowledge. All that I have told you was accepted by the Holy People. My prayers were answered, and the game was placed there in front of me.

I left from home with my older brother. We hunted together in those days. We are almost alike.

We rode horses up over the ridge to the top of the mountain. The snow was packed knee deep. Up there we tied our horses and went forward on foot. New snow had fallen. There were no tracks, only smooth white snow. Rocks stick up out of the mountain over on the sunny side. There we expected to find what we had come for.

As we came to a small dip, we found tracks. They were old and partly covered by new snow. I followed these tracks, plowing on ahead of my brother. They led on up over the mountain to where the rocks are big as this house and the pine trees grow all around.

There is a place where the rocks hang over. Below is a clear place where nothing grows, although pine and fir trees stand on all sides. I thought that we would find something under these rocks, even though the tracks were old and covered with snow. I kept on walking ahead of my brother to get there first.

He was still far behind when I came to the edge of the rocks. There by a big pine tree I could see a dark spot. There he was, lying in the sun. He was the one who had made those tracks. Now he rested below those rocks.

His antlers seemed very big. As I looked he turned his head, and the light fell across them. They shone, wide and thick, curving far out. Such things are rarely seen. This was the great buck that we call *deek'áliitsoh*.

He shook his head. Right then it seemed that the Holy People were whispering to me. "Look what we have placed in front of you. See him!" It was as if they were whispering into my ear, telling me to shoot my arrow down in there.

I didn't tell my brother. I walked around right above where he lay. There, straight below, he was. Very near. Then I shot my arrow down.

I shot my arrow into him, and it struck right below the foreleg. It touched the tip of the breast bone, came out the other side and went into the ground. I watched him roll over. My brother started running towards me. He carried an old gun. He got to the edge and fired *"ch'el, ch'el."* I don't know what he was shooting at, but none of his bullets ever hit.

I watched him roll over. A cliff rose bush grew there covered with snow. He rolled down against that and stopped. I waited for him to move again, so I could shoot my second arrow.

When he lay still, we went down to where he was. Then I saw how big his antlers really were. The snow was red where the arrow had come out.

We skinned and butchered him right there according to the holy way. I threw the large intestine toward home, for it is said that it will become a deer again.

My older sister had said as we left home, "The neck will be mine." She must have had some power, because you have never seen such a neck. The hind legs were as big as a horse. The ribs were huge.

My brother took the skin and hind legs. Even though I wanted them, I gave them. If you are selfish, your hunting partner may speak against you and you will not kill again. Also it is said that

the one who kills does not keep the skin. On the first hunt the hunters gave the skin to Talking God and Black God in payment for the ceremony. To this day hunters may not keep the skin.

We picked up the meat, piece by piece, and carried it to the horses. That is a time to pray and sing. You may ask for valuable things—soft goods, jewels, turquoise. Today perhaps people ask for cars.

These songs and prayers are from the oldest times when the first hunters returned home from the first hunt. So we, too, let our horses walk, and we sang all the way down the mountain. So we, too, brought the meat down to our homes, just as the sun also went down.

My sister came by for the neck she had asked for. My father, *Ayói Anílnézí* (The Very Tall One), knew a great deal about hunting. He told us we really had taken a *deek'áliitsoh*. He told us we had done everything right—the way it should be done.

Usually you remove the antlers while you are still up in the mountains, along with the head. The antlers must be laid out on the east side beneath a juniper, pinon, fir, or cliff rose. As you sprinkle them with corn pollen, you tell Talking God and Black God to provide you with another deer.

A long time ago, when there was a lot of starvation, people would bring the head back. They would eat the head. So it was that we boiled the head and ate the meat and the brains.

You eat everything. You eat all the meat off the bone until the bone is white. You must waste no part of the one you have killed. The Holy People themselves have warned us. If you waste their gift, they will not send you another.

When all was finished, we took the head and bones back to the forest. We laid them out in the holy way beside a juniper tree and blessed them with pollen. We said the prayers to Black God and Talking God, asking for another gift. That was the end of the ceremony that began in the sweathouse.

My brother and I did not hunt again that winter. But even when the game was very scarce, we always found one. Maybe it was because we did all the things we were told to do. We kept things holy. We spoke only the language that was used a long time ago. We followed the words that were spoken by the Holy People. We followed those. We used only those things. Maybe that is why we have always come home singing.

*Note: Tł'ááshchí'í Sání* told his hunting story to Frank Harvey of Lukachukai on January 29, 1980. Even though he told the story in the winter, he said that students could hear it at any time of year.

# BIGHORN SHEEP

Dibé Nitsaa, *Big Sheep Mountain, marks the northern edge of Navajo Country. For the last two hundred years and more, this mountain has guarded a land of Navajo sheep and Navajo shepherds.*

*But* Dibé Nitsaa *was not at first a shepherd's mountain. It got its name far far back in time from a different kind of sheep.* Dibé Nitsaa *is the mountain of the wild bighorn sheep, the* Tsétah Dibé, *the Sheep-Among-the-Rocks.*

*There was a time when wild bighorn sheep roamed all over Navajo Country. The Anasazi drew their pictures on rocks and caves and left behind white bones of sheep they had killed with spears. Stories from the Night Chant told by Navajo elders say that one of the Holy People,* Gháá'ask'idii, *is in charge of the bighorn sheep, and that they follow him wherever he goes.*

*But the Sheep-Among-the-Rocks are gone from Navajo Country. Few Navajos alive today have ever seen a bighorn sheep on Navajo land.*

*These inscriptions may be seen at Tsé Bik'i Na'astséli, a rock wall northwest of Rock Point, Arizona.*

- *Why did they go?*
- *What does a wild sheep or any other wild animal need to live?*
- *Will they ever come back?*

On the far western edge of the Navajo Reservation, the Colorado River and its smaller cousin, the Little Colorado, begin cutting the deep canyons that join to make Grand Canyon. You can go west across the Painted Desert and never guess that the rivers are there at all, until the trail stops at the edge of a crack in the earth so deep that the bottom looks blue like distant mountains. It seems as if the land just broke there by accident like pottery, and you can't believe that your trail doesn't keep going on the other side.

A thousand feet below is a rocky world quite different from the world on top. It is thought to be the last possible hiding place for bighorn sheep in Navajo land.

In the winter of 1979 at least one young ram did live in the canyon of the Little Colorado. He roamed the rocks and coves from Blue Water Spring down to the salt spring on the Colorado near the place where the two rivers join.

During lambing season, wild rams leave their ewes and wander to different ranges in separate herds, but the young ones almost never go alone. Now there were no others, no old and wise sheep leading his herd of bachelors. All alone in the dark days of February, when the sun almost never shone in the bottom of the canyon, this last young ram dreamed of better times.

He was dreaming in this way when an evil wind carried the real smell of real sheep to his wild nose. He followed the smell easily, because he stood at the foot of the "Salt Trail," one of the only places where walking creatures can enter or leave the main canyon of the Little Colorado. For centuries people have come that way to gather sacred salt from the salt spring further down. The ram climbed easily to the bright land above and ran on toward the smell of other sheep and into a world where he usually would never go.

☆  ☆  ☆

Hoskie Tso[1] had brought his sheep back to the corral early that day because of the cold. He was inside his hogan heating up coffee when he heard a rattling and banging from the corral. He ran outside. There was the wild bighorn ram stamping and snorting and butting the corral fence.

Hoskie couldn't believe his eyes. He set down his coffee cup and stamped and shouted a little bit himself, but the ram did not go away.

Hoskie looked carefully at the low winter sun. Did he have time to drive back to Tuba City and get a gun before dark? Heck, why not try? An hour later Hoskie's pickup roared into Tuba City where some relatives lived in a trailer home. In minutes he and his cousin were back on the highway with a deer rifle on the gun rack.

☆  ☆  ☆

The young ram could not figure out what to do about the strange herd he had found in the corral. To him they smelled like sheep and even looked a little like sheep. There was even a ram among them, but he was small and weak. But worst of all this new herd seemed to be caught and could not follow him back to the canyon.

For a long time he roamed around the corral, stamping and butting. Sometimes he ran a little way back to the canyon, hoping that the others would follow, but they did not.

Hours passed, and the purple winter twilight swallowed up the canyon and the hogan, the corral and the low hills that ran east to the Painted Desert. All was quiet . . . but not quite. In the distance a pickup rattled and roared over the dusty road.

The wild sheep stood like a rock and listened. The fire of headlights grew in his eyes. For a moment the world at last was silent. The rifle cracked then, and broke the wild ram's heart forever. His dreams ran out with his blood and made the sand by the corral black in the twilight.

☆  ☆  ☆

1. Although the story is true, this person's name has been changed.

47

"Good shot, man!" said Hoskie. "Look at those horns."

"I'd like to keep them," said his cousin.

"No way, man! I found this boy. I'm keeping the horns."

Hoskie's cousin dropped the rifle on the seat of the pickup. "Cool down," he said. "Let's just split them."

So the two cousins butchered the sheep and smashed his skull with an axe so each could take one of the great curved horns.

Days passed after that, and Hoskie bragged about his adventure over his CB. The news of the wild ram's death traveled all over the reservation.

Even in places like Kayenta where there is no wildlife at all and coal miners from Black Mesa live side by side in their trailers, people argued about the wild sheep.

Some said, "I sure wish I had some horns like that!"

Others were angry. "Why do people want to kill everything that is rare and beautiful!" they said. "That guy didn't need the mutton."

So the news ran here and there until at last it came to the Navajo Tribe's Department of Fish and Wildlife. The people in this department are hired by the Tribal Council to protect wildlife on the reservation. Long before hearing about the ram from the Little Colorado, they had been looking for places where wild sheep might be able to survive again on the reservation.

Nearly thirty years had passed since anyone had reported a wild sheep. Ken Foster, a Navajo ranger from Sheep Springs, had seen it. "There used to be a small herd that roamed the Carrizo Mountains," he said. I used to see them there in those black rock canyons. Then, one by one they all disappeared. The last one was around for quite a while, but I guess somebody finally got him too. I might have been one of the last people to see him, but that was back about 1950."

Mike Walker, a wildlife biologist who had followed a herd of bighorns for two years in southwestern Arizona, thought the north side of Navajo Mountain looked good for sheep. Few people ever went there, and wild sheep had been seen across the river to the north.

The Fish and Wildlife Department hired a helicopter to fly over that area to check for signs of wild sheep and look for plants that sheep eat.

After a morning of flying back and forth over the rocky slopes of Navajo Mountain, the helicopter flew on to Page for gas. As he took off his flight suit, Mike shook his head and spit tobacco on the runway. "It's good sheep country all right," he said. "But there's nothing up there but burros and goats that people have let go wild. There won't be any room for bighorns."

So people in the Fish and Wildlife Department were both happy and sad to hear about the ram from the canyon. Navajo rangers set off to find Hoskie Tso, even though they knew his relatives would try to hide him. Mike Walker went to the Little Colorado to look for more sheep.

The rangers tracked Hoskie to the trailer home in Tuba City. He knew he had broken a tribal law, and the officers' badges at the door scared him. The rangers made him tell his story, but they did not arrest him. The sheep was dead forever, and punishing Hoskie would not bring him back. They wanted Hoskie to understand how sad it was that he might have killed the last wild Navajo sheep. They talked to him a long time about how in the old days people respected wildlife and didn't kill it off without reason. Hoskie and his relatives agreed that a terrible thing had happened, and the rangers left, hoping they would never have to come back with handcuffs.

No more sheep were found that year in the Little Colorado Canyon, although Mike Walker went there on foot and by helicopter. "It's first-rate sheep country, though," he said. "Plenty of food, plenty of rocks and cliffs where a sheep can escape its enemies, and no burros or goats. There could be a small herd there again. Sometimes I dream about it. Sometimes I hope it never happens. Why have such beautiful animals in a place where people might just gun them down for the hell of it?"

# WILD PLACES AND WILD LIFE

Just as herder and medicine man know where to find plants they need, the hunter knows where to look for the deer. The ranger knows where wild sheep can live.

By knowledge of how animals choose their homes and use the land, the ranger can protect wildlife. By that knowledge the hunter fed his family through a hungry winter.

The area where an animal, or a person, makes its home is its *habitat*, which means "living place". A mouse's habitat may reach only ten yards from its hole. The grassland habitat of an antelope may cover miles.

Animals, like plants, are *specialized* for life in different habitats. Pinon-juniper country and mountain forest are the deer's habitat. His favorite food grows there. His color hides him there. Bighorns are *specialized* to live among rocks were a deer cannot. Steppe-colored antelope eat steppe plants that would kill deer and have speed to escape across plains without hiding places.

Habitats, like plant communities, are *limited*. Plants in one habitat can feed a certain number of animals and no more. If bad weather cuts the food supply, some must leave or starve or have fewer babies. It is the same for people. No work at home means looking for jobs elsewhere.

Each animal in a habitat must have a "job", a place in the Circle of Life. This is called its *niche*. Often an animal's niche depends on the food it eats. There are grass-eaters (grazers), bush-eaters (browsers), meat-eaters (hunters), eaters of dead things (scavengers), etc. All are *interdependent* and necessary for the Circle of Life.

In the story of the bighorn, the goats and donkeys north of Navajo Mountain angered the ranger because they filled the *big*-horn's *niche*. They eat the same food and climb nearly as well. Wild sheep are too shy to push them out of that habitat.

The picture on this page shows three habitats and some of the animals in them.

Cliff

Steppe

High Country Forest

51

# PEOPLE AND ANIMALS

Our hunter in his mountain cabin has not forgotten the lesson that all hunters once knew. "Respect the game or starve." He sees clearly that he and the deer are part of the same Circle of Life.

"You will live in a land that is hard and flat like a rock, a desert area, a place where life is hard," he warns those who do not follow the old wisdom. But such warnings did not save the last bighorn from a careless shot.

And bighorns are not the only wild animals that are now gone or almost gone from Navajo Country. In the last 150 years many animals that once lived everywhere have nearly disappeared. Even the deer are in danger.

In the old days, before there were hunting laws and rangers, the hunter's wisdom protected the wildlife. It was not wasted. Trouble began when hunters began killing without understanding or reason.

By 1950 Navajo deer were almost completely wiped out, and a medicine man from Lukachukai named Dinetsosie asked the Tribal Council to do something. That spring the Council passed the first hunting laws and hired rangers to enforce them. Deer were brought from Colorado to restock the reservation.

On the Chuska and Carrizo Mountains and the Defiance Plateau, these deer survived, because the rangers protected them. On the Shonto Plateau, where regulations were not enforced, they were quickly killed off.

By 1980 the deer everywhere were in trouble again. More people had moved into their mountain habitat. More people shot them carelessly, and more livestock left less food for the fawns born each spring.

Here are some of the animals that are gone or nearly gone from the reservation. Is our land richer or poorer without them?

**DESERT BIGHORN SHEEP**
*Tsétah Dibé*

**WOLF**
*Ma'iitsoh*

**GRIZZLY BEAR**
*Shashtsoh; Shash Na'ałkaahii*

**ELK**
*Dzééh*

**BLACK-FOOTED FERRET**
*Dlǫ́'ii*

**PRONGHORN ANTELOPE**
*Jádí*

53

# ANIMALS AND PEOPLE

Hunting is not the only way people change the lives of wild animals. People raise livestock and have dogs. People build roads and fences, cut down trees, and drill wells. People can change their habitat in many ways.

But a very specialized animal like the bighorn sheep cannot change its way of life when people change its habitat. The picture here shows what happens to wild sheep when people and their livestock move into their habitat. It's bad for bighorns.

But there is another animal in the picture who is not sorry, the coyote. According to the old stories he has sacred power. He can survive almost any disaster and does not suffer much from people. In fact we often make his life better, even when we don't mean to.

This raises many questions. Do we think about wild animals when we make our own homes? How are we ourselves different from these animals? When our lives are changed (when our habitat is changed), do some of us survive better than others? And why?

- Noises and smells of people scare bighorns.
- Goats in the cliff habitat fill the niche bighorns would use.
- A windmill allows stock to live where otherwise only wild sheep might survive.
- Camp dogs usually do some hunting on the side.
- Grazing livestock often change the plant life over a wide area.
- Dumps often contain poisonous trash.
- Highways and fences scare bighorns and keep them from moving to water, lambing areas, winter shelter, and new grazing areas.

# THE HUNTER TRADITION

The knowledge of the hunter goes back to the edge of human understanding. He came long before the farmer, and the oldest signs of people in Navajo Country are his weapons that once killed giant animals.

The monsters of Navajo legend were not unlike the mammoths, bison and cats that once roamed where sheep now graze. There were also wild horses, camels and sloths, and hunters followed them all. Spearheads like the most ancient ones seen in Navajo Country have been found with their bones.

What destroyed the giants of the past? Weather and plant life have changed some, but that does not explain everything.

Why did horses disappear 8,000 years ago? When Spaniards brought them back centuries later, they survived easily. Camels also disappeared but survive in other parts of the world and happily ate the plants of Navajo Country when the U.S. Army sent a camel train through it in 1857.

Some blame the ancient hunters. Did they kill off these animals or somehow break the circle of life that kept them alive? Who were the hunters? Were they ancestors of today's people, or a tribe that disappeared?

The answers lie buried forever, but every time a hunter takes aim at wild game, he writes another line in a story tens of thousands of years old.

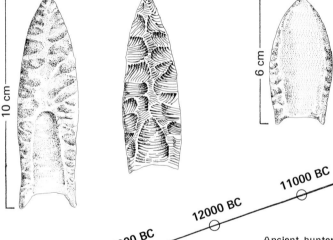

10 cm

6 cm

Clovis and Folsom points made

9000 BC

10000 BC

11000 BC

12000 BC

13000 BC

14000 BC

15000 BC

16000 BC

17000 BC

18000 BC

Animal bones and bone tools 30,000 years old have been found in Alaska, and new findings may prove that people hunted in the Americas 20,000 years or more before that. Alaska and Siberia were connected then. Did people cross that way from Asia? Who? Were there other paths? Did anyone cross the other way?

Between 40,000 years ago and 10,000 years ago ice covered most of Canada. Alaska itself stayed ice-free. A strip of land down the east side of the Rocky Mountains only froze for 3,000 years about 21,000 years ago, so that people could have traveled between continents easily. Navajo Country was probably wetter and cooler than it is now and rich in wildlife.

Ancient hunters made spear points in a special way—hollowed out where they fit into the spear. The two at the left are "Clovis" points, first seen among mammoth, camel and horse bones near Clovis, N.M. The one on the right is a "Folsom" point, first seen among giant bison bones near Folsom, N.M. Folsom and Clovis points, 10-12,000 years old, have been found in Navajo Country near Sanders, Tanner Springs, Kayenta and the Hopi town of Mishongnovi.

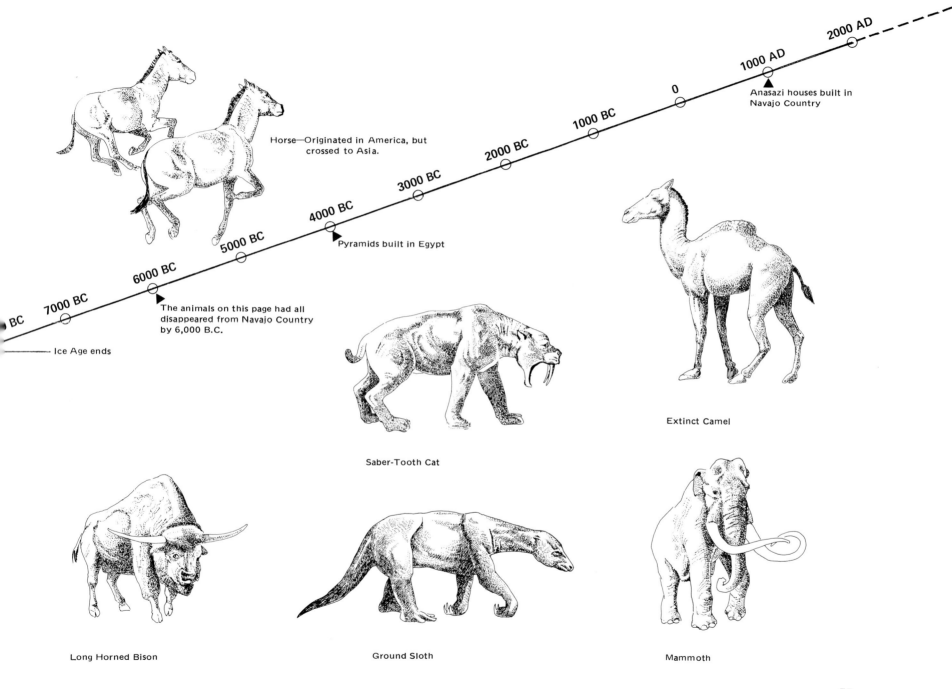

2000 AD

1000 AD

0

Anasazi houses built in Navajo Country

1000 BC

2000 BC

3000 BC

4000 BC

Horse—Originated in America, but crossed to Asia.

5000 BC

6000 BC

7000 BC

Pyramids built in Egypt

The animals on this page had all disappeared from Navajo Country by 6,000 B.C.

BC

Ice Age ends

Extinct Camel

Saber-Tooth Cat

Long Horned Bison

Ground Sloth

Mammoth

57

# ANASAZI

# ANASAZI

*Yes, there was a people who became the Anasazi, the Ancient Tribe. But now you only see the ruins of their homes. Over there, where the sand is, the broken pieces still lie. Against those rocks too. They were there. So it is everywhere, even far up into Utah. Wherever you go, the broken pots and stones and signs of the Anasazi are there before you. You can see that their numbers became large and crowded—like the Navajos are becoming crowded today.*

*What took them? Maybe the holy ones they lived by. Nothing survives alone. It is the same for sheep and horses. There is no rain, so they die away. The Anasazi were taken and afterwards we Navajos came.*

—Hashk'aan Ts'ósí

Since the beginning of time many people have crossed Navajo Country, gathered the plants, hunted the game, and farmed the soil. The land still keeps the ruins of their ancient houses and villages. We see these things and wonder, "What did these people of the past live by? How did they become so many? Why did they leave? Did they leave behind a lesson for us?"

They are remembered as the Anasazi, which is really the Navajo word *Anaasází*, the Ancient Tribe. We know them from pictures scratched on canyon walls, from ruined houses, pots, and jewels that the land has kept down to our own times.

From the ruined houses and broken pots, many people have tried to understand who the Anasazi were and how they lived. Books have been written about them, and museums display their crafts and their clothes. But these do not tell all of Anasazi history.

Navajo tradition has many stories that describe things that happened when the ancient ruins were living towns. Stories living people tell about their lives can be handed down from parent to child and so last through generations. They may change in the telling, but no more than the pot that broke, the string of beads that scattered, the old trail that filled with sand. Such stories may tell something of how the ancient tribe lived and passed on, and they hold many lessons for everyone who has followed the Anasazi into this land.

The story here is a small piece of a legend that would take several long winter nights of telling and fill several chapters this size. Many details and side stories are known only by certain people, and the story itself has different forms. The part here tells only enough to show how history lives on in our land and our traditions. It is up to the reader to find out more.

It all happened in Chaco Canyon, which cuts a dry mesa halfway between Mount Taylor and Shiprock: A thousand years ago Anasazi built apartment houses there as large as any in the world at that time. Their ruined walls still show their greatness. Some say the hero of the story was a Navajo. Others say he was Anasazi himself and that the people from Chaco Canyon later joined the Navajos. The truth could be either or neither.

62

## THE GREAT GAMBLER

Giants and monsters still roamed the country when the people first built their homes. Because of this, they moved from place to place building houses that can still be seen. From time to time they heard of other lands of little snow and plenty of wild seeds for food. For this reason, too, they kept moving on. Always some stayed behind, but at last a great number of them and their chief came to Chaco Canyon, to a place called *Tsé Bíyah Anii'áhí* (Braced Up Rock).[1] There they built a house and lived well. They planted crops and gathered the wild seeds that grew richly everywhere.

It is said that these people brought with them a great wealth of turquoise and shell beads and beautiful goods that they held sacred. And first among all these things was a great round turquoise, as tall as a man, with twelve bright feathers around it.

According to their traditions, the chief of these people never stepped out into the sun. And so it was that the Sun became jealous of this chief that he had never seen and wanted the beads and the great turquoise for himself.

Near the house of the chief lived a poor woman named *Asdzą́ą́ Tł'ohdeii* because she lived from the seeds of *tł'ohdeii* (goosefoot). She was of the *Hadahoniye'* Clan[2] which does not exist today. The Sun visited this woman secretly, and she bore him a son.

The mother taught her boy to run great distances, and he grew handsome and tall. However, because his mother was poor and his father was unknown, people laughed and made fun of him. Thus, he was sad and felt very sorry for himself. He should not have worried. One day his father lowered the rainbow to earth and raised the young man up to his home.

Now the Sun wanted all the beads and riches of the people, together with their chief whom he had never seen. For this he had a great plan.

First he gave his son two turquoise earrings as clear and perfect as the sky itself. Then he taught the young man all the gambling songs and chants, and also a chant for pulling people to himself.

Eight games, the Sun taught his boy. He also gave him the dice sticks, rings and other things he would need to win them.

When the young man came back at last to Chaco Canyon, he at once started to gamble. For a time people tried to buy his turquoise earrings, but he would always say, "If you win them, you can have them." When he chanted, the people came to him and gambled their wealth. Soon he was known everywhere as *Náhwíiłbįįhí*, the Great Gambler, the Winner, or *Náhwíiłbįįhí Dine'é*, the Winner of Men.

He won everything. He even won the children and women and men for his slaves. They worked for him building the great houses that can still be seen in Chaco Canyon. He won the Male Rain, the Female Rain, the Rainbow, the rivers, the mountains and all the earth. The rest of the land went dry for it only rained where he lived. He had good corn and beautiful flowers. He even won the wife of the chief and the chief himself together with his prayer sticks and beads.

Last of all the Gambler played for the great round turquoise as high as a man, and this, too, he won from the people. Then the Sun came down and said, "My son, this I want. You may have the rest, but the great turquoise is mine." The Gambler, however, had become very sure of his power. He only smiled slyly at his father the Sun and said, "Now I will gamble with you!!"

The Sun did not answer but went angrily back to his home. There he again made plans to get the great turquoise of the people. On the mesa near where Farmington is today lived another woman of the *Hadahoniye'* Clan. Now the Sun visited her, and soon she also had a son. This boy grew as strong and tall as the first and at last went to his father's home. There he, too, learned the eight games, and his sister shaped him into the exact twin of the Gambler.

The Gambler, however, had become so powerful that he could not be beaten without help. "Make me an offering," the Sun told the second young man, "a white shell basket filled with chips of precious stones. Offer it with a prayer." Next he told the young man the offerings he must make to the Wind Spirit (Nílch'i), and the different animals he would need to help him.

The young man gave a buffalo robe to Bat, which Bat still wears. To Big Snake he gave a red stone. Measuring Worm got a piece of black jet. Rat's gift was white shell. For mixed chips of stones the Wind Spirit would help him see the Gambler's mind. Woodpecker joined the plan for a red stone that he also still wears. Dark Wind and Cut Worm were also asked to help.

The young man was to have two beautiful girls to bet against the Gambler. They would be the daughters of Haashch'éélti'í (First Talking God) and Haashch'ééhoghan (Second Talking God). The two Holy People let their daughters be part of the Sun's plan, but only for a short time.

Now everything was ready. They dressed the young man exactly like the Gambler from feet to head and set out for the Gambler's house. On their way they met Mountain Rat. "Why have you kept this secret from me?" he asked. So they gave him white beads to please him. Just then Owl hooted ahead of them. He also was angry because he had no part in the plan. To Owl also they gave beads, and to this day gamblers put beads in the nests of rats and owls to bring luck in their games.

On they went with a large crowd of people. Dark Wind went ahead to blind the Gambler's spies with a dust storm. Bat also went ahead to hide in the roof beams of the house where the first game would be played.

Before meeting the Gambler face to face, the young man wanted to "split his mind," to make him feel weaker and unsure of himself. So the young man hid himself by the well where the Gambler's wife came for water. She of course thought he was her husband, because the two men looked exactly alike, but when she returned home, the Gambler heard her story and at once became jealous and angry. "Who is this person?" he thought.

"I will have to win him too for a slave." But from that time on, he was worried and afraid.

Dark Wind now blew up a terrible dust storm so that the Gambler and his spies saw nothing until the young man and the people crowded around their door. The Gambler's wife smiled when she saw the young man, and again jealous thoughts worried the Gambler. But before he could speak, the young man stepped up to him and said, "Brother, I come for the great turquoise."

The Gambler slowly stood up and looked around him at the young man and the crowd of people. "Spies!" he said, "Why did you not warn me that these people were coming?" But the spies had seen nothing because of the dust.

## THE FIRST GAME

Then he turned to the young man. "So you wish to gamble!" said he, and he brought out his basket of dice sticks and shook it. "First we will bet our wives." He said this because he had seen the beautiful daughters of the two Holy People.

The stick dice game uses seven sticks that can fall either white side up or black side up. The Gambler, however, had sticks that were white on both sides.

"Throw your sticks high up to the roof," said the young man, "and we will watch the ground to see how they fall."

The Gambler then shook his basket and said, "Mine is white. Mine is white," and threw them to the roof beams. Bat, however, caught the Gambler's white sticks and threw down the young man's seven black ones.

The Gambler cursed. "This time mine is black. Mine is black," he said, and threw them again. But Bat caught the black sticks and threw down the white ones. "Ha! You lost with your own sticks," said the young man. For the first time the Gambler began to fear, but he doubled his bets and asked for the hoop and pole game.

## THE SECOND GAME

In the hoop and pole game, called na'azhǫǫsh, the players roll a ring down a track and race after it. As the ring stops rolling each player throws a stick and tries to make the ring fall on his stick. "We used your dice," said the young man. "Now we will use my ring."

The Gambler picked up his stick and began to exercise his arms and legs. He chanted in a whisper:

> *I walk among the beautiful goods,*
> *The white bead stick in my hand.*
> *It is tied with white bead string.*

> *I walk among the beautiful goods,*
> *The white bead stick in my hand.*
> *The white bead ring is on my stick*
>
> *Today luck is on my side.*

The two men stood at the end of the track. The young man threw the ring and the race was on. The Gambler ran ahead and threw his stick first. Then the young man threw his stick. As all the people watched, the ring rolled over the Gambler's stick and fell on the young man's. Why? Because Big Snake was inside the ring holding his tail in his mouth.

Again the Gambler cursed and tried to grab the ring. But the young man grabbed it first to save the snake. "Oh no you don't!" said he. "The people you beat did not take your ring."

## THE THIRD GAME

The young man bet all that he had and all that he had won. The Gambler bet an equal amount and brought out his rainbow-shaped stick for the third game. "No," said the young man. "I won the last game, so we will use my stick."

When thrown into the air, the rainbow shaped stick would land points down, then fall to one side or the other, the way a coin will fall heads or tails. High in the air went the young man's stick, but Measuring Worm was in the stick and he would not let it fall on the Gambler's side.

By now the Gambler was soaked with sweat. He had lost three times, but once more he bet for all that the young man had.

## THE FOURTH GAME

Next came the ball game. To win, the young man had to hit a ball through the door of a house. He made a great show of exercising his muscles and chanting. "Ball, don't miss. Go straight through the hole." The Gambler sat to one side chanting, "Miss the hole. Miss the hole."

The young man swung his club with mighty force, but he was careful to hit the ground just behind the ball, because Rat was inside the ball. Rat, of course, bounced straight for the open door, and the Gambler lost for the fourth time.

## THE FIFTH GAME

By now the young man had won a great deal, but the Gambler still had enough to match his bets. They now began the guessing game. For this the Gambler drew a picture of one of the sacred beings he had won.

"Now my friend," said the Gambler with an evil smile. "Tell me the meaning of my drawing."

The young man waited a second until the Wind Spirit that knows and sees everything whispered in his ear. "That," he said, "is Water Boy who guards the water jars. He has four beautiful flowers in each hand."

"Yes," said the Gambler, "but do you know the rest? And one by one he pointed to the water jars by the picture of Water Boy.

One by one the young man named them. "Beside Water Boy stand eight jars. The first four hold the male rain—Black, Blue, Yellow and White. The next four hold the mists and the female rain—black, blue, yellow and white."

"Oh, my friend, you are better than most. Is that all?" said the Gambler, still smiling in his evil way.

The young man waited for the Wind Spirit to whisper. "No," he said at last. "The eighth jar holds more than the white female rain. It has the flowers and their pollen as well."

When he heard that, the Gambler's smile disappeared and drops of sweat broke out all over his body. "And the last great jar?" he asked, pointing to the last circle of his picture. This last jar held all his magic. He shook with fear as the young man opened his mouth to answer.

"That jar holds . . . ," began the young man. But he didn't finish, for at that moment the white bird that guarded the Gambler's magic flew up from the jar. "Well, my brother," said the young man. "You are the loser,"

The Gambler hung down his head. He no longer looked so fresh and proud. His hands shook and his breath caught in his throat.

## THE SIXTH GAME

Again the bets were twice as large as before. To win, the young man had to kick a stick to three different marks on the ground and then over the great house itself. This he did with no trouble at all, because Woodpecker was in his stick. "I lose. I lose," sobbed the Gambler, but once again he doubled his bets, because he still hoped to win.

## THE SEVENTH GAME

In the seventh game two sticks were planted in the ground. The men raced and grabbed the one they thought was planted loosely. The other one could not be pulled up. The Gambler of course knew which stick to choose and laughed to himself when the young man ran for the wrong stick. However, the young man pulled the stick easily from the ground because Cut Worm had cut it free. When the Gambler tried the other stick, it threw him back. Dark Wind had caused roots to grow on it, and it could not be moved. "Give up," said the young man. "You can pull all day, and you will still be the loser."

## THE EIGHTH GAME

This was the last bet. The two men bet everything, the Rain, the Holy Beings, the Sacred Turquoise which the Gambler had won. When the bets were made the Gambler spoke: "Now we will race. If I lose again, my life goes also. Kill me. If I win, I will kill you."

They raced to a hill where a ruin now stands, circled it and headed back to the start. Four times the Gambler went ahead, but when the young man passed him once more, the Wind Spirit whispered in his ear, "Jump high, he's going to shoot."

The arrow passed below him, and the young man picked it up. "He shoots high. Lay flat," said the Wind Spirit. The arrow passed over him, and the young man picked it up.

"Duck!" said the Spirit. "He'll hit your heart." Again the arrow missed, and the young man picked it up.

"Your head!" warned the Spirit. "Hit the dirt." And so the young man picked up a fourth arrow.

"Now," said the Spirit, "he is out of arrows. Let him pass and do the same to him." Four times the young man shot, hitting the Gambler in the leg, the back, the shoulders and the head. "Now pass him," said the Spirit, "but don't let him touch you or he will become strong again."

At the finish line there was a little hill. The young man ran up on the winner's side. The people cheered and blew their flutes. The young man waited, the sweat and dust shining on his body, until the Gambler came up. "My friend," he said, "You are the loser."

"I lose everything," said the Gambler, "even my life. Kill me while I am still warm." He brought a stone club from his house, gave it to the young man and threw himself on the ground broken hearted.

The young man raised his arm to strike the Gambler dead, but at that moment the Sun spoke. "Don't kill him," said the Sun. "He, also, is my son, and he has nothing left on earth but his life."

The Sun threw down the Dark Bow, and told the young man to put the Gambler on the string. In this way the Gambler was shot up into the sky. As he rose out of sight he called back twice, "Long ago I died in the center of the earth. My spirit will return." A third time he spoke, but the sound was almost lost in space.

The games were finished. Turning to the Sun, the young man said, "Father, the Sacred Turquoise is yours. There it is."

"I thank you," said the Sun. "I thank you." Then he turned to *Haashch'ééhoghan* and said, "Let us send our children to *Dził Ná'oodiłii* (Huerfano Mountain). They shall go above the eight rings of the mountain where there is a house. That mountain is the earth's heart, and it can be their home forever." So the young man took the girl for his wife and made plans to go.

But before he left, he went into the Gambler's great house and pointed to the jars in the picture on the wall. He ordered them to go back to all parts of the world. "From you the people of the earth will have rain, clouds and mist."

As he left the house, he found the people who had been the Gambler's slaves. They were weeping, because they did not know what would happen to them. "Be cheerful," he told them. "I am a different kind of person than the Gambler was. You may go back to your own countries or wherever you wish."

"These are the kindest words we have heard in a long time," they said. That day all the people moved away from Chaco Canyon to whatever places they had chosen for their homes. Some went back where they came from. Others said, "We have always dreamed of a new country. We know of one. We will go there."

And as to the Gambler. Some say that his last word was "Adios" and that he returned as a Spaniard. They say the moon took pity on him and gave him livestock of all kinds, great riches and a new people to govern. From him, they say, the Spaniards increased and in time some of them came up from Mexico and built towns along the Rio Grande.

[1]Navajos use the name *Tsé Bíyah Anii'áh í* for Pueblo Bonito and often for Chaco Canyon itself. It means "Braced Up Rock." For centuries a large piece of the cliff behind Pueblo Bonito threatened to fall over. The Anasazi built walls to brace it up. It fell on January 22, 1941 and smashed 30 rooms of the ruin below.
[2]*Hadahoniye'* is usually translated "mirage stone." It is a thin, polished white rock shaped like a cucumber. It has bands around it like the layers of mist that make a mirage. The Anasazi had many of these stones and today Navajos use them also in ceremonies.

Many different versions of the story of *Náhwiiłbįįhí* have been told by medicine men, and several were written down nearly 100 years ago. These written versions were collected by Aileen O'Bryan and retold as "The Story of Noqoilpi, the Great Gambler," in *The Diné: Origin Myths of the Navajo Indians*, pp. 48–63.

# ANASAZI: A People Who Changed

The old houses and other signs of the Anasazi show that they did not always live in the same way. The story of the Gambler says that at first they moved from place to place, building houses and looking for wild seeds. Then they stopped moving, planted crops, and built large houses. In the time of the Gambler himself, people from far and wide became his slaves and worked for him. When he lost, they scattered and left their great houses.

Things left by the Anasazi show that changes like these really happened. The first Anasazi did not have bows and arrows. They did not plant crops, build long-lasting houses, or live in towns. But in time they began to do these things.

Most of the changes in Anasazi life happened in less than 800 years--a very short time in world history. Few people have ever changed so fast until modern times.

People change for many reasons. They may invent new ways to use the land and protect themselves from weather. They may be guided by religion. They may learn from their neighbors or even from distant peoples.

As people change their way of life, however, they may change their niche in the habitat around them and even change the habitat itself.

This happened as the Anasazi changed. It happened as the Navajos followed them. And it happens today.

## The Beginning

The earliest signs of Anasazi show that they needed little to live (a small niche). They knew about corn and squash, but wild plants and animals were their main food. They hunted with traps, clubs and spears which they threw with a stick.

They moved often and did not crowd the land. They did not cut big trees or break stones to build houses. Only their rock-lined storage pits can be found in caves. They wove baskets and moccasins from yucca and other plants. They made no pottery.

Archaeologists have divided Anasazi history into sections. This first part is called "Early Basketmaker" or "Basketmaker I & II". It begins about 1 A.D.

## The First Steps

After a few hundred years, the Anasazi learned new ways to use the land (a larger niche). This part of their history lasted from about 450 to 700 A.D. It is called "Modified Basketmaker" or "Basketmaker III".

With better corn seed and a new crop, beans, they planted bigger fields and grew more food with less work. They made pottery and boiled food (like beans) that they couldn't have cooked easily before.

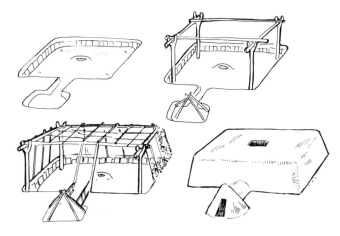

They built "pit houses" dug partly into the ground. With more ways to get more food from the same land with less work, they stopped moving and began living in pit house villages.

Bows and arrows made hunting easier.

## The Builders Come

In time pit house villagers tried building in new ways. House walls of poles, brush and mud were put straight up and down so two rooms could fit together. Later they used rock laid in rows. These and other ideas give this part of Anasazi history the name "Developmental Pueblo", which some divide into "Pueblo I & II".

They planted cotton and wove it on looms like those used by Navajos today. They started using hard cradle boards that flattened the backs of their heads.

They built row houses, first partly underground, then above ground. A pit house often stood in front of the row house, just as a hogan often stands by Navajo houses now. In time it was changed into the ceremonial "kiva" still found in modern pueblos.

They raised tame turkeys. They made fine black and white pottery and rough, gray cook pots.

71

## The Great Pueblos

The Anasazi population grew quickly. In places like the Chinle Valley they built villages everywhere they could. This began about 950 A.D. This part of Anasazi history is usually called "Great Pueblo" or "Pueblo III". By 1200 there were more Anasazi people and towns than there ever would be again.

In time, many houses were built high in caves. Did people fear enemies? Maybe, but other towns were still built on level ground, and some Anasazi still built pit houses.

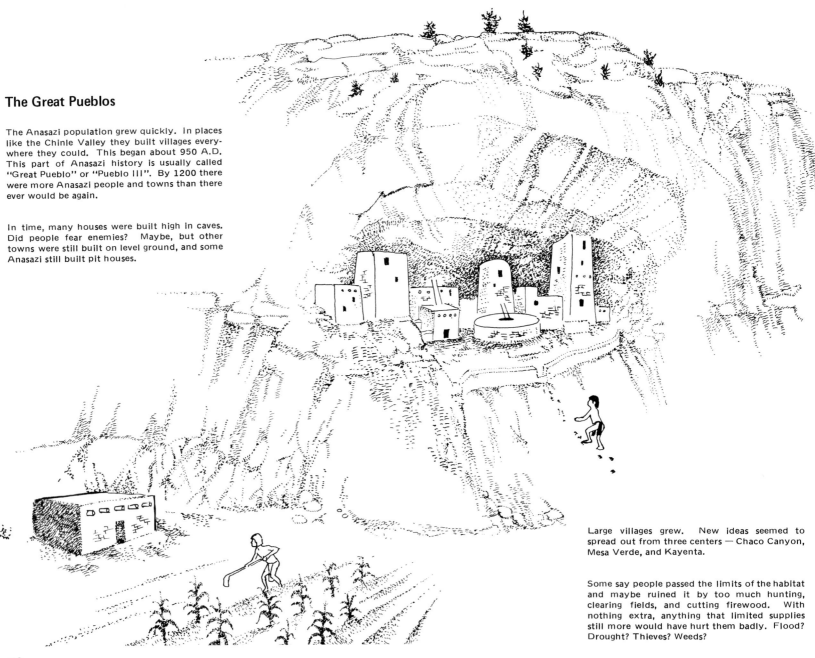

Large villages grew. New ideas seemed to spread out from three centers — Chaco Canyon, Mesa Verde, and Kayenta.

Some say people passed the limits of the habitat and maybe ruined it by too much hunting, clearing fields, and cutting firewood. With nothing extra, anything that limited supplies still more would have hurt them badly. Flood? Drought? Thieves? Weeds?

## The Empty Land

For some reason, most of the Anasazi left their land. Some built large towns again on the edges of their old territory — near the Hopi Mesas, Zuni, and the Rio Grande Valley. This time is usually called "Regressive Pueblo" or "Pueblo IV".

They left quickly. Although Chaco Canyon was nearly empty by the year 1200, most other Anasazi moved out in the 50 years between 1250 and 1300, leaving land they had known for over 1,000 years.

People and tribes mixed and changed as the Anasazi moved. Few of the new towns had the huge houses and fine stonework of the old ones. Pottery changed into many new styles, some finer and some rougher. Languages and clans no doubt changed as well. Yet Anasazi traditions still live among the many tribes of Navajo Country today, and stories of them are still told.

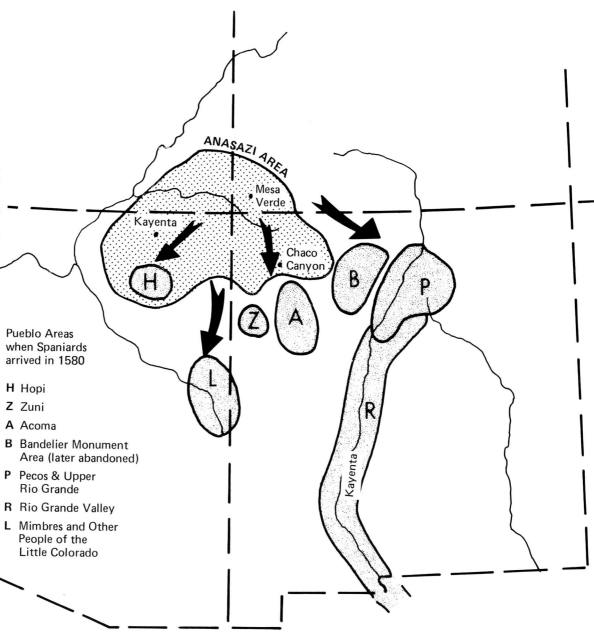

Pueblo Areas when Spaniards arrived in 1580

H  Hopi

Z  Zuni

A  Acoma

B  Bandelier Monument Area (later abandoned)

P  Pecos & Upper Rio Grande

R  Rio Grande Valley

L  Mimbres and Other People of the Little Colorado

73

# CHACO CANYON

The Great Gambler story says much about the riches of Chaco Canyon. It tells of "a great wealth of turquoise and shell beads and beautiful goods... and first among all these things a great round turquoise, as tall as a man, with twelve bright feathers around it."

The Gambler won all that and more. "He won everything. He even won the children and women and men for his slaves. They worked for him building the great houses that can still be seen in the canyon. He won the Male Rain, the Female Rain, the Rainbow, the rivers, the mountains and all the earth. The rest of the land went dry, for it rained only where he lived. He had good corn and beautiful flowers...."

Was the story true? Has anything been found in the canyon to prove it?

Maybe. At least no one can say that the story is not true, and many things have been found that show Chaco Canyon had a very different history than any other place where Anasazi people lived.

74

# THE GREAT HOUSES

Nothing like the stone houses of Chaco Canyon has ever been seen north of Mexico. The walls of Chaco houses are thicker and stronger than any others built by the Anasazi. The work of finding, carrying, cutting and stacking all that rock was enormous. Who did it? Rich people or poor? Slaves?

The builders used a forest of logs for the roofs of the houses. They cut huge trees to hold up the ceilings of the great kivas. Most of the wood came from the Chuska Mountains 75 miles away. Corkbark fir logs that grow only on the *tallest* mountains are found. Who cut them? Why?

Most Anasazi towns grew one room at a time. Most Chaco towns were planned first, then built quickly. Some, like Pueblo Bonito were built in several parts, and it is easy to see where the plans changed. What leaders (or what Gambler) made the plans and organized the workers?

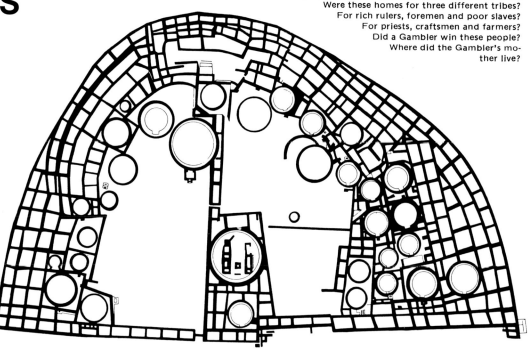

There are three kinds of house in Chaco Canyon. Were these homes for three different tribes? For rich rulers, foremen and poor slaves? For priests, craftsmen and farmers? Did a Gambler win these people? Where did the Gambler's mother live?

The drawing on the left shows a line of columns that were later filled to make a wall. At that time Mexicans built columns to hold up the roof over cool shady areas in front of houses. But Anasazis *never* built columns--except at Chaco. Who brought the column idea from Mexico? Who filled them in?

## Pueblo Bonito

The biggest houses like Pueblo Bonito are often "D", "E" or "O" shaped. The walls are of thin flat rocks. A wide plaza often has round "Great Kivas" in it.

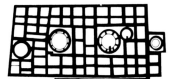

## Kin Kletso

Other large houses are built of thick, square blocks and have smaller rooms--like some houses north of the San Juan River. These people wanted no plazas or great kivas. They put small kivas in the middle of other rooms.

## Tse Tso House

Many small houses were built without any plan. The stonework is rough. They have small kivas both inside and outside the main house.

75

# TRADE

More people crowd into modern towns than the land nearby can possibly feed. Yet the towns grow bigger because the people buy, sell, and trade to fill their needs.

Anasazis, especially Chaco People, traded for the same reason. Ruts of ancient roads go out from the canyon in all directions. Pots, flint for tools, food, logs and jewels came from far away. Because of trade, the canyon was probably home to more people than it could feed by itself.

What was bought? What was paid? How did Chaco Canyon come to be so rich a place?

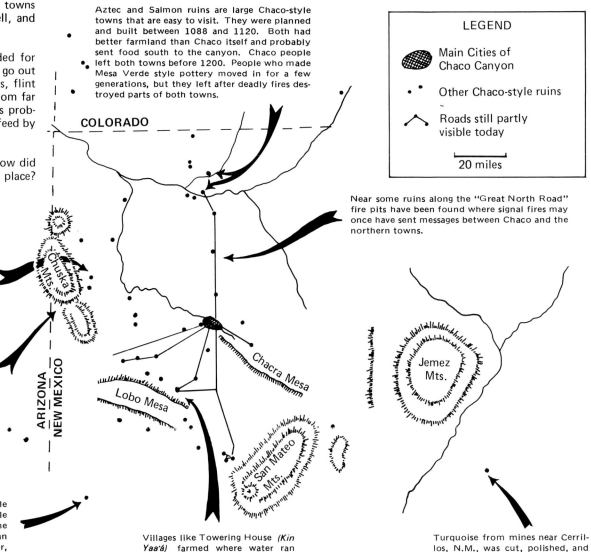

Aztec and Salmon ruins are large Chaco-style towns that are easy to visit. They were planned and built between 1088 and 1120. Both had better farmland than Chaco itself and probably sent food south to the canyon. Chaco people left both towns before 1200. People who made Mesa Verde style pottery moved in for a few generations, but they left after deadly fires destroyed parts of both towns.

COLORADO

LEGEND

Main Cities of Chaco Canyon

Other Chaco-style ruins

Roads still partly visible today

20 miles

Near some ruins along the "Great North Road" fire pits have been found where signal fires may once have sent messages between Chaco and the northern towns.

Most pottery found in Chaco Canyon in fact came from small villages below the Chuska Mountains.

Chuska Mts.

Red flint for arrows and tools came from Washington pass — Red Flint Pass in Navajo *(Béésh Lichíí' Bigiizh).*

ARIZONA
NEW MEXICO

Chacra Mesa

Lobo Mesa

San Mateo Mts.

Jemez Mts.

Far from Chaco Canyon itself, Chaco-style pottery and ways of building show that people had close contact with other Chaco towns. The "Village of the Great Kivas" near Zuni is an example. Further west and north, however, other Anasazi towns had different styles.

Villages like Towering House *(Kin Yaa'á)* farmed where water ran off Lobo Mesa onto the plain.

Turquoise from mines near Cerrillos, N.M., was cut, polished, and drilled by Chaco craftsmen.

## Turquoise, Shell Beads and Bright Feathers

The Gambler's story says the Chaco People had a wealth of turquoise, shell beads, and bright feathers. Indeed, shell from California, feathers from deep in Mexico and many thousands of turquoise beads have been found among the ruins of Chaco.

Did the turquoise pay for all the things that came across the roads to the Canyon? Even now in Navajo Country, sky-blue stones are loved more than gold or silver.

If Chaco people were the main turquoise traders of their time, is it surprising that they could build such fine towns?

The map shows how the Chaco traders might have done their business.

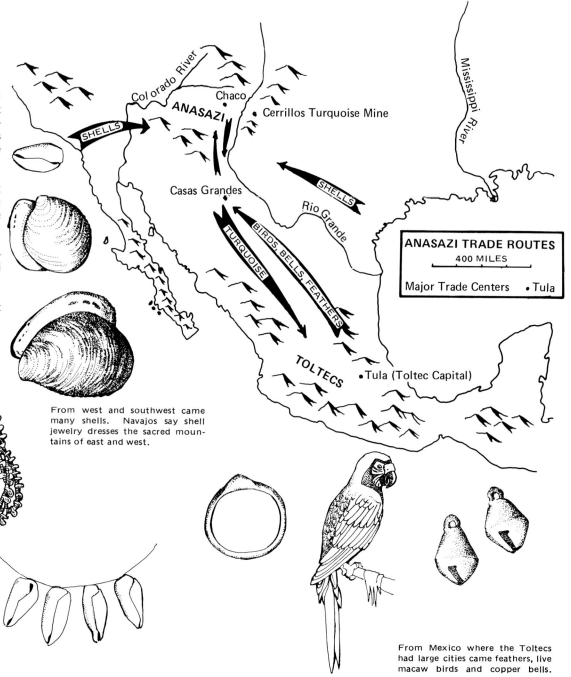

Colorado River

Mississippi River

SHELLS

Chaco

Cerrillos Turquoise Mine

ANASAZI

Casas Grandes

SHELLS

Rio Grande

TURQUOISE

BIRDS, BELLS, FEATHERS

TOLTECS

• Tula (Toltec Capital)

**ANASAZI TRADE ROUTES**

400 MILES

Major Trade Centers    • Tula

From west and southwest came many shells. Navajos say shell jewelry dresses the sacred mountains of east and west.

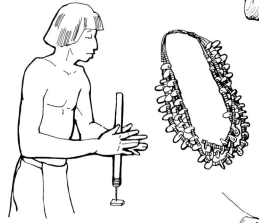

Craftsmen cut and polished turquoise into beads. A 2,500-bead necklace has been found. How they drilled so many small holes is a mystery. Some say they used a cactus pricker. How many hours (how many prickers) would 2,500 holes take?

From Mexico where the Toltecs had large cities came feathers, live macaw birds and copper bells.

# THE END OF CHACO

Rich and fine were the houses of Chaco. Yet under their greatness lay weakness. In 1150 the canyon walls echoed with life. Fifty years later, wind and sand blew through empty rooms.

In the story, only the evil power of the Gambler held the people together at the end. When the hero broke that power, they left.

The story may be true, but it doesn't answer all questions. People had lived in the Canyon for 500 years and had become rich and powerful. Why didn't anyone stay behind? Why couldn't some other people become rich again on the same land? What in our own times could turn a lively city into a ghost town?

We only know that mistakes are made by people, not land. People choose how they wish to live and cannot blame the land if they fail. The ecology of a canyon full of towns is hard to understand. We can only guess where the Chaco people went wrong and look for wisdom in the ruins they left behind.

CHACO LIFE WAS A CHAIN OF MANY LINKS

From Earth, Air, Sun and Rain come all life. The Chaco people wasted little. They caught water running from the cliffs after storms for irrigation. Their houses faced the sun to catch the warmth. They did all they could to fit more people into the canyon habitat.

**People Made the Chain. Only People Could Keep it Together.**

Chaco people were interdependent. To plan, build, irrigate and farm meant sharing work. All suffered if anyone failed. Who chose the diggers, the builders, and planters? How were the crops and riches shared among the workers?

Chaco reached its limit when the food and firewood began to run out. Planting more crops meant using poorer, drier land. Getting supplies from elsewhere needed the special talents of traders, craftsmen and load carriers.

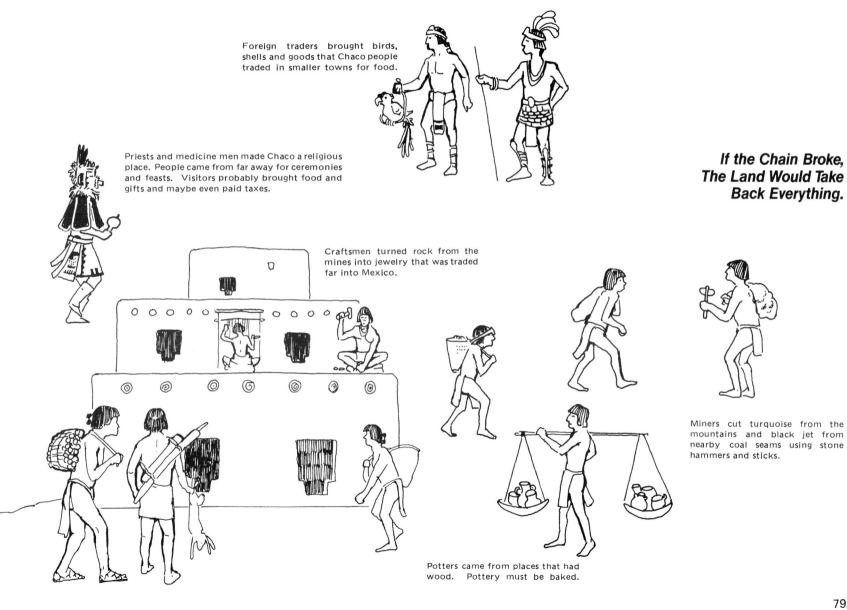

Foreign traders brought birds, shells and goods that Chaco people traded in smaller towns for food.

Priests and medicine men made Chaco a religious place. People came from far away for ceremonies and feasts. Visitors probably brought food and gifts and maybe even paid taxes.

**If the Chain Broke, The Land Would Take Back Everything.**

Craftsmen turned rock from the mines into jewelry that was traded far into Mexico.

Miners cut turquoise from the mountains and black jet from nearby coal seams using stone hammers and sticks.

Potters came from places that had wood. Pottery must be baked.

# ANCESTORS

On the box: SWEET POTATOES

GEN. GALLUP SUPPLY CENTER
CONTRACT NO. NDUC-1439-2760
GALLUP, NEW MEXICO 8780

MANUFACTURED IN ONE
NET WEIGHT: 47 LBS.

# ANCESTORS

*My grandfather, a well-known medicine man, used to say he didn't understand why people speak of the Anasazi as some foreign race. "We ourselves are Anasazi," he would say. He believed that pure Navajos once existed, but from time to time across the years they were joined by others who were refugees or had left their homes to find food. And surely some people always moved from place to place and did not settle in towns. In time they all came to speak Navajo and so called themselves Navajos. This can be seen in the stories of Navajo clans.*

*There are supposed to be four original Navajo clans, but there is no agreement on these. Other clans we know came from other people in other places. They carry the names of ancient ruins, of other tribes and the clans of other tribes. So you can't point back in time and say, "Here the Anasazi ended and there the Navajos began."*

—Barney Mitchell

Stories of the beginning of this world are known. The elders sing of the Holy People and how living beings came up from worlds below this one. In winter they tell how First Man and First Woman found a baby on top of *Ch'óol'í'í,* Gobernador Knob, and how this baby grew to be *Asdzą́ą́ Nádleehí,* Changing Woman, mother of the Hero Twins who cleared the land of monsters.

Those are sacred stories. The stories of Changing Woman are the heart of *Hózhǫ́ǫ́jí,* the Blessingway, which many believe is the oldest and most sacred of Navajo ceremonies. Parts of these stories, told by different singers and medicine men of the past, have been printed in books.

This book, however, will not try to repeat them. If you have ever looked through the smoke of a cedar fire as the cold stars of January slipped past the chimney hole of a hogan, if you have ever heard an old man tell how your world was made as if he had been there himself, then a few pages of English translation will teach you nothing.

Storytellers in different families have their own ways of explaining these things. However, most agree that after life between the Sacred Mountains had been put in order, Changing Woman left for a new home in the western sea. Some beings stayed behind. As the story is usually told, Changing Woman made four women and four men in the west and sent them back to her old country. After many adventures, those eight people did return, and from them came the first four clans of the people that called themselves *Diné,* Navajos.

The stories here come from a time after the first four clans were made. They only try to show how people lived long ago and how much of that ancient experience is part of our lives today.

According to the clan tradition, children belong to their mother's clan and should not marry someone of their own or their father's clan. Today dozens of clans exist. Most of them came from women who joined the Navajos at later times—as orphans and slaves, as wanderers running from enemies or hunger, or as wives of Navajos who lived a while among other tribes and passed new clans on to their children.

Today when people meet, they name their clans. One may say, "I am *Kin Yaa'áanii,* the Towering House Clan, born for *Kin Łichíi'nii,* the Red House Clan (father's clan). My mother's father was *Tó'aheedlíinii,* the Waters Flow Together Clan, and my father's father was *Áshįįhí,* the Salt Clan. Then that person will be called "brother," "cousin," or "grandson" by people he has never seen before. By the history of his clans he is related to many strangers and to many tribes and places.

The two stories here are not complete clan histories. However, they do show where the roads back into history lead. They tell how the *Diné* lived when they first began to spread across the land, and how from the very beginning they were joined and strengthened by others they met.

Whoever wishes to know more will seek out the history of his own clans.

84

# THE TOWERING HOUSE

*John Barbone is a Blessingway Singer from Borrego Pass, New Mexico. His clan is Tł'ógí; he is born for Kin Yaa'áanii. Here he tells how one group of Changing Woman's people, his father's ancestors, came into the country of the Chaco Anasazi and became known as the Kin Yaa'áanii—the Towering House Clan. Ruins of the Towering House itself are not far from his home.*

Long ago the Anasazi people lived all over the old Navajo Country, the *Diné Tah*. They lived underneath the cliffs and in dangerous places in the cliffs. Where water ran down over the rocks they hung yucca ropes, they say, and the water ran down the ropes to their homes. In this way they lived until they argued among themselves, separated and moved on. Among them were people who moved down to *T'iists'óóz Nídeeshgiizh*, Narrow Cottonwood Pass, where the town of Crownpoint is today.

On the plain at the foot of the mesa they built a great house that stood up into the sky, planted their fields, and lived.

As our ancestors wandered from place to place, a group of them crossed over the mesa and saw the tall house and the Anasazi people scattered on the plain below. Our ancestors had no horses. They carried everything on their backs. They had no clothes, only shoes, and we do not know how their shoes were made. They had never seen corn or planted a field. Their only weapons were arrows and clubs.

They hunted deer by driving them into pits where they fell on sharp sticks. They killed rabbits with clubs and lived on meat which they cut into thin strips and dried.

Some of our ancestors came down from the mesa and settled among the Anasazi people of *Kin Yaa'á*, the Towering House. From then on they also were known among the *Diné* as *Kin Yaa'áanii*, the Towering House People.

The Anasazi of the Towering House had turkeys for pets. A turkey shook its feathers and corn fell out, white corn first, and then all the different kinds of corn. "How did this happen?" our ancestors wondered, but they planted it. Rain came and it grew gently. So it was that corn came from the turkey, and the Towering House People were the first of our clans to plant it.

They lived peacefully for a while until some *Diné* killed some of the people of the pueblo. They moved on, but every now and then they would meet again.

The true Towering House Clan was small, but many others joined them. The *Shash Dine'é*, Bear People, and *Tązhii Dine'é*,

Turkey People, became their relatives; so did the *Dził Tł'áá Dine'é*, Mountain Cove People, and many others. You will find them everywhere in Navajo Country. My own father was of the Towering House. My mother was *Tł'ógí*, the Weaver Clan, which comes from Zia Pueblo.

The Towering House itself, *Kin Yaa'á*, can still be seen standing into the sky from the plain by Crownpoint. But the high hollow tower is only a ruin now. The house itself has fallen, and the sand blows freely over the place where our ancestors got their name.

*Kin Yaa'á*

John Barbone told his story in July, 1980, to Rex Lee Jim from Rock Point. Rex's grandfather was also a *Kin Yaa'áanii*.

# WANDERERS

*Navajo life changed over the centuries, just as Anasazi life changed. The Navajos, however, never became townspeople. They kept moving freely over the land. The next passage tells how people like the wanderers who came to the Towering House lived from day to day. A medicine man described it this way in a story he told 100 years ago.*

Long ago near *Dziłk'i Hózhónii*, Beautiful Mountain, by the Carrizo Mountains, lived a family of six: parents, two sons and two daughters. They did not live in one place all the time, but moved from place to place. The young men hunted wood rats and rabbits, for that was their meat. The girls gathered the seeds of wild plants.

After a time they went east to *Tsé Bit'a'í*, Shiprock. They camped, and the oldest brother went to look for water. He could see a sandy hill covered with plants, and when he got there he noticed the ground was damp. He had not dug far with his digging stick when water rushed into his hole. He hurried back to tell the family. The spring he found is still there and is called *Tó Bináák'is*, One-Eyed Water.

The family had one water bottle, a basket covered with pine gum. The wife wanted to move close to the spring, since it was her job to carry the water. But her husband wanted to stay where they were, since it was his job to build a shelter, and there were building materials nearby. They argued about it for a long time, but finally the woman won and they moved down near the spring.

The eldest son said they should build their home down in the ground for more warmth and protection. So the old man chose a sandy hill and began to dig out one side, while the boys went to get poles.

They had a stone ax head. They bent an oak branch around this and tied it with yucca to make a handle. With this axe they chopped all day, and at night they returned with four poles. The next day they chopped all day again, and at night they returned with four more poles, while their father continued his digging. So they continued for four days, bringing home twelve poles in all, and finally their shelter was finished.

They made mats of grass to lie on and another one to hang across the door. They covered themselves at night with mats of cedar bark, for in those days the *Diné* did not weave. The soles of their moccasins also were made of grass and the tops of yucca.

The young men worked hard to find meat, setting traps by the holes of small animals. Sometimes they hunted far from the camp, sleeping at night near their traps, while their sisters searched all over the surrounding country for wild plant seeds.

In spite of all their work, they found it hard to make a living in that place. The land was barren. Even rats and prairie dogs were scarce, and there were few seed-bearing plants. Only four days after their shelter was finished, they talked about it and decided it would be better to move on to the San Juan River.

They broke camp and moved on to the river, gathering *chiiłchin*, sumac berries, and *tł'ohdeii*, goosefoot, along the way. At last they came to a place along the river called *Tsétaak'á*, where much salt is found. They cut some out from under a great rock and put it in bags made from the skins of small animals.

They went on up the river to a place called *T'iisyaa Hózhóní*, Beautiful Under the Cottonwoods, where they stayed one day and killed two rabbits. They skinned the rabbits and crushed them between two stones, bones and all, so that nothing would be wasted. Then they put them into an earthen pot to boil, and when they were cooked they added some powdered seeds to make a thick soup. This made a tasty meal. The *Diné* in those days had no horses and so could not carry grinding stones. They ground their wild seeds on stones that they found around them wherever they were.

They searched now for a place to cross the river, for they planned to travel on toward *Dibé Nitsaa*, Hesperus Peak, where they would hunt deer.

So they lived.

This is the way a medicine man began his story of the origin of *Dziłk'ijí*, the Mountain Top Way. He told his story in the 1880s to Washington Matthews, who wrote it down in *The Mountain Chant: A Navajo Ceremony*, pages 387–389.

# STORIES

Many of the stories in this book go back a long way. They show what ancient Navajo life was like. They are, nevertheless, only small pieces of what a person can find by seeking his own stories.

Before languages were written down, before cameras and tape recorders, storytellers kept the history of nations and did it well. If a 70-year-old elder teaches clan history to a 20-year-old student, the story passes down 50 years. Only twenty tellings carry the story 1000 years. Families may tell the stories differently after twenty tellings, but the heart of the truth has probably survived as well as many records written in ink. Some stories, especially those connected with ceremonies, are carefully guarded and may be told only under certain conditions. These safeguards help assure that they will be told carefully and well.

The storytelling chain will never break as long as someone carries the story forward. In the past many were willing. Today, however, we depend too much on books, tapes and pictures. Learning a story is hard, and stories and songs seem cheap because we live among magazines, TV, and radio all the time.

In fact, however, the value of old stories grows year by year, for if they are lost, our past will be lost forever. The elders saw clearly that knowledge of the past gave them strength for the future, and they took their learning seriously. The history of your own clans and your own family can give you strength for the future. Try it for yourself. Seek out an older clan relative and learn the history of one of your clans well enough to tell it to someone else.

*"When you want to hear a story, when you want to have a story told to you, this is the proper way of going about it:*

*"If you really want to have a story told to you, and if you really want to learn, you would go to the storyteller's place and you would put on a pot of coffee. You would lay out mountain tobacco. Then you would roll one, using a corn husk, and give it to the storyteller, and you would light it for him, saying, 'I want you to tell me the story. I want to know this. . . .'*

*"Then he will tell you. Coffee will be boiling. Maybe you might even make* haníígaii, *stew with corn. And you would ask him, 'Now tell me the story.' If you are the person who is saying, 'I want to know this story,' if you really are sincere about it, then you would do this.*

*"The storyteller will tell you a story here, then skip one or two and tell you another story, then tell you another. If there were another person there, he would tell that person the part that he didn't tell you, and the part that he told you, he will not tell to him. Then after he has finished telling you everything you wanted to know, he will say, 'GO, go tell each other the stories that I have told you.' In that way, the complete story does not come from his mouth. So no two people hear the complete story from one man. That is the way it is.*

*"You cannot tell everything. You MUST not tell everything. This protects you and shields you. You walk behind this shield. It protects you, and you walk behind it. It is like that."*

—Clan brother of George Blueeyes

# WHO ARE THE DINÉ?

Chaco Canyon was almost empty by the year 1200. In the rest of Anasazi Country the settlements lasted for another hundred years. But time ran out for them, too.

By 1300 the houses stood empty. The end came quite quickly. Ruins, pottery, rock drawings, and other things still seen on the land tell part of the story. Some Anasazi towns burned. Ashes and signs of war are found. There are also signs of sickness, drought, and ruined farmland.

Why all this happened is still a mystery. Stories give almost the only way to trace wanderers like those who came to Towering House or camped near Shiprock. Much can be learned by studying stories such as the Great Gambler tale and the account of the Towering House, even though families may disagree. Some families tell stories of the end of the Anasazi.

How much did Navajos of long ago travel among Anasazi, as the Towering House story claims at least one group did? Should Anasazi be considered relatives or foreigners?

The mysteries of the past will always be there to teach, guide, and warn that the future will not be like the present. How long did it take us to become the people we are?

# WAYS OF LIFE

Although the Anasazi moved out of the heart of Navajo Country, they did not disappear. They survived among the Pueblo tribes that still live side by side with the Navajos.

Pueblos and Navajos have raided and fought now and then for centuries. Yet, like animals in the same habitat, townspeople and wanderers also depend on each other. From towns the wanderers got things like corn and cotton cloth. Townspeople got meat and skins and help when war or drought forced them also to leave home and wander.

Wandering people are called "Nomads". Nomads wander still across many parts of the world, just as Navajos once did. But wherever nomads wander, there are also towns where they trade.

Nomads cover lots of land, but never ask one place to feed them very long. That way they can live where townspeople would starve. In Navajo Country lack of water also limits the size of towns.

Townspeople use much less land. They survive by making that land grow a lot of food and by trade. By trading with nomads, they can have things from places where they could not live. Townspeople and nomads are *specialized* for life in different habitats, but both live better by trading.

# LANGUAGES, CULTURES AND MIGRATIONS

The map shows Navajos and Apaches speaking languages like those of tribes far to the north. This "Athabascan Language Family" is large. Did Navajos come from Alaska and, before that, from Asia? Or did the Alaskans come from the South? Did all come from Changing Woman across the ocean?

Most Athabascan tribes are hunters and wanderers. Were they once one tribe? Did Athabascan tradition keep Navajos from building towns? Maybe, but languages don't tell the whole story.

Today's Pueblos surely come from the Anasazi, but all Pueblos don't speak the same language. Some are related to tribes that never lived near Anasazis or remember their culture.

What did the Anasazi speak? Were there several Anasazi tribes? How were they related to each other and to the Navajos by blood or tradition?

Such questions can be asked about people anywhere. Look up the history of English or Spanish. The encyclopedia shows that all languages have very twisted roots.

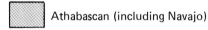 Athabascan (including Navajo)

 Uto-Aztecan

 Kiowa-Tanoan

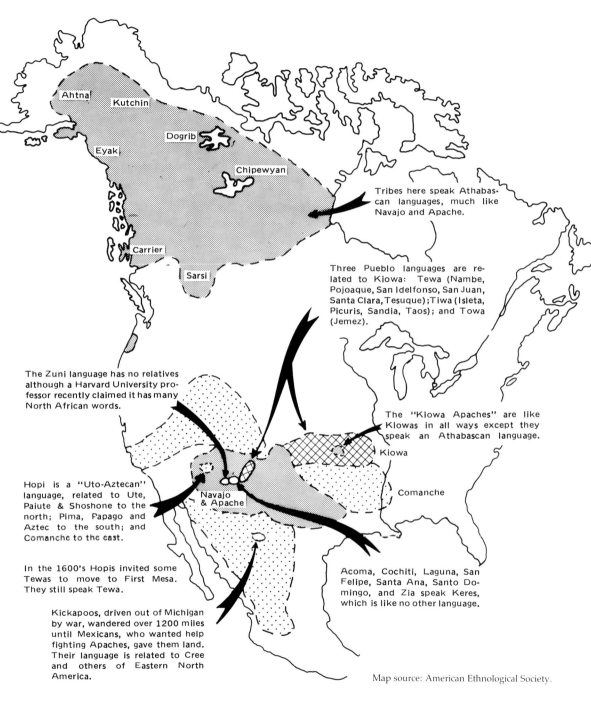

Tribes here speak Athabascan languages, much like Navajo and Apache.

Three Pueblo languages are related to Kiowa: Tewa (Nambe, Pojoaque, San Idelfonso, San Juan, Santa Clara, Tesuque); Tiwa (Isleta, Picuris, Sandia, Taos); and Towa (Jemez).

The Zuni language has no relatives although a Harvard University professor recently claimed it has many North African words.

The "Kiowa Apaches" are like Kiowas in all ways except they speak an Athabascan language.

Hopi is a "Uto-Aztecan" language, related to Ute, Paiute & Shoshone to the north; Pima, Papago and Aztec to the south; and Comanche to the east.

In the 1600's Hopis invited some Tewas to move to First Mesa. They still speak Tewa.

Acoma, Cochiti, Laguna, San Felipe, Santa Ana, Santo Domingo, and Zia speak Keres, which is like no other language.

Kickapoos, driven out of Michigan by war, wandered over 1200 miles until Mexicans, who wanted help fighting Apaches, gave them land. Their language is related to Cree and others of Eastern North America.

Map source: American Ethnological Society.

92

# EUROPEAN LANGUAGES

Two thousand years ago most of the people of Western Europe spoke Celtic languages. Modern French, Spanish, English, and German did not exist as we know them.

The map at right shows where today's languages had their roots. There are many blank spaces because the history of many ancient tribes has been lost.

The maps of course tell only about language. They say nothing about the mixing of culture and blood.

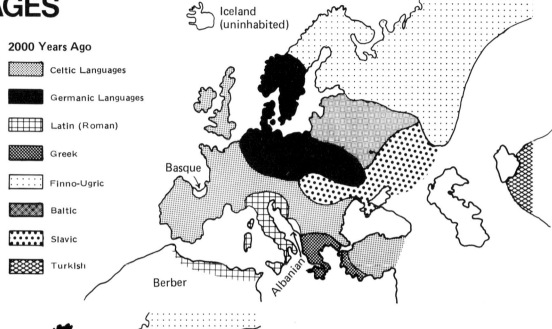

**2000 Years Ago**

- Celtic Languages
- Germanic Languages
- Latin (Roman)
- Greek
- Finno-Ugric
- Baltic
- Slavic
- Turkish

Iceland (uninhabited)

Basque

Berber

Albanian

**Today**

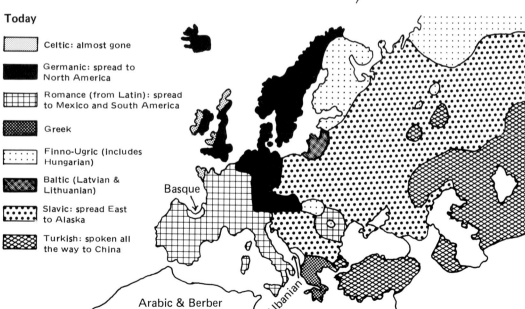

- Celtic: almost gone
- Germanic: spread to North America
- Romance (from Latin): spread to Mexico and South America
- Greek
- Finno-Ugric (includes Hungarian)
- Baltic (Latvian & Lithuanian)
- Slavic: spread East to Alaska
- Turkish: spoken all the way to China

Basque

Arabic & Berber

Albanian

Today Celtic languages exist only on the tips of France and the British Isles. No one speaks Latin now, but French, Italian, Spanish, Portuguese, and Romanian are related to it. The German languages have become modern German, Dutch, English, and the Scandinavian languages. Slavic languages are spoken in Russia, Poland, Czechoslovakia, Yugoslavia, and Bulgaria. Long ago a German king brought Hungarians from the northeast to help fight Slavs. They speak an Ugric language.

Each tribe and nation is different, but history has stirred them together in the same stew many times.

# ATHABASCANS

Navajo and the Apache languages all belong to the Athabascan language family. The San Carlos, White Mountain, Chiricahua, and Mescalero Apaches understand Navajos if they speak simply and repeat often. Jicarilla is further from Navajo, but a Navajo speaker can learn it in a few months.

Athabascan languages in Canada and Alaska are also like Navajo in many ways. In Sarci, *ts'aal* is moss, used for diapers. A baby is *ts'aalt'ah sidá*, moss pocket sitter. In Navajo, *awééts'áál* is a cradleboard or the cliffrose, used for diapers. *Tah* means "among"; *sidá* means "he sits".

Here are words from six Athabascan languages.

| Navajo | Sarci* | Chipewyan* | Beaver* | Carrier* | Tsekani* | Ahtna | English |
|---|---|---|---|---|---|---|---|
| chaa' | tsxa | tsáá | cháá' | tsaa | tsá' | tsa' | beaver |
| deeł | dáł | deeł | -- | deł | deeł | dael | crane |
| tsé | tsáh | tthee | chée | tthee | tsee | ts'es | stone |
| yá | naak'os | yaa | yaa | yaah | yaa | yaa | sky |
| tł'oh | guutł'owí | tł'og | tł'ógi | tł'ooh | tł'óo | tł'ogh | grass |
| gah | -- | gah | gaah | goh | gah | ggax | rabbit |
| tó | tútii | tuu | chúu | tuuh | chúu | tuu | water |
| tin | nistiní | tvn | istÝni | tvn | tvn | ten | ice |
| k'os | k'os | k'oth | k'os | k'vs | k'os | k'os | cloud |
| sǫ | sÝn | tthÝn | sÝn | svm | svm | son' | star |
| kǫ | kuu | kon | kÝn | kvn | kon | kon' | fire |
| yas, zas | zas | yath | yas | yvth | yas | yaas | snow |

*In these languages the "v" is similar to "u" in the English word "put."

†The "th" in these languages is usually written "θ."
Source: Young & Morgan, *The Navajo Language.*

# NEIGHBORS

Storytellers often speak of other peoples using names forgotten today. Here is a list of neighboring nations and pueblos.

**Apache**

| | |
|---|---|
| Chiricahua | *Chíshí* |
| Jicarilla | *Beehai* |
| Mescalero | *Naashgalí* |
| San Carlos & White Mt. | *Dziłghá'í* |

| | |
|---|---|
| **Comanche** | *Naałání* |
| **Havasupai & Walapai** | *Góóhníinii* |
| **Paiute** | *Béyóodzin* |
| **Papago** | *Kégiizhí* |
| **Pima** | *Kétł'áhí* |
| **Mexican** | *Naakaii* |
| **U.S. (Anglo)** | *Bilagáana* |
| **Ute** | *Nóóda'í* |
| **Yavapai** | *Dilzhí'í* |

**PUEBLOS** — *KIIS'ÁANII*

**Tiwa**

| | |
|---|---|
| Isleta | *Naatoohí* |
| Picuris | -- |
| Sandia | *Kin Łigai* |
| Taos | *Tówoł* |

**Tewa**

| | |
|---|---|
| Nambe | -- |
| Pojoaque | -- |
| San Idelfonso | *Tséta' Kin* |
| San Juan | *Kin Łichíí'* |
| Santa Clara | *Naashashí* |
| Tesuque | *Tł'oh Łikizhí* |

**Towa**

| | |
|---|---|
| Jemez | *Ma'ii Deeshgiizh* |

**Keres**

| | |
|---|---|
| Acoma | *Haak'oh* |
| Acomita | *Tó Łání Biyáazh* |
| Cochiti | -- |
| Laguna | *Tó Łání* |

| | |
|---|---|
| San Felipe | *Séí Bee Hooghan; Tsédáá' Kin* |
| Santa Ana | *Dahmi* |
| Santo Domingo | *Tó Hajiloh* |
| Zia | *Tł'ógí* |

| | |
|---|---|
| **Zuni** | *Naasht'ézhí* |

**Hopi**

| | |
|---|---|
| 1st Mesa | |
| Walpi | *Deez'áají'* |
| Sichomovi | *Ayahkin* |
| Hano (Tewa) | *Naashashí* |
| 2nd Mesa | |
| Mishongnovi | *Tsétsohk'id* |
| Shipaulovi | *Tsétsohk'id* |
| Shongopovi | *Kin Názt'i'* |
| 3rd Mesa | |
| Old Oraibi | *Oozéí* |
| New Oraibi | *Oozéí* |
| Hotevilla | *Tł'ohchin Tó* |
| Bacabi | *Tł'ohchin Tó Biyáázh* |
| Moencopi | *Oozéí Hayázhí* |

# CLANS

Here is a list of clans from the Navajo dictionary written by William Morgan and Robert Young. Many are so closely related that they treat each other as relatives. Others have several branches with the same name but different histories. These relationships are so complicated no one can possibly know them all. However, by knowing a bit about your own clans, you can find relatives anywhere in Navajo Country.

Some clan names come from other tribes. Others have taken in people from other tribes, and some clan members still trace their blood to them. You can see which names from the list of tribes turn up among the clans, and any expert on clan history will have a great deal to say about which clans have taken in new people.

Clan relationships are taken seriously by all tribes in Navajo Country. At Jemez Pueblo on feast days, Navajos of the *Ma'ii Deeshgiizhnii* Clan will find a special welcome. The same is true among the Mescalero Apaches, Hopis, and others when they meet Navajo relatives.

*Áshįįhí,* Salt Clan
*Áshįįhnii,* Salt Clan (extinct)
*Bįįh Dine'é,* Deer People
*Bįįh Bitoodnii,* Deer Spring Clan
*Bįįhtsoh Dine'é,* Big Deer People
*Bit'ahnii,* Within-His-Cover Clan
*Bit'ąą'nii* (extinct)
*Deeshchii'nii,* Start of the Red Streak Clan
*Dichin Dine'é,* Hunger People
*Dibé Łizhiní,* Black Sheep Clan
*Dzaanééz Łání,* Many Burros Clan
*Dziłt'ahnii,* Mountain Cove Clan
*Dził Ná'oodiłnii,* Turning Mountain Clan
*Gah Dine'é Táchii'nii,* Rabbit Clan (division of the *Táchii'nii*)
*Haltsooí Dine'é,* Meadow Clan
*Hashk'ąą Hadzohó,* Yucca Fruit Clan
*Hashtł'ishnii,* Mud Clan
*Honágháahnii,* He-Walks-Around-One Clan
*Hooghan Łání,* Many Hogans Clan
*Iich'ąh Dine'é,* People that have Fits Clan
*Jaa' Yaalóolii,* Sticking-Up-Ears Clan
*K'aa' Hináanii,* Living Arrow Clan
*K'ai' Ch'ébáanii,* Gray Willow Line Clan
*Kin Lichíi'nii,* Red House Clan
*Kin Łitsonii,* Yellow House Clan
*Kin Yaa'áanii,* Towering House Clan
*Lók'aa' Dine'é,* Reed People
*Ma'ii Deeshgiizhnii,* Coyote Pass Clan (Jemez)
*Naaneesht'ézhí Táchii'nii,* Charcoal-streaked division of the *Táchii'nii* Clan
*Naakaii Dine'é,* Mexican Clan
*Naashashí,* Bear Enemies, the Tewa Clan
*Naashgalí Dine'é,* Mescalero Apache Clan

*Naasht'ézhí Dine'é,* Zuni Clan
*Naayízí Dine'é,* Squash People
*Nát'oh Dine'é,* Tobacco People
*Nihoobáanii,* Gray-Streak-Ends Clan
*Nóóda'í Dine'é,* Ute Clan
*Nóóda'í Dine'é Táchii'nii,* Ute People division of the *Táchii'nii* Clan
*Séí Bee Hooghanii,* Sand Hogan Clan
*Tábąąhí,* Water's Edge Clan
*Táchii'nii,* Red Running into the Water Clan
*Ta'neeszahnii,* Tangle Clan
*Tó'áhani,* Near to Water Clan
*Tó'aheedlíinii,* Waters Flow Together Clan
*Tó'ászólí,* Light Water Clan
*Tó Baazhní'ázhí,* Two-Came-to-Water Clan
*Tó Dích'íi'nii,* Bitter Water Clan
*Tótsohnii,* Big Water Clan
*Tł'áashchí'í,* Red Bottom Clan
*Tł'ízí Łání,* Many Goats Clan
*Tł'ógí,* Weaver Clan, the Zia
*Ts'ah Yisk'idnii,* Sage Brush Hill Clan
*Tsé Deeshgiizhnii,* Rock Gap Clan
*Tsé Nahabiłnii,* The Sleep Rock Clan
*Tsé Níjíkiní,* Honey-combed Rock Clan
*Tsé Táá'aanii,* Rock-Extends-into-Water Clan
*Tsézhin Nidii'aaí,* Slanted Lava Spire Clan
*Tséikeehí,* Two-Rocks-Sit Clan
*Tsi'naajinii,* Black Streak Wood Clan
*Tsin Sikaadnii,* Clumped Tree Clan
*Yé'ii Dine'é,* Monster People
*Yoo'í Dine'é,* Bead People

# SPANIARDS

# SPANIARDS

*It is often said among the Navajos that the four sacred mountains are the posts of a great hogan. For years the Navajos, Hopis, Zunis and other tribes lived along together inside that hogan. They fought, traded and suffered drought, but the world outside the four mountains mattered little to them.*

*A day came, however, when Spaniards from across the oceans pulled the blanket from the hogan door, and winds from the four corners of the world blew inside. According to the legend, the people of the Gambler had come back.*

*The stories in this chapter show how the coming of the Spaniards made Navajo Country part of a world much bigger than the four mountains. The story of Navajo Country from that time on cannot be told by itself. It is part of the history of the whole world. Nothing that has happened in Navajo Country from then until today can really be understood without also knowing what has happened elsewhere.*

*And what did happen in Navajo Country? The Spaniards brought war, blood, sorrow and change to many. Nevertheless, the Navajos did not die away. In fact the tribe became bigger, richer and more powerful. Some even say that the coming of the Spaniards really helped the Navajos. Who can say now for sure after nearly 500 years have passed.*

*Here is a story of those times.*

## THE STRANGER

In July of 1691, ninety-seven years after the Spaniards first settled in New Mexico, a Navajo man dressed in rags walked into Jemez Pueblo. He was not an old man, but hard times were written on his face. He had no teeth, and at first the Jemez people thought that might explain why he spoke Navajo so badly.

Navajos often traded at Jemez in those days, and many Jemez knew the language and the Navajo Country well. All morning the Navajo man went from place to place in the village asking for news of his father. Finally at midday he found someone who could help him.

An older Jemez man leaning against the wall of his house stared long and hard as the Navajo worked his way slowly down the row of houses. He said nothing when he heard the Navajo's question, but his shoulders moved and his eyes sparkled as if the question made him laugh deep inside for a secret reason.

Then this Jemez man leaned his head back and covered his eyes like someone digging into the very bottom of his memory. "There was a man once called *Naat'áaniiłbáhí*," he said. "But he's gone now."

The Navajo sighed and looked down. "Gone?" he said. "That's probably right. Where are his people now?"

"They say," said the Jemez, and he smiled secretly again, "that his people have fields and livestock in Largo Canyon. I expect they're there. But brother, you look hungry. You must eat with us."

As the Navajo stranger sat with his Jemez friend, he told a long story of his life and how he had come back to his land from far beyond the sacred mountains. It was a good story and he told it well, but he could not tell the whole history of his adventures. History is like a blanket that covers the land. It is woven from many stories.

## THE GOVERNOR

In 1659 a long train of wagons and pack mules came north to Santa Fe along the Royal Road (El Camino Real in Spanish) bringing guns, gunpowder, hammers, nails, plows, tools, window glass, church bells, books, needles and fine cloth. All of these were things a Spaniard might need for a good life.

In this dusty train of squeaking wheels and sweating mules rode the new Spanish governor of New Mexico, Bernardo López de Mendizábal and his beautiful wife Teresa de Aguilera y Roche.

The governor on his horse did not look quite like the other dusty, thirsty soldiers guarding the wagons. His spurs were not rusty. They were silver. His boots did not bang his shinbones like stove pipes. An expensive boot-maker had made them fit soft and close. The soldiers' ponies had burrs in their tails. López rode a tall horse that a servant brushed twice a day. The fine white cloth of his shirt, the careful stitching of his leather jacket and the heavy ring on his hand all showed that he was governor indeed.

López had been born in Mexico, but he did not call Mexico his home. No sacred mountains, oceans or rivers marked his land. "My home," he often said, "is the Spanish Empire. Wherever a Spanish king has power, I will go." He had gone far. As an officer in Spanish ships he had sailed to the richest cities of the world. In Italy, 7,000 miles away, he had married a Spanish woman. Spanish armies had conquered Italy some time before, and her father was a high official in the city of Naples.

And now Teresa López, wife of the governor, sat silently on the back of a mule-drawn wagon reading an Italian book. Her long dress with its lace collar had turned yellow in the dust. Big circles of sweat darkened her armpits. But she sat very straight and turned the pages of her book carefully. López remembered watching her sit like that in the cool, quiet rooms of her father's palace in Naples, 7,000 miles away.

She was reading about the seven circles of hell, and as the day grew hotter in the low valley of the Rio Grande, he began to think that even the seventh circle of hell might be better than New Mexico. New Mexico was a poor rough territory. He would rather have been governor of some place else.

"Well, maybe I'm lucky," he thought at last, "Most people only get to hell as slaves, but I get to go as governor. What would the devil do with a chance like this?"

He laughed at his joke and spurred his horse along the sweating mule train. In his mind he could see long lines of slaves coming back to Mexico and wagons full of cotton cloth, buffalo hides, salt and pinon nuts. All of that would be his to sell. He meant to buy a fine house in Mexico City for his old age.

A blue-robed friar (a Catholic Missionary of the Franciscan Brotherhood) in a forward wagon coughed in the dust kicked up by Bernardo's horse. Fray Juan Ramírez was in charge of the missions in New Mexico.

## THE FRIAR

Fray Juan Ramírez, born in Taxco south of Mexico City, was the son of a silver miner. Early in his life he had decided several things. He did not want to be a miner. He did not want to be poor. He did not want to spend all his life in Taxco. And he did not want to be forgotten when he died. Getting what he wanted, however, was not easy. His family was not rich or powerful. They could not help him become a governor or high official. In Mexico in the 1600s priests and missionaries led very good lives. At age 16 Ramírez joined the Franciscan brotherhood and began studying to become a priest and a servant of the Catholic Church.

The Church and the Franciscans did help him. He got a higher education. He traveled all over Mexico. He became a powerful official. Finally he was put in charge of the missions in New Mexico and started north with his train of wagons and the new governor. Fray Ramírez and Governor López were very different. López looked richer than the other soldiers. Ramírez, however, looked poorer than the other friars. He was not poorer. He worked harder. His boots were not cheap, but they had holes in each toe. His robe was fine wool, but it had holes at each elbow. His

head, which had little hair on it, was baked the color of saddle leather. He thought wearing a hat slowed him down. He could sharpen a razor on the palm of his hand.

His fierce black eyes watched Governor López gallop easily by on his tall horse. "God forgive me," he said to himself, "but I hate that man and his silver spurs." Few missionaries or silver miners' sons enjoyed silver spurs, tall horses and fine women, and Ramírez knew it.

He put his hand over his eyes. "God forgive my jealousy," he said, "but he can have his spurs. One day we'll find out who is the better man."

## THE CAPTAIN

The Navajo leader *Naat'áaniilbáhí* (Gray Leader) and his people soon knew of the new governor of New Mexico. As soon as Bernardo López got to Santa Fe, he started to organize an army to hunt Navajos. Governor López himself did not go. He had other greedy plans to keep him busy. He ordered his captain, Juan Domínguez y Mendoza, to take an army of 40 Spaniards and 800 Pueblo Indians up the Chama River northwest of Santa Fe to the valley of the San Juan River where Navajos were harvesting corn.

Domínguez had done the same thing for other governors. He had come to New Mexico as a soldier when he was only 14. Now he was 30 and could look back on 16 years of fighting. It was the only work he knew.

On the morning of September 4, 1659, his little army gathered in front of the governor's palace in Santa Fe. There was great ceremony. Governor López, dressed all in silk and velvet, gave a speech about punishing the savages of Navajo Country. "Dios y Santiago (God and Saint James) will guide and protect you!" he said at the end. Teresa López put flowers in the bridles of the officers' horses. Domínguez saluted her and spurred his horse. But he stopped again at once.

He was a fighting man, but he never forgot his god. "Where's the priest?" he asked. "Wasn't he supposed to bless us?"

Governor López spat in the dirt. "The devil take Ramírez! He's weeping in his church, because you're not staying around to protect him. 'Let the friars sweat!' I say. They're too fat and lazy anyway."

Domínguez wasn't satisfied. "Somebody should bless the troops," he said.

López patted the captain's knee. "My dear captain," he said. "Don't worry about blessings. Just remember Our Lord's commandment, 'Thou Shalt Not Kill'. Bring them back alive, if you can. We can't sell the dead ones."

Domínguez flashed a smile, gave a shout and the army started off. They surprised the Navajos in their fields, killed many, made some slaves, took all the corn they could carry and burned the rest. *Naat'áaniilbáhí* lost a brother and one of his wives. He himself was away hunting at the time.

But his crops were lost, his hogans burned; his metal axe, his blankets and buckskins were all stolen. The winter came on long and cold. Many older people died. When spring came, starvation hunted everyone.

## THE MASSACRE

Some weeks before planting time in the windy days of spring, a Jemez runner came to *Naat'áaniilbáhí's* camp with a message from Governor López himself.

The Governor wants peace," said the runner. "He attacked you last fall because he had heard many stories of Navajo raids. But now he wants peace, and he might even give back some of the people he took with him. He will meet with you at Jemez at the next full moon."

*Naat'áaniilbáhí* listened well to the Jemez runner and joined many others who moved south to meet with López.

The Navajos camped near Jemez until the Governor and his men arrived. The next morning, the leaders went to see him. A warm sun made everyone think happily of planting and summer.

Captain Domínguez welcomed the Navajos. A cow was butchered, and the soldiers and the Jemez began to trade with the Navajos. At last Domínguez invited the leaders to meet the governor in a small room near the church.

The Navajos stepped into the dark room from the bright spring sun. They could not see the soldiers lined up inside. They did not see the knives. The meeting was a trap. In less than a minute 15 Navajos lay dying in their own blood. Waving bloody swords the soldiers rushed from the room, jumped to their saddles and galloped for the Navajo camps, shouting "Santiago!" the Spanish battle cry. Nobody could stop them.

The youngest son of *Naat'áaniilbáhí* had not gone to Jemez with his father. He had spent the morning with the women and other children playing around the campfire.

The people in the camp saw the riders gallop out from town, then drop from sight behind a hill. Too late, they recognized the shining leather and steel of enemies. The quickest ones escaped, but the small son of *Naat'áaniilbáhí* stood by the fire crying. He went to Mexico in the slave train of Governor López.

## THE HOMECOMING

The strange Navajo who walked into Jemez 29 years later was of course that youngest son of *Naat'áaniilbáhí*. In his old age his people called him *Hastiin Béésh Ligaii* (Mr. Silver) because he told stories about silver. The story he told the old Jemez man was the story of his days in Mexico.

He had been sold to a rancher near the Mexican town of Parral (El Parral it was called then). He worked there herding sheep and cattle until the rancher grew old and sold the ranch.

"I was free then," he explained, "but I needed a way to live. Miners were paid well in Parral, so for several years I worked under the ground digging rock with an iron pick. Water covered the floor of the mine. A sheep grease lamp gave the only light. We always feared that falling rock would bury us alive.

"Last year my friends at the market asked me to carry a message to El Paso. As soon as I put my foot on the road north, I knew I would not stop until I came home. I can tell you that from El Paso down past Parral everything is burning. There's even talk among Apaches of taking El Paso itself."

"I know how it is," smiled the Jemez man. "Over there by that kiva, there is a grave. A Spanish priest is buried there. Father Juan de Jesus he called himself. He and his soldiers used to chase us into the church. They whipped old men like me if they heard us singing in the kiva.

"So we sent him away to the heaven he used to talk about and put his bones by the kiva. Now he can hear us forever. We hated him for the things he did to us, but he believed he had to do it. He was not afraid to die. His god gave him strength for that."

*Hastiin Béésh Ligaii* looked at his friend. "Pray for that strength yourself," he said. "The Apaches may talk about taking El Paso, but the Spaniards will not be beaten. There is a new governor in El Paso named de Vargas. He talks about coming back to Santa Fe, and he gets what he wants. He will come here, too."

The Jemez nodded. "We know that. The Spaniards will come back. Not long ago they came as far as Zia and killed some people there, but they didn't have the strength to go on. Now we are the weak ones. Our leaders sit in the old governors' palace in Santa Fe. And the villages hate them like they hated the Spaniards. The Spaniards will come back and take us one by one the way a man goes around his field picking corn.

"It will be like it was in my grandfather's time when the Spaniards first came. Some of the towns will welcome them. Other towns will fight. Jemez will fight. Will anyone help us? Who knows? If we lose, we will run away, but we will not stay away forever. We Jemez get homesick for our valley. We will not be slaves of the Spaniards. We are slaves of the land itself. We always come back to that. After every war and drought we rebuild our houses, plant our crops, and hold our ceremonies. We could leave here and live like the deer, moving from place to place as

"The rock we carried out of the mine went to the 'patios' where it was ground to powder and the silver was taken from it. As soon as I could, I found work there so I could be in the sunlight again. I learned all there is to know about silver, and in the end they paid me very well. But death was in the air at that place. The workers at the patio grew old quickly. My gums began to bleed and one by one my teeth simply fell out. See now how my hands shake.

"The best years of my life were gone when we heard in Parral that the Indians of New Mexico had killed all the Spaniards here. The news rolled across the country like blowing dust. Soon all the land between Parral and El Paso was at war. The ranch where I grew up was burned. A thousand cows and horses were taken. At the mine there were people who spoke and dressed as Spanish as the governor himself, but one by one they wandered away. I was one of them. Indians who came to market in Parral asked me to spy for them. I could help them, because the Spaniards told me everything. I was one of them.

Navajos do. But this valley will always be home. We will live here, even if we live with the Spaniards."

"Well," said the Navajo, "if all your bad dreams come true, you may join us and live like the deer for a while."

"I will," said the Jemez. "Do you know who I am?" Again he smiled his secret smile.

"No, tell me. Have I met you before? Maybe in a dream?"

The Jemez man smiled again. "Do you remember a slave your father had called *Ma'ii Yáázh?* I was that slave. I remember you well. The winter before López came, your father traded me back to my own people for corn. Your relatives still visit me when they come to trade. We are friends."

## THE RECORDS

All that is known about the story of *Hastiin Béésh Ligaii* comes from things written by Spaniards or found on the land itelf. A careful eye can still see where Navajo hogans were built in Largo Canyon. A Spanish friar wrote how starving Navajos came to Jemez in the winter of 1658–59 to sell back slaves like the Jemez man in the story. The old records tell how Captain Domínguez attacked camps in Largo Canyon and how Governor López murdered fifteen Navajo leaders at Jemez. They tell how the body of Father Juan de Jesus was found with an arrow in his back by the kiva at Jemez.

The records also tell what history did to the others in the story.

## GOVERNOR LÓPEZ AND TERESA

The governor and his wife had a very unhappy time in Santa Fe. Teresa suffered more than her husband. She tried to make the governor's palace a fine home like the one where she grew up. She couldn't. The slaves working in the palace stole her silver candlesticks. Other Spanish women hated her for her education and Italian ways. Her husband left for weeks at a time, and she heard gossip about him that she knew was true.

To forget her troubles, she spent many hours reading her favorite Italian books. She often read out loud just to hear the sound of the language. Nevertheless she looked forward to better days ahead. She would come back from New Mexico rich. She would live well among friends into high old age. She wasn't so lucky.

In 1662 Fray Ramírez brought another wagon train from Mexico with a new governor and a warrant to arrest López and Teresa. They would get no riches from their slaves and wagons of cotton, salt, piñon nuts and buffalo hides. They went back to Mexico in chains with the slaves themselves.

Adult slaves were set free. Children like *Béésh Ligaii* were kept to grow up as Christians. A special church court called The Holy Office of the Inquisition tried to show that the governor and his wife had tried to hurt the work of the church in New Mexico and were not good Christians. Ramírez and his friends said the governor had broken church rules 257 times and his wife 40 times.

Some of the charges were not true. The judges were told that Teresa's Italian books were probably Jewish (not Christian) and were probably dirty since they made her laugh.

Other charges were more serious. Fray Ramírez told the court that López' slave raids turned the Indians against the Church. He said López' men worked the Pueblos so hard they could give nothing to the Church.

Week after week the judges questioned the governor and his wife about their lives in Santa Fe. At first López shouted back that he was not guilty. His enemies had lied about him, he said. But month after month the questioning went on. López' voice became weaker. He grew thin and his hands shook. Finally, after nearly two years in prison, he died in his cell.

Teresa survived. She cried many tears when she heard the terrible things said about her in the court, but she pointed her finger right back at her enemies, including Ramírez. Finally, after her husband had died, the court decided that she was in fact innocent. But she had lost her property, lost her friends, and lost her dream of a fine life forever.

## FRAY RAMÍREZ

Juan Ramírez did not cry when Governor López died in prison. He believed that the church was always right. Proud Spanish governors and Indian medicine men were all the same to him. They both hurt the work of the church. The medicine men deserved the whip and greedy governors deserved prison. The church had laws against taking Indian slaves and laws against reading Jewish books or singing in kivas. Church members who broke these laws should be punished. Ramírez had no doubt.

But the people he punished became his enemies. Even other members of the Franciscan brotherhood whispered against him. They greeted him with polite smiles, but his black eyes looked back fiercely. He knew they were out to get him. He was right.

Not long after the Holy Office of the Inquisition arrested Governor López and Teresa, it arrested Fray Ramírez himself. He had

106

... "Great has been the greed of the governors of this kingdom. They say they are fighting enemies. That is an excuse for sending the king's armies to capture Indians to sell at the mines of El Parral. (Governor Don Bernardo López de Mendizábal is doing that now. He has already sent 70 men and women to be sold).

This is a thing which the king and his officials have forbidden. The law calls for strong punishments. But no one pays attention to the law because so much money can be made. Therefore God our Lord is losing the souls of the Indians. Because of the slavehunting, they have a great hatred for our religion and for the Spanish nation ..."

*(Letter to the Holy Office of the Inquisition, Sept. 8, 1659 signed by Juan Ramírez and six other Franciscan Friars)*

punished too many people for breaking church rules. Now his enemies had caught him breaking four rules himself. They said: He had blessed holy water in a pot he once used as a bathroom. He had held a church service in a cart where he also ate and slept. He had not put the proper things on the altar during the service. He had given meat to his friends at a time when church law said they shouldn't eat it.

For that Ramírez spent a year behind bars and never again did important work for the Franciscan Brotherhood or the Church. The law was the law, and it didn't matter who broke it.

## CAPTAIN DOMÍNGUEZ Y MENDOZA

Well, it was not quite true that the law treated everyone the same way. The records say a great deal about Captain Domínguez, and nearly all of it is bad. Even in times of peace, he murdered innocent Indians more than once. He led attacks on Apaches and Navajos for another 20 years after the massacre at Jemez. By Spanish law he should have spent most of his life in jail. Many other Spaniards complained of his cruelty, but no one touched him.

When the Pueblos did fight back and killed hundreds of Spaniards, Domínguez was among the lucky ones. He escaped to El Paso with most of his property. He wanted very much to become governor at El Paso, but even his friends probably did not want such a blood-thirsty leader. He tried at least once to fight his way back into New Mexico anyway, but failed. After that history says nothing about him.

But history did not forget him. The cruelty of Domínguez and people like him began a war with the Apaches and Navajos that lasted more than 200 years. It was a war the Spaniards could never win. Even though they built towns and missions, Europeans would not travel safely through Navajo Country for a long, long time.

## DE VARGAS AND JEMEZ

Just as *Hastiin Béésh Ligaii* and his Jemez friend feared, the Spanish governor at El Paso, Diego de Vargas, did come back up the Rio Grande Valley and pick off the Pueblos like ripe corn. With 40 Spanish soldiers and 80 "Indian Allies" (from other Pueblos), he came to Jemez the evening of July 23, 1694.

About half the men, led by Captain Eusebio de Vargas (no relation to Diego), hid behind the mesa where the old village stood. Diego hid the rest below the main trail in front. Both groups attacked at dawn. Later Diego de Vargas wrote:

> The barbarians ran to fight Captain Eusebio de Vargas and his crowd and in the fighting lost twelve to fifteen dead. At the same time our men, because they were shooting, were heard. Even though the Indians shot many arrows, hurled stones, and loosed some boulders, our men withstood and parried them and swiftly climbed the slope, so effective was their shooting. When the rebels recognized that our men were near and about to enter the pueblo, seven threw themselves over the edge.

> . . . I then climbed the rock and found our forces still locked in combat. From holes in the walls of houses some of the enemy shot many arrows, wounding some of our people. After fires were set in the houses, it was found that four Indian men and one woman had died inside, choked by the smoke, and burned.

> . . . There had been 55 other deaths in this battle. Two of the enemy* were captured, and I ordered likewise that they be shot. Thus on this day, the 24th, all told 84 died. The whole mob of captives numbered 361, persons of all ages, women and children.

> Having entered the plaza and pueblo on the mesa . . . I acclaimed the King Our Lord for the victory won by his royal arms, shouting, "Long may he live!" . . .

> That night, Saturday the 24th, was the eve of the feast day of the glorious apostle Santiago, patron of the Spains. . . .

*One of these was an Apache or perhaps Navajo. See Espinosa, Manuel, *Crusaders of the Rio Grande*. Chicago, Illinois: Institute of Jesuit History, 1942. (p. 200)

108

Many Jemez people did escape, however, and joined the Navajos. The old man, *Ma'ii Yáázh*, may have been among them. Or he may have been shot by the firing squad with his Navajo friend. There has been close kinship between the Navajos and the Jemez since that time, however. Many Navajos of the *Ma'ii Deeshgiizhnii* Clan (Coyote Pass People, the Navajo name for Jemez) are descended from the Jemez who joined the Navajos after de Vargas burned their town.

Today the ruins of Pueblo-style houses and forts can still be seen in Largo Canyon. Navajos and Pueblos working together built them. And Navajo storytellers, farmers, weavers and medicine men still use knowledge brought by the Pueblo people.

*Ruin of Pueblo-style fort in Largo Canyon.*

Note: This story is based on historical facts documented in a series of articles by France V. Sholes in the *New Mexico Historical Review*, volumes 5, 10, and 15. Other background information came from reports and books by Correll, de Vargas, Espinosa, and Hackett. See bibliography.

# THE ROYAL ROAD  *El Camino Real* in 1650

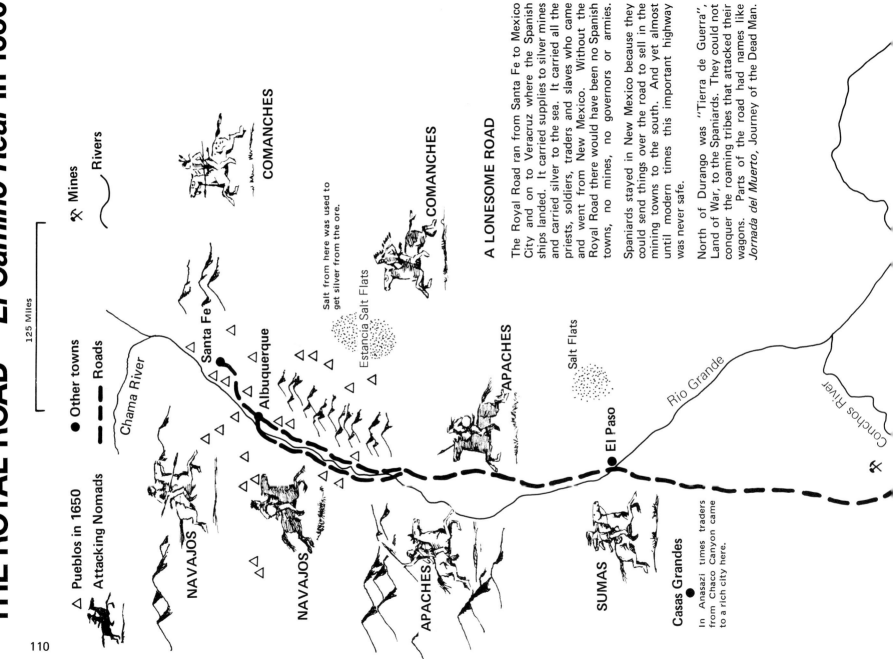

△ Pueblos in 1650    ● Other towns    ⚔ Mines

Attacking Nomads    ▬ ▬ Roads    Rivers

125 Miles

**COMANCHES**

**COMANCHES**

Salt from here was used to get silver from the ore.

Estancia Salt Flats

Chama River

**Santa Fe**

**Albuquerque**

**NAVAJOS**

**NAVAJOS**

**APACHES**

**APACHES**

**SUMAS**

**Casas Grandes**

In Anasazi times traders from Chaco Canyon came to a rich city here.

**El Paso**

Salt Flats

Rio Grande

Conchos River

## A LONESOME ROAD

The Royal Road ran from Santa Fe to Mexico City and on to Veracruz where the Spanish ships landed. It carried supplies to silver mines and carried silver to the sea. It carried all the priests, soldiers, traders and slaves who came and went from New Mexico. Without the Royal Road there would have been no Spanish towns, no mines, no governors or armies.

Spaniards stayed in New Mexico because they could send things over the road to sell in the mining towns to the south. And yet almost until modern times this important highway was never safe.

North of Durango was "Tierra de Guerra", Land of War, to the Spaniards. They could not conquer the roaming tribes that attacked their wagons. Parts of the road had names like *Jornada del Muerto*, Journey of the Dead Man.

110

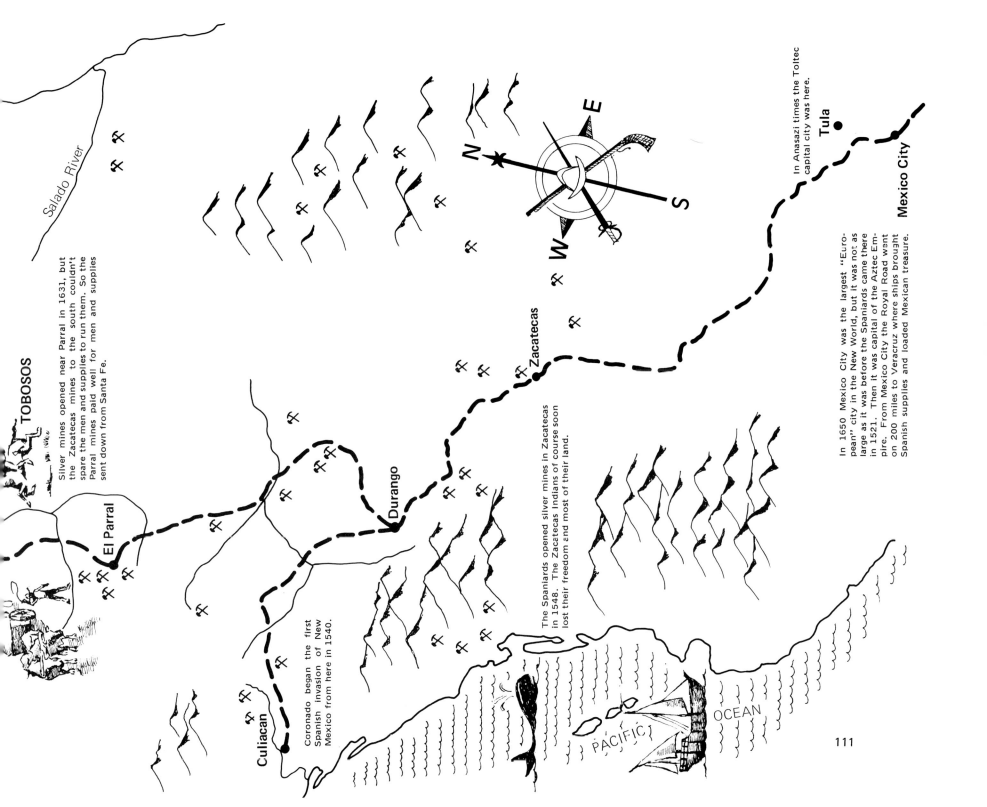

Salado River

TOBOSOS

Silver mines opened near Parral in 1631, but the Zacatecas mines to the south couldn't spare the men and supplies to run them. So the Parral mines paid well for men and supplies sent down from Santa Fe.

El Parral

N
E
S
W

Tula

In Anasazi times the Toltec capital city was here.

Zacatecas

Durango

The Spaniards opened silver mines in Zacatecas in 1548. The Zacatecas Indians of course soon lost their freedom and most of their land.

In 1650 Mexico City was the largest "European" city in the New World, but it was not as large as it was before the Spaniards came there in 1521. Then it was capital of the Aztec Empire. From Mexico City the Royal Road went on 200 miles to Veracruz where ships brought Spanish supplies and loaded Mexican treasure.

Mexico City

Coronado began the first Spanish invasion of New Mexico from here in 1540.

Culiacan

PACIFIC OCEAN

111

# RICHES, GREED, MONEY AND BLOOD

Why did Governor López do what he did? Why did the kings of Spain want all that silver and gold?

They wanted to become rich, of course. López wanted a fine house in Mexico City where he could spend the rest of his life without working. The kings wanted to make Spain the strongest and largest empire in the world.

Greedy people sometimes get caught, however. López died in prison. The kings lost their empire and Spain itself became a poor nation.

True riches are made when something useful is created. It may be a poem, a prayer, a tool or a field of corn. When useful things are bought and sold, traded and shared they make life richer. Money by itself does not.

The word "useful" is the key. Who today makes or does useful things in Navajo Country? Who is poor? Who gets rich by greed? Who is like López? Who like the Spanish kings?

## López The Exploiter

Exploitation means robbery. An exploiter gets rich by making other people poor. But exploitation cannot go on forever. It stops when there is nothing left to exploit or when the poor fight back as the Indians of New Mexico did in the Pueblo Revolt. Unfortunately that came too late to save many of them.

Here Fray Ramírez tells how López got salt from dry lakes near Estancia, southeast of Albuquerque. The miners in Parral used it in taking silver from the ore.

**Fray Ramírez wrote:**

*As soon as López came, he ordered the natives to make nine wagons, and to pull them he has taken nearly 200 oxen. . . . To load the wagons, he forced Indians of the pueblos of the salt flats\* to carry salt on their shoulders. . .ninety miles one way, without pay, to the Royal Road . . .and did not even feed them.*

*He sent officials to some of the pueblos to take their grass mats, which were their bedding. From others he took buckskins and moccasin leather. . . . He paid nothing. In Taos Pueblo alone he took 40 buckskins and many cow hides. . . for whips, straps and covers on the wagons.*

*. . .The officials made the Indians, and some Spaniards, take the wagons to El Parral without pay. As the salt is sold along with the wagons themselves and oxen, the Indians stay there homeless, away from wives and children, until they are lost.*

*. . .Taking the salt has caused serious illness. Some are disabled completely in the Pueblo of Cuarac.*

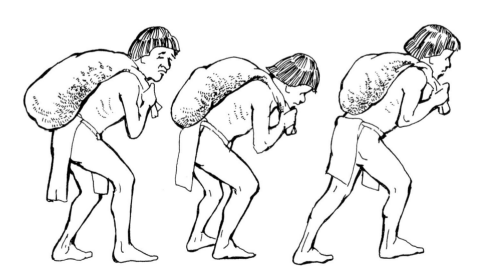

\* Chilili, Tajique, Cuarac (Quarai), Abo, Quivira, and Jumanas were Tewa, Tiwa, and Tompiro towns. Because of exploitation, they died away completely before 1680. The names (except Jumanas) still show on road maps. Check Route 14 north and south of Mountainair, New Mexico.

Riches gained by exploitation and fed to the dragon of war spread poverty.

## The King's Mistake

The mines of Mexico, Bolivia and Peru seemed like never-ending money machines to the kings of Spain. The world had never seen such treasure. Poor Spain became rich Spain. A weak kingdom became a powerful empire.

The Spaniards were not the only Europeans who believed that silver and gold would get them everything, but they were the only ones unlucky enough to find it.

The treasure that built the Spanish empire was lost. Silver that paid soldiers and bought weapons in foreign countries did not help Spaniards or Indians become better farmers or craftsmen or live better lives.

Riches that came from exploitation were spent on war. Nothing new or useful was created. When the mines ran out of ore and the soldiers lost their wars, rich Spain became poor Spain again, and its empire broke up.

The Spaniards did not go away like the Anasazi, but Spain lost its power in the world and in Navajo Country to other nations.

The people of Navajo Country may think hard about the problems of the Spanish kings. Today Navajo Country has rich mines of coal and uranium. Where do these riches go? Do they stay in Navajo Country? Are they exploited by others? Is anything new or useful done with them? For whom?

Just as plants and animals help each other in a circle of life, true riches grow in a circle of trade. Each member is a giver, a taker and a creator. Each depends on the others.

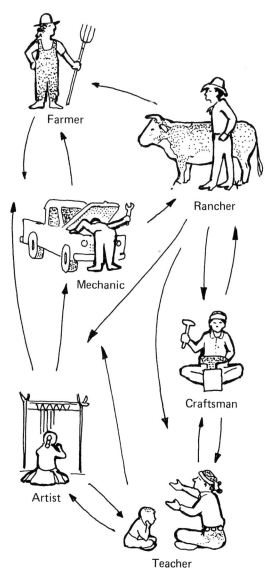

113

# NOMADS, PUEBLOS AND EUROPEANS

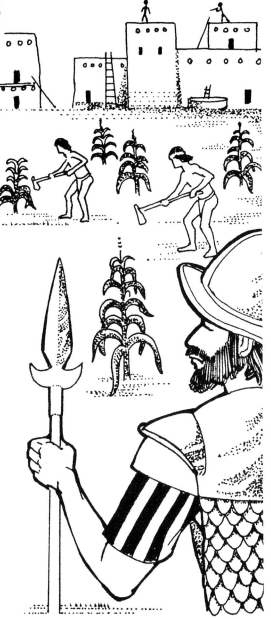

An earlier chapter talked about the difference between nomadic people and town people. The Jemez man thought of that difference when he said he could "live like the deer" and move from place to place with Navajos, but his valley would always be home.

Navajos and Jemez did live differently. Like plants in the same community, they lived together because they lived differently. Europeans upset this community like a new animal might upset growing plants.

Pueblos were sweet grass to the Spaniards. A few soldiers could boss a whole village, because the people would not leave homes and fields. So soldiers took food, cotton, etc., and made people work. Often "work" meant fighting Navajos. Remember 800 Indians who hunted slaves with Captain Dominguez.

In return the Pueblos got measles, small-pox, flu and poverty and died by the thousands.

Navajos, however, grew stronger because their way of life was specialized to survive. They lost a few slaves, but took horses, livestock and steel weapons. They lived far from each other, so European diseases hurt them less. And Spanish armies only wasted time chasing people who could always move.

For 300 years Navajos took more than they lost from the "Web of Empire". Then in 1864 the United States forced them onto a reservation. What have they gained since then? What have they lost?

# THE PUEBLO REVOLT

The Indians of New Mexico spoke many different languages and often fought among themselves. However, they all suffered together from the Spaniards. When they agreed to fight together, they won.

In 1675, the Spanish Governor tried once too often to wipe out Pueblo religion. He arrested 47 medicine men, hung three, whipped the rest and planned to send them to Mexico in chains. However, 70 Tewa warriors marched into Santa Fe and rescued them.

That day, one of the medicine men, Po'p'ay of San Juan, began plans for a real freedom fight. Working from Taos, he spent five years getting the trust of other leaders.

Then one night his runners left Taos for the other Pueblos, carrying knotted ropes, a rope for each village and a knot for each day until the attack.

Four days before the time, the Spaniards caught two runners at Tesuque, tortured the

secret out of them, then killed them. But Indian news traveled faster than Spanish news. Not waiting for knots, the villages attacked at once on August 10, 1680. Within two weeks Pueblos, Apaches and Navajos took Santa Fe. Some Spanish survivors made it back to El Paso, but fighting spread far into Mexico as other tribes heard the news.

Twelve years later the Spaniards did return and "picked the Pueblos like ripe corn", but they learned to rule less roughly.

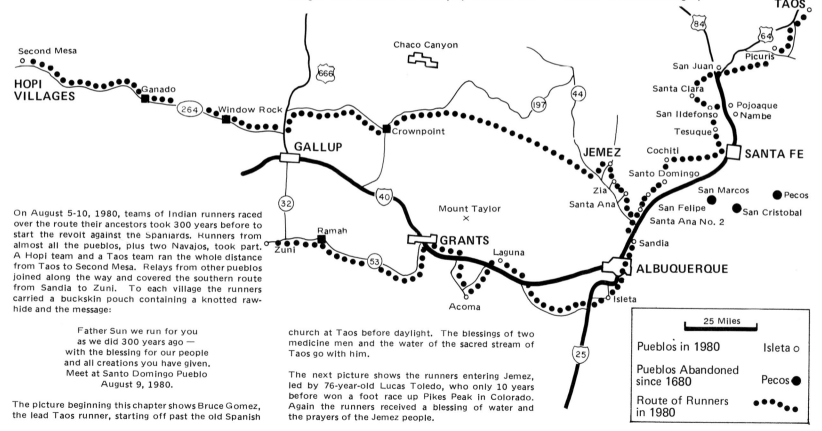

On August 5-10, 1980, teams of Indian runners raced over the route their ancestors took 300 years before to start the revolt against the Spaniards. Runners from almost all the pueblos, plus two Navajos, took part. A Hopi team and a Taos team ran the whole distance from Taos to Second Mesa. Relays from other pueblos joined along the way and covered the southern route from Sandia to Zuni. To each village the runners carried a buckskin pouch containing a knotted rawhide and the message:

Father Sun we run for you
as we did 300 years ago —
with the blessing for our people
and all creations you have given.
Meet at Santo Domingo Pueblo
August 9, 1980.

The picture beginning this chapter shows Bruce Gomez, the lead Taos runner, starting off past the old Spanish

church at Taos before daylight. The blessings of two medicine men and the water of the sacred stream of Taos go with him.

The next picture shows the runners entering Jemez, led by 76-year-old Lucas Toledo, who only 10 years before won a foot race up Pikes Peak in Colorado. Again the runners received a blessing of water and the prayers of the Jemez people.

# THE WEB OF EMPIRE

This map shows the Americas in 1700. Then four European nations, Spain, Portugal, England and France claimed huge pieces of land. Empires* were growing. Those countries, plus Russia and Holland were taking land all over the world.

Besides the Americas, all Africa, India, Australia, and Asia except Japan and parts of China were taken over by European countries.

The wars and trade of empires tied the world together in a huge spider web. Whatever shook part of the web shook it all.

The web caught **Béésh Łigaii** and other Indians of New Mexico along with everyone else. By making silver, **Béésh Łigaii** helped spin the Spanish part of the web. His silver paid soldiers in France, Holland and Italy. It traveled to India, China, the Philippines and Japan in trading ships.

The empires of that time have nearly all disappeared, but the web still ties the world together. Navajo soldiers fight wars in Japan or Vietnam. Uranium dug from sacred Mount Taylor may make electricity in Germany or bombs in England.

**Béésh Łigaii** and his Jemez friend did not talk of such things, but they had already fallen into the web, and their children would never escape it.

*When the government of one country rules many other countries also, that is called an empire.

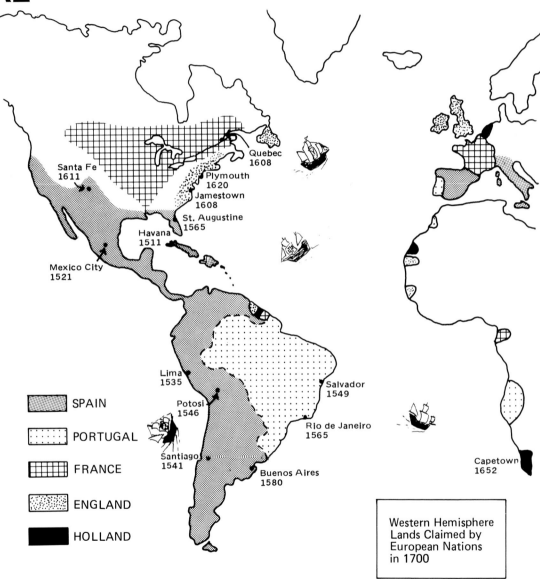

Santa Fe 1611
Quebec 1608
Plymouth 1620
Jamestown 1608
St. Augustine 1565
Havana 1511
Mexico City 1521
Lima 1535
Salvador 1549
Potosi 1546
Rio de Janeiro 1565
Santiago 1541
Buenos Aires 1580
Capetown 1652

▨ SPAIN

⠿ PORTUGAL

⊞ FRANCE

⠂ ENGLAND

■ HOLLAND

Western Hemisphere Lands Claimed by European Nations in 1700

116

## ACROSS LAND AND SEA

Not only war traveled across the "Web of Empire". Knowledge, religion, food plants, tools and other things passed quickly from one side of the world to the other, changing the lives of people everywhere.

The corn and beans that fed the people of Navajo Country long before the Spaniards came soon grew on every continent. According to the *World Book Encyclopedia,* Mexican turkeys (cousins to Navajo Country birds) were carried to Spain, traded to England and Holland, and *came back* to *America* with the Pilgrims for their famous Thanksgiving party.

On the other hand, Navajo fried bread is made with European wheat. The blood of Spanish sheep, taken in raids, or given to Navajos in 1868 after the Long Walk, still runs in Navajo herds.

These things happened after Europeans learned to sail the oceans. But in fact they only wrote one more chapter in an old story. Columbus was not the first to cross between continents. The land itself holds proof.

## HORSES AND SHEEP

Navajos have a story that says sheep and horses were created at the home of the Sun a very long time ago. Bighorn sheep once roamed parts of Navajo Country, and many still live in ancient rock drawings.

The first Europeans to visit Navajo Country saw no horses. They said Indian horses came from Spain. However, horse bones older than any found in Europe have been dug up in North America, some of them near Navajo Country.

People studying these bones believe the world's first horses did live here, somehow wandered into Asia, and survived until Spaniards brought them back. Were Navajos here when American horses died out (or were hunted down) 8,000 years ago?

## COTTON

Native Americans in the Southwest had cotton cloth before they saw a Spaniard. Cotton has been dug out of Anasazi ruins 1,000 years old and from South American ruins 3,000 years older than that.

Spaniards first saw cotton when Arab armies carried it into Spain from North Africa. In America they took all the Indian cotton they could find because it was just as good.

Now plant scientists say without doubt that the ancient American cotton is in fact half American wild cotton and half African cotton. That means someone probably brought cotton from Africa by boat 4-5,000 years ago. Later American cotton spread to many islands in the Pacific Ocean.

Ocean-sailing boats were built by both North Africans and South American Indians long before Columbus decided the world was round. They could have carried cotton seed.

Now American cotton grows world wide, but the questions remain. Who mixed African and American Cotton? Who figured out how to weave it? How did the idea get to Navajo Country? What else came the same way?

# WILD THINGS AND EMPIRES

The "Web of Empire" brought new people, gods and ideas to Navajo Country. Mines, roads and cities now mark the land in ways never seen before on this side of the oceans. The history of Navajo Country is now part of world history.

But the wildest, most forgotten corners of the land show best what the "Web of Empire" really means. Winds and seasons have carried changes even there.

The wild things on this page all come from other continents, and they are not the only newcomers. Everywhere you go in Navajo Country, plants and creatures that Hastiin *Béésh Ligaii* never saw will be there before you. Europeans brought them, but who now could send them back?

THE HOUSE SPARROW came from England. From New York City it spread across the country and is now the most common sparrow. The small brown birds you see hopping around houses, camps and garbage dumps are probably house sparrows.

BARBARY SHEEP look like bighorns, but they grow smaller, straighter horns and have long hair under their necks. They come from North Africa and can live where the roads, noises and smells of people would kill bighorns or drive them away. They also need less water. They come from North Africa and were put in Largo Canyon in 1956.

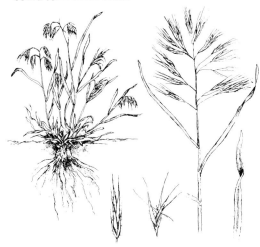

CHEAT GRASS, sometimes called brome tec for its Latin name *bromus tectorum*, grows early, but by late June it dries out and turns almost purple. Its sharp seeds will stick in your socks and the lips of animals. Some places, as between Lukachukai and Round Rock, it is almost the only grass growing, but it comes from southern Europe.

TAMARISK or SALT CEDAR grows along the washes everywhere in Navajo Country. In late summer and fall it has beautiful purple flowers. It comes from Spain. Navajos often call it *gad nahalinigii* because it looks like juniper (gad).

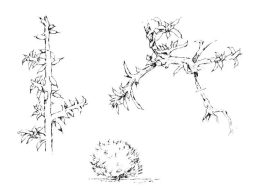

TUMBLEWEED or *ch'il deenini* (prickly weed) in Navajo grows everywhere in Navajo Country. It is a terrible pest, even though livestock can eat it if they are hungry enough. It comes from Russia and is also called Russian Thistle.

# SILVER: A Deadly Beauty

Long before Governor López' time, silver was known in Mexico. Today, 300 years since Hastiin *Béésh Ligaii* went down into the mines of Parral, you will find the bright white metal wherever you find Indian people, from the Rio Grande to the Colorado River.

In the hands of the best smiths in all the world, the beauty of the land itself is melted, hammered and polished into silver and worn proudly by young and old.

Getting pure shining silver from gray mountain rock, however, is difficult and dangerous. The drawings below show how this was done in Parral. There are people alive today who still remember this method.

Hastiin *Béésh Ligaii* lost his teeth because of the mercury that was used to make the silver pure. Mercury is a deadly poison. Today cyanide is used, also deadly, but easier to use safely. Many have died young because of silver.

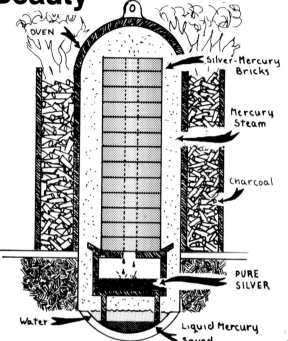

Silver ore came from mines to the "patios" in Parral. There, two sets of millstones (1) ground it to pebbles, then to sand. Next it was mixed with water, salt (from the north), copper sulphate (mined nearby), and mercury (from Spain). For several weeks horses walked around on this mixture (2) until the silver joined the mercury. (The mercury also slowly killed the horses.) The mixture was then washed in tubs (3). The silver-mercury mix went to the bottom. The worthless rock was taken off the top. The silver-mercury part was put in sacks, squeezed in a press (4), and dried into bricks. The bricks were stacked under a bell-shaped metal oven and cooked (5). The mercury boiled away, and pure melted silver ran down into a pot. Running water under the oven turned most of the deadly mercury steam back into liquid so it could be used again.

The world's biggest mercury mine was (and still is) in Almaden, Spain. The lives of miners poisoned there must be added to the price paid by the miners and patio workers for the silver of Mexico.

# WAR AND
# RESERVATION

# WAR AND RESERVATION

Navajo Country, like any place where many tribes and nations cross the same land, has seen as much war as peace. Especially in the time between 1800 and 1864, stories of war and raids among Navajos, Utes, Hopis, Zunis, Comanches, Apaches and Spaniards are nearly endless. Those were truly the days of the Wild West.

Last of all came the U.S. Army. In 1848 they marched into Santa Fe and made the Mexican towns of New Mexico part of the United States. The Navajos' turn came in 1864. Soldiers led by Kit Carson rounded up some 8,000 Navajos, marched them to *Hwééldi*—Fort Sumner in Eastern New Mexico—and kept them there for four years.

This book will not retell the story of the "Long Walk" to Fort Sumner because many other books tell it.[1] Instead, this chapter takes a look at the fighting that came before the Long Walk and the peace that came after it. The stories raise many questions:

- Why did the fighting take place?
- What did people want from the land they fought over?
- How did people feel about their homeland?
- Could wiser people have kept the peace?
- How did the Navajos survive as well as they did?

After the Long Walk and four years at Fort Sumner, the Navajo reservation was created and a line was drawn around it. Navajos were not supposed to leave it. The new rules and lines slowly ended the shooting, but they did not change the way people felt about the land. A few old wars still go on under the new rules. History shows how people came to feel the way they do.

Tales of raiding between Utes and Navajos open the chapter. They come from Ken Foster of Sheep Springs on the east side of the Chuska Mountains. The elders of his family tell many such stories because enemies from all directions crossed the pass above Sheep Springs.

In the next story Mexican slave raiders from the Rio Grande attack Navajo camps near Rock Point, Arizona. Emma Lee Jim, great-granddaughter of the heroine, tells the story. Her son Rex, who learned to write Navajo as a student at Rock Point School, wrote down her words and has published her story in a Navajo supplement to this book.[2] His English translation appears here.

The rocks in the area where the raid actually happened add an interesting note to the story. On a wall covered by ancient Anasazi and Navajo drawings are the words *"Blas Lucero Año de 1860"* and *"Navajoe Expedition October 21st, 1860."* Military records mention Lucero often as an Indian fighter and slave raider. Colonel Canby of the U.S. Army led the Navajo Expedition and hired Lucero and his men as a "spy company." No doubt they knew the area and raided camps there more than once.

According to the records, the Navajo Expedition camped a few miles further down the valley at a place called *Tó Dilhil* (Dark Water). The short piece titled "A Navajo Warrior" is printed as told by the warrior's grandson, *Tó Dilhil Biye'*, who comes from that place.

The last story tells of the birth of the Navajo leader Chee Dodge during the wars between the Navajos and the U.S. Army. It comes from the records left by the U.S. Army and the memories of his descendants, especially his son Tom Dodge. The many stories about Chee do not agree in every detail. However, all paint a strong picture of how people lived and fought, even though the whole truth may be hidden forever by the dust of war.

Each of the stories is a thread in the history of our land. Such stories are told in many families by the descendants of the raiders and warriors and heroes who lived them. They are part of us forever.

[1]See bibliography.
[2]*Naakaiitahgóó Tázhdííyá*, by Emma Lee Jim, transcribed by Rex Lee Jim, Rock Point Community School, Chinle, Arizona, 1981.

# STOLEN HORSES

*There are two sides to every war, as this story told by Ken Foster of Sheep Springs shows. Foster's clan is Kin Yaa'áanii; he is born for Kin Lichíi'nii. The elders of his family knew many tales of Utes, Comanches, Mexicans and others.*

One day a young man was herding by himself out near Burnham. When he came back home, he found his horses gone and his uncle dead with an arrow in his chest.

For a while he did nothing, just kept on living as usual, but his aunt began to nag at him.

"What kind of a man are you anyway?" she said to that young fellow. "You're supposed to get revenge for your uncle. People will call you a coward for the rest of your life. You can't just leave things like that."

So the boy started off, tracking his uncle's horses toward the north until he came to the San Juan River. On the other side he could see the Utes, and there were hundreds of them. They were cutting down greasewood and brush for a corral.

That night the boy sneaked in there so quietly that the dogs didn't even bark. He knew of one wild horse in the herd that led all the rest, but it had never been ridden. He climbed up on the corral and waited for the lead horse to come close. Then he jumped. He hoped that if he stayed on, the horse would cause so much commotion that the herd would break out of the corral. So he hung on with all his strength, and sure enough, the horses pushed over the brush and broke for their own country across the river.

The Ute horses were grazing down by the river. The boy steered his herd right through them, so they all came too. He kept the lead horse galloping until he was out of danger; then he slipped over onto one of the tame horses and slowed the herd down.

The next day he got back to his aunt's place with all those horses and the Ute horses too. She was happy. "Well, I guess you're a man now," she said. After that they moved away.

That's how things were between the Navajos and Utes. Years later, after the Navajos came back from Fort Sumner and there was no more fighting going on, Utes used to come down to Sheep Springs to trade peaceably. When they got together with the Navajos there was always a lot of boasting going on.

At one of those meetings an old Ute man said, "Oh, the Navajos are such cowards. We used to come down here and round them up like sheep and take their horses. Navajos are cowards. Everyone knows that."

Well, there was a Navajo there, and he wasn't going to hear that, so he said, "No, the Utes are the cowards. They always travel around in a big gang. Then they act tough. But alone they are cowards. It's well known that some Navajos carry around a big stick that looks like a gun because they know a Ute won't get close enough to find out if it's real. I've killed many Utes in my time, and it was easy."

The Ute didn't believe it. "Who did you kill?" he barked.

"Well," said the Navajo, "I killed two Utes over on the Carrizo Mountains one time. I just tracked them along, and when I found them I shot them. Then I also killed one up near Mesa Verde. There were a lot of Utes around hunting. I shot one of them in the chest with my arrow, and after he fell over I shot him again in the back of the head. Then I took his horse."

When the Ute heard that story he said something in Ute to one of the ladies there, and pretty soon she began to cry. "That man you killed was her brother," he said. "When we got back from driving the deer, he was missing and also the horse of one of the other men. When we went back, we found him just like you said, with an arrow in the chest and another in the back of the head."

Then the Utes had to believe what the Navajos were saying about them. That's the way it was. The Utes always came in a big bunch, but sometimes the Navajos got even with them anyway.

# A NAVAJO WARRIOR

*Hastiin Tó Diłhił Biye' (Dark Water's Son), of Rock Point, Arizona, tells of his grandfather, Deeshchii'nii Atsidí, who grew up in the war years before 1864.*

My grandfather went to *Hwééldi* (Fort Sumner), but even in his old age he carried a steel spear head as long as your forearm. He would wave it about saying, "This is a warrior's spear, a *tsii'détáán*. Do you have a *tsii'détáán*, my grandson? I have a *tsii'détáán*."

He would say that and show it off. When he slept, he put that spear head under his own head as a pillow.

"In the days before *Hwééldi*, I used to make arrows," he would say. "I made the heads of steel as long as my finger and feathered them with eagle feathers. No enemy shot by such an arrow could survive. Often people said to me, 'We cannot take your arrows out of the bodies. We leave them.' "

My grandfather told of how he fought. "Sometimes enemy riders would surround you," he said. "They had guns and arrows, but you would run around in the circle of horses and shoot at them. Sometimes you were alone. If you were not good, they would strike you behind the head with a *tsii'détáán*, and you would fall at once.

"A person inside the circle of enemies must stampede them or push them back to a mesa or canyon where escape is possible. Sometimes, somehow you would escape. Sometimes you were wounded.

"The Navajos then had amazing strength. Two of them together were dangerous indeed. We used to kill running horses. Stories were told about the bravest and best."

That is how my grandfather used to talk.

126

# CAPTURE BY MEXICANS

My name is Emma Jim. My clan is *Kin Lichíi'nii;* I am born for *Kin Yaa'áanii.* My mother's father was *Honágháahnii;* my father's father was *Áshįįhí.*

I will tell the story of my great-grandmother, who was taken among the Mexicans from her home near Rock Point. My mother used to tell it to me.

## THE RAID

They say that a long time ago there were homes in the alcove near *Tsé Biná'áz'éli* (Rock Washed Around by Floods). My great-grandmother, *Asdzą́ą́ Atsidí,* started out from there one day to visit a younger brother near *Tsé Ahił Halne'í* (Rocks Talking to Each Other).

"I'm going to tell them that we should meet and travel together over to Black Mesa," she told her family.

Along the way she came across some *tł'ohdeii* (goosefoot) and stopped to gather seed. That took time, so she left the plants, planning to pick them up on her way back.

When she reached her brother's place, she found them baking bread in the ground. "We'll start for Black Mesa as soon as the bread is out of the ground," they told her. "You start too as soon as you get back home. We'll meet over at *Dibé Bichaan Bii' Tó* (Sheep Manure Spring)."

So she went back, stopping only to pick up the *tł'ohdeii* that she had left.

Nearing home she heard gun shots. Quickly crawling into a greasewood bush, she hid until everything was quiet, then crept carefully on to her camp. As she came closer, she heard someone hammering. At that time they had a brush shelter, and the hammering came from inside.

Her heart went faster, but inside she found only her ten-year-old son happily hammering away. "Where did the others go?" she asked him.

"Oh, they went down the wash," he said, as if nothing special had happened. "Some Mexicans are chasing them on horseback. As for me—I got tired of running and crawled under a bush. They just went on by."

So that boy had just wandered on back and was happily hammering away in the shelter while the Mexicans chased his father and brothers on down the wash.

*Asdzą́ą́ Atsidí* at once grabbed her son and set out for a cave she knew of near *Tséch'iltsoh* (Big Oak). But on the way they saw the tracks of a pack rat running into a hole.

"Let's take it out," the boy urged.

"No! Hurry up! Let's go!" his mother said, pushing him on.

But they did stop and poked a stick into the rat hole. The rat ran out, and they clubbed it.

"Let's go on now!" *Asdzą́ą́ Atsidí* felt like shouting, but when they got to the top of the mesa, the boy said, "Let's roast this rat so we'll have strength to go on."

"No! Let's go!" she cried, but again the boy had his way and they roasted the rat in the ground.

As they were taking it out, they heard shots again—right near by! Finally they started running. Down in a small alcove they crouched behind a tiny sumac bush. The Mexicans rode by above them. Silence.

But as they crawled from their hiding place, one of the riders saw them. "Come on out, you two!" he said, raising his gun.

"No! Let's stay here!" whispered the little boy, crying and pulling back, but his mother answered, "We must go out or he'll shoot us."

So the Mexican took them to his camp on the plain near Big Oak. The fires were lit and coffee was boiling. The captured Navajo women were put to work cooking. "Who's going to eat this well at home?" some of them even said as they made tortillas and stew.

The relatives *Asdzą́ą́ Atsidí* had visited that morning were among the prisoners. A fat Mexican took her son away from her. The boy spent the night with him, and the Mexican didn't allow her to come anywhere near.

She might have run away that very night. Her other children, a brother, and her husband who was of the *Kin Yaa'áanii* Clan, had out-run the Mexicans and escaped to the north towards *Tó Diłhił* (Dark Water). Yet she stayed there with the Mexicans because of her youngest boy.

## ON TO THE RIVER

The following day they started out. They went northwest over the mesa, through the place called *Tó Hahaas'nilí* (Water Taken Out), and on to Dennehotso and Kayenta. Then they turned south through Chilchinbito. Near there they captured some Paiute children and babies.

From there they moved on past Rough Rock. Somewhere before Many Farms they stopped for the night at a place called *Tséta'* (Gap). There a band of Paiute warriors almost caught up with them. Four of the captured Paiute children saw them and ran away in the night. They left behind the babies, who were carried on to Mexican country.

On they went past Many Farms and along the edge of Canyon de Chelly to *Sǫ' Silá* (Sonsela—"Lying Stars"). As they traveled, the Mexicans captured more people. Some ran away as soon as possible, but because of her son, *Asdzą́ą́ Atsidí* stayed.

On they went through valleys and over mountains, and way on somewhere they ran out of food.

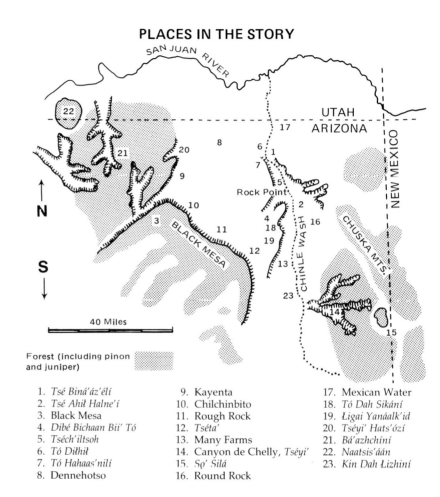

PLACES IN THE STORY

Forest (including pinon and juniper)

1. *Tsé Biná'áz'éli*
2. *Tsé Ahił Halne'í*
3. Black Mesa
4. *Dibé Bichaan Bii' Tó*
5. *Tséch'iltsoh*
6. *Tó Diłhił*
7. *Tó Hahaas'nilí*
8. Dennehotso
9. Kayenta
10. Chilchinbito
11. Rough Rock
12. *Tséta'*
13. Many Farms
14. Canyon de Chelly, *Tséyi'*
15. *Sǫ' Silá*
16. Round Rock
17. Mexican Water
18. *Tó Dah Sikání*
19. *Łigai Yanáalk'id*
20. *Tséyi' Hats'ózí*
21. *Bá'azhchíni*
22. *Naatsis'áán*
23. *Kin Dah Łizhiní*

A very ugly Mexican among them had taken a beautiful young Navajo woman. She cried a lot because of him. "Just run away from him," she was often told. But she always replied, "At night he ties me to himself." So she cried all the time because of that. "Men in other places have said, 'Give me this girl,'" she would weep, "But my relatives always said 'No!' I think they were saving me for this ugly creep."

One morning the ugly creep went around with a bowl asking for food, but there was none so he butchered a donkey. Others who had run out of food stole some of the meat, and the Navajo women teased him about it, saying "Our in-law killed a donkey for us!"

They ate and went on their way through mountains and onwards until they ran out of food again.

The Mexicans could barely walk and used their guns as canes. They ate weeds and grasses soaked in water, and chewed sinews cut from dead stinking horses they passed. The Navajos should have clubbed their captors right there instead of just letting them lead them along.

One Mexican wove a small bag for a Paiute baby. He hung the bag from his saddle horn and put the baby inside. The baby gnawed on tortillas while the Mexican led the horse. Even though that baby messed up everything, the Mexican loved him and would clean him up.

Finally food was sent to them by wagon, and after some time they came to a river. The water was not running high, so they crossed easily. They had reached the Mexican country.

## AMONG THE MEXICANS

Mexicans were living there in tents, they say. They kept *Asdzą́ą́ Atsidí* in one of the only buildings. The other Navajos were taken to different places, but *Asdzą́ą́ Atsidí* lived there in the house of the fat Mexican's mother, along with two other Navajo girls who had been captured two years before and knew some Spanish.

The fat Mexican took her son and only brought him there during the day. She thought, "If he is left here overnight, we will escape." But her son never was allowed to stay. And so the boy got used to life over there. The Mexican bought him good clothes and shoes. He dressed him well and took him wherever he went.

*Asdzą́ą́ Atsidí* herself was pregnant at that time, and after about two months she gave birth over there in the Mexican country. The fat Mexican's mother and her household carried the baby all

around. When somebody came down the road, the fat Mexican's mother would run off with the baby calling, "Let them look at the baby!" They ran around so much with that baby that they killed it. And so *Asdzą́ą́ Atsidí* was alone again.

Once the fat Mexican did take her home with him. She spent the night there and he took her to the top of a mountain. "Do you see that reflection over there?" he asked her. "That's the ocean."

One day the people in her household told her, "There's a ceremony going on. Let's go!" So she went along with them to a long building full of people—ladies on one side and men on the other. Even the doorway was crowded. A board table stood in the middle with a long covered box on it. Two women walked around it, crying all through the night. Everyone sang. When the ladies finished singing on one side, the men started on the other.

Later she learned that the women cried for their mother who had died and was laid out in a coffin on the table. The ceremony went on all night, and the next morning they had the burial.

That night *Asdzą́ą́ Atsidí* recognized a Navajo lady of the *Kin Lichíí'nii* Clan sitting in front of her. The Mexicans had cut her hair up to her ears.

The fat Mexican sat next to *Asdzą́ą́ Atsidí* and noticed that she had seen a friend. He called over a slim Mexican who spoke Navajo. He interpreted for the fat Mexican, who said, "Maybe you long for your relatives. Do you want to go back to them?"

She replied cautiously, "Who would I go back to? My relatives are all gone. You have taken them all. Why should I go back there just to die of thirst or starvation?"

But he said, "We'll give you a horse with a pack and everything in it. We will even give you some cows to take along too, so when you get hungry you can just kill one."

"No!" she answered. "How would a lady like me kill a cow? Why should I go back there? I don't want to go back!"

*Asdzą́ą́ Atsidí* was no fool. The Mexican interpreter whispered to her in Navajo, "If you say yes, they will sell you across the sea as a slave. That's why they offer you those things. Your friend here tried to run away. They caught her because she couldn't cross the river. That's why they cut her hair."

Later the slim Mexican interpreter spoke to her again. "Why should you be a slave, my mother? Forget it! Run away! A slave's life is hard. I know. I spent some years over there near a place called Big Oak." He mentioned all the places *Asdzą́ą́ Atsidí* knew, from Round Rock to Rock Point and on towards Mexican Water. "I was a slave of a man named *Hastiin Ts'ósí* for many years, but I never got used to things there," he said. Then she remembered she had in fact often seen that man with *Hastiin Ts'ósí*.

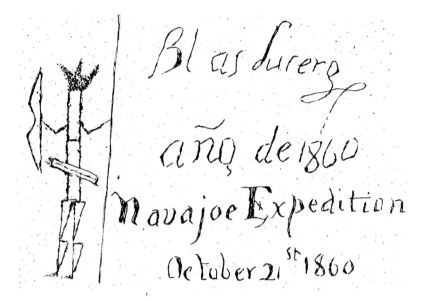

*These inscriptions in Spanish and English can be seen on a rock near Rock Point, Arizona, not far from the place called Big Oak where the heroine was first taken after her capture.*

**THE ESCAPE**

That day she began to plan her escape. To get in shape, she jogged back and forth in the building where she stayed. At first she bled and was sore, but she kept on training.

The next time the fat Mexican brought her son, she stayed with him a while, but her mind went back to home. "Forget this!" she thought. "I'm going to run away. My son is not suffering here, and I have other children at home to think of." And so she decided to leave him among the Mexicans.

For days she sewed clothes and collected things for the trip. Her bundle held flour, knives, needles and thread, moccasins, a large jar of water, and a rope and a big knife she had found.

Then one summer night she cut the wooden bars of her window with that big knife, tied the rope to her bundle and lowered it down, and, carrying the jug of water, she lowered herself.

Quietly she walked. Not even the dogs noticed her. As soon as she passed the settlement, she started jogging and kept on until at dawn she came to a big mountain. She hid there all day.

When she came to the river, she found it ran too deep to cross. For seven days she walked along the bank each dawn looking for a shallow place. After a week she noticed a huge black thing lying across the water on the far side of the river in the distance. It lay like that all day. She had heard the Mexicans say, "We will have another raid in seven days." Had they now come?

All day she watched the mysterious black thing from her hiding place, but as it hadn't moved by late afternoon, she started cautiously towards it.

It was a pine log that had fallen into the river. She took off her clothes, wrapped them in her bundle and started into the water, carrying the bundle on her back. *Asdzą́ą́ Atsidí* carried corn pollen at all times. Now she placed some on the water, praying, "Even though there be nothing in my land, even though my relatives be gone, I go back now because I long for my land. May I travel peacefully, unharmed by Mexican or Ute."

Then, using a stick as a cane, she felt her way across the river. Once the water lifted her, but she reached the log and walked safely to the other side. There she slept a while, and woke to find that the water had risen even more and no enemy could hope to cross after her. From then on she traveled during the day and as far into the night as she could.

She came back by her memory of where she had traveled before. She mixed her flour in a small bowl and ate it without frying or baking it. They say that you should not finish all of your food, but should put a bit under a bush for luck so you will never run out. That she did all the way.

One night as she traveled beneath a bright moon, a loud noise broke from the bushes beside her. *"Ts'iłiizh! ts'iłiizh!"* Twigs and branches were breaking under something heavy. "Not the Mexicans!" she prayed.

132

Then whatever it was cried out. "Shoo, that's the voice of The One Who Walks the Mountains," she thought. "The Bear!"

She prayed to that bear the way she had prayed to the river: "Grandchild, I pray no enemy sees me as I go to my land. Though I have no relatives, though they all be captured, even so I go home because I long for my land." Thus, talking and praying, woman and bear walked together through the night. And always the bear's voice answered her.

At dawn, exhausted, she slept for a while, but she jumped up after sunrise and started walking. Her water was gone.

Finally she reached the rim of *Tséyi'* (Canyon de Chelly) and sat down to rest, but on looking down she saw people far below. "Friends or enemies?" she wondered as always. Late in the afternoon she tired of waiting. "Why hide now?" she thought. "This is my own country!" And indeed, down in the canyon she found her own uncle and his wife collecting *Tł'ohdeii*.

"My dear mother!" cried her uncle as she rushed to him. "Where are you coming from?" And so they welcomed her to their home. The woman ground the seeds of *tł'ohdeii* and made bread. The man had two rabbits, and they ate until they could eat no more. She told the whole story of her adventure—where she had gone and how she had escaped, and she gave them some of the things she carried—knives, clothes and shoes.

"Stay here with us!" they begged. But she ran away one day when they were off gathering *tł'ohdeii*.

## HOMECOMING

She left Canyon de Chelly, and down near Many Farms she scrambled up a hill to a place called *Tó Dah Sikání* (Standing Water Barrel). Nearby, at *Náát'ezhí Sikaad* (Wild Currant Thicket), she found that the *náát'ezhí* were ripe. Making bags from her supplies, she picked as many as she could carry. Then passing *Ligai Yanáalk'id* (White Hill) and Rough Rock, she went along the foot of the mountain.

At Chilchinbito, near an old brush shelter, she found some old deer bones under a bush. She cleaned and boiled them and drank the juice. It gave her strength to go on. But of course she carefully put the bones back in their place as one must do with the bones of a deer.

North of Kayenta, she came to *Tséyi' Hats'ózí* (Narrow Canyon). There she found several horses with big packs on their backs tied beneath a juniper tree. Some ladies sat nearby, and a huge woman seemed to be wiping the last bits of food from a bowl with her fingers.

Soon she came to a cliff. Below on the plain she thought she could see a spring, but she could find no way down. For a long time she walked back and forth searching until the bear's tracks led her to a sand dune against the cliff. "That's where the bears go down," she thought.

Speaking again to the bear, she said, "You, grandchild, walk down there, but I will go this way!" And she squatted down and slid all the way to the foot of the cliff. She had guessed right about the spring and so filled her jug and pushed on.

Crossing the mountains she came to *Sǫ' Silá*. There platforms were built in the trees because of wolves. Perhaps others running from slavery had built them. She slept there without fear.

The huge woman called out when she saw *Asdzáá Atsidí*. More people appeared, and then two girls, the very same Paiute girls who had run away from the Mexicans! They said something in their own language to the huge woman who was their grandmother. She flung herself on *Asdzáá Atsidí* crying, "My beloved Ancestor! Where have you come from? They have taken all my children!"

"Yes, they took them back to Mexican country, even the babies," *Asdzáá Atsidí* told her, and all the Paiute women cried, because those were their children.

"We've been to the San Juan River to pick *chiiłchin* (sumac berries)," said the Paiute grandmother, and she held out a bowl of ground berries. But *Asdzáá Atsidí* asked for an empty bowl and filled it herself with *nááťezhí*. The Paiutes had never seen them. As they gobbled them down, they kept trying to say the Navajo name, but pronounced it wrong: *"Nááťesh! Nááťesh!"*

Then one of the women looked up. "Let's go," she said. "More Paiutes are coming, and some of those boys are rough."

"But where are my sons and husband?" *Asdzáá Atsidí* asked them.

"West and north of here in Paiute Canyon at a place called *Báʼazhchíní* (Born for Him), Navajos and Paiutes are harvesting fields," they told her.

"Oh! That's where I'm going," cried *Asdzáá Atsidí*. "That's why I came back all this long way!" And tears of hope ran down her face.

*Asdzáá Atsidí* set off on foot, but the Paiutes all rode. They had to lift the huge grandmother into the saddle, and there she sat among great bags of mountain tobacco which they meant to trade in the canyon.

They traveled on towards *Naatsisʼáán* (Navajo Mountain) until they came to the edge of a deep canyon and looked down on fields of corn, beans, squash, and wheat. The Paiute boys fired shots in the air and shouted as they started down the trail.

But when *Asdzą́ą́ Atsidí* got to her relatives' fields, she found no one. The shots had scared them all away.

As she stood there alone, a woman slowly crept from hiding. It was her brother's wife. They rushed together, crying for joy. When the others came out of hiding the questions began. "Tell where you have been and how you came back!"

"Your real home is on the mesa," they told her. "Someone must run and tell them." The next morning *Asdzą́ą́ Atsidí* left for home with a woman sent down by her relatives. As they reached the camp, a family elder called *Hastiin Náá' Ádiní Sání* (Old Mr. Blind Man) said to the waiting relatives, "Stop! Even though you long for her, leave her alone! You also wait there!" he called to *Asdzą́ą́ Atsidí*.

And there, just outside the home of her loved ones, the old medicine man made her stand and tell her whole story. She laid before him every detail.

Then yucca soap and fresh clothes were brought, and the blind man washed her, dried her with corn meal, and sang over her as he led her into the hogan.

Her two sons—the boys who had escaped—were both there, and their father too. One brother had died.

And so right away they had a Blessing Way Ceremony for *Asdzą́ą́ Atsidí*. The people brought kneeldown bread and meat, and still more people came the next day. And so she was accepted back among her relatives and was welcomed back to her land.

One day in a mound of Anasazi pottery, *Asdzą́ą́ Atsidí* dug up a jar. When you find something like that, they say you shouldn't open it right away. You should cover your eyes as if you are crying, then cover the jar. Only then open it. If you do that, they say, there will be something in it. She did that and found white corn right to the top of the jar.

She took the ancient jar of corn home and gave half to her brother. "Make these your planting seeds," she told him. But he only gave them to his wife to grind.

But *Asdzą́ą́ Atsidí* hid her corn, and when spring came, she planted it.

In the Chinle Valley before you come to Valley Store there is a mesa where ladies dig up *dleesh* (white clay) for cooking. On that mesa she built a small stone house. To this day the place is called *Kin Dah Łizhiní* (Black House on Top). In the valley below she planted the white corn, and it grew richly.

Just as her crops were ripening, people began coming back from *Hwééldi*. They came to her from all directions, asking for her corn, and she fed them with kneeldown bread and they ate.

Her brother came to her several times too for corn, but she chased him away saying, "You go back and get your wife to grind something for you."

*Asdzą́ą́ Atsidí* lived for many years, and that is the way she told her story, they say.

## AFTERWARDS

Soon after *Asdzą́ą́ Atsidí's* return, most of the Navajos went to *Hwééldi* (Fort Sumner), but her family did not go. For a while she lived near Dennehotso with a brother and his wife. They had no livestock and traveled on foot.

# CHEE DODGE

*This is a story of the birth of Chee Dodge, an orphan who in modern times became Navajo Tribal Chairman and a protector of Navajo land. His mother was* Ma'ii Deeshgiizhnii *Clan, descended from the Jemez Pueblo people who joined the Navajos to escape from Spaniards. According to Chee's children, his father was a Mexican who chose to live and die as a Navajo. Chee's ancestors did not leave their own people to join a weak or cruel nation, and the strength and generosity of the Navajos was richly rewarded by his leadership. He was 100 percent Navajo in everything he did.*

The last and most cruel of the Navajo wars had already begun. The Navajos were bitter about slave raids and killings and New Mexican herds on their land. The New Mexicans also hated the Navajos for the livestock they stole. Into the middle of it all marched the U.S. Army to build Fort Defiance at *Tséhootsooí* (Pasture Rock).

They filled it with soldiers and to feed the soldiers put out cattle on the grassland north and south of the fort. The land was used by the Navajo war leader *Hastiin Ch'il Haajiní* (Manuelito), and he owned the stock which the soldiers killed to make room for their own. Few could hope for peace. By the fall of 1859, all sides knew that the future would be bloody.

One dark January morning when the horses' hooves rang like bells on the frozen ground, a wagon started to haul wood for the camp near *Tségháhoodzání* (Window Rock) where the army herd was kept. A whizzing of feathers cut the air. There was a shout, perhaps, and three of the men in the wagon lay full of arrows on the ground. Two hundred or more Navajos then galloped toward the cattle and drove away all they could before the guards found their weapons.

Clan: *Ma'ii Deeshgiizhnii*
Born for: *Naakaii* (Mexican)

136

In the end the soldiers saved themselves by sending a message to the fort tied to the neck of a dog. The first big fight of the winter ended in a tie, but the commander of the fort was angry.

Major Shepherd had a terrible temper. That night eyes watching in the darkness could see him walking back and forth in his room as he talked to his officers. His face grew red in the candlelight and he shook his fists like a man in a trap.

He knew that his men could not stay at the fort through the winter without their cattle. He also knew that he could not fight back, because his own commanding officer had sent all the cavalry and their horses to Fort Wingate. Soldiers without horses could do nothing. Shepherd could not even call for help.

"Gentlemen," he said at last. "At least we must find out who's against us, where their camps are, and who is leading them. We'll visit them with powder and shot when we get some cavalry."

"Only one man can tell you that," came the answer from a sergeant at the back of the room.

"Speak!" said the Major.

"The interpreter, sir" said the sergeant. "Juan Anaya. The men say he was seen with the ones who led the attack this morning, sir."

The Major stopped in his tracks. "Juan?" he said, "He's Mexican. He's their slave. What's he doing leading raids on us? Didn't he used to work for Captain Dodge out here before Dodge was killed? I heard he was a guide for the cavalry just last year."

"Maybe he was a Mexican once, sir," laughed the sergeant, "but he's Navajo now, he and his brother both. They're married into the family of some chief, sir."

"Interesting," said the Major. "What changed him?"

"Same as the rest, sir," answered the sergeant. "He walked out of here right after we killed Manuelito's livestock last year. The next time we saw him, he was carrying messages for the enemy."

"But he did guide our troops last winter," said the Major.

The sergeant laughed again. "Yes. He came in here with a peace message from some chief and we locked him up. We caught his brother too and their women. We told Juan that he and his brother had better work for us, or their families would never leave the fort alive."

"I see," said the Major, "Can we catch him again?"

Juan Anaya[1] was indeed a Mexican. He and his brother Torivio had been taken in a raid as small boys. They grew up as Navajos, and even though they knew their families and friends still lived in Santa Fe, they chose to stay with the Navajos.

There had been a time when both Navajos and Americans hoped for peace. At that time Juan did work as interpreter for Captain Henry Dodge, an officer at Fort Defiance.

Dodge himself almost became a Navajo. He, too, married a Navajo woman and knew all the Navajo leaders from the Rio Grande west to the Colorado. As long as he lived in Navajo Country, he and Juan managed to keep the peace. But Dodge was killed by Apache raiders near Zuni in 1856. Two years later when war broke out over Manuelito's livestock at Fort Defiance, Juan chose the Navajo side.

While the angry Major at the Fort made his plans, Juan had a night visitor at his camp not far away at *Tsé Naní'áhí* (Natural Bridge). *Bilį́į' Łání* (Many Horses), the son of another Navajo leader *Tótsohnii Hastiin* (Ganado Mucho), warmed his hands over the coals that still glowed red in the dark hogan. "The officers at the fort are talking," he said. "They will be out like bees in the morning. I would be far away, if I were you."

"My wife is pregnant," said Juan. "Her time may come any day. But I am not afraid. The army has no cavalry. They can't do much without horses. And remember," he added with a smile. "I was

---

[1]In some versions of the story he is referred to as Juan Cosinás.

born Mexican. I am still useful to them. They might shoot you on sight. They will only arrest me."

"True," said *Bilíį' Łání*, "and I am worried. This is Manuelito's fight and we to the west don't want to suffer for it. My father plans to move all his people and stock south towards Zuni until the trouble is over."

"Go," said Juan. "I will watch the fort. In a month or two signal me from a safe place, and I will give you the news."

A few days later Major Shepherd did send soldiers from the fort to arrest Juan. They took his pregnant wife and locked her in the guard house. Juan came with her.

☆   ☆   ☆

Juan often wondered why Major Shepherd wanted him there. Shepherd said he would kill him if he told lies but did not trust him if he told the truth. But nothing really mattered, because Shepherd had no horses and could not send his men far on foot.

Three weeks after his first raid on the cattle, Manuelito attacked again. This time, however, many well-armed men were guarding the herd, and the Navajos got nothing.

So the winter wore on. Both soldiers and Navajos seemed to give up the idea of war until spring. Major Shepherd got nothing from Juan, and Juan gave him nothing. He thought less about war and more about his family. Late one February night his wife told him her baby was on its way. Some time after midnight, with only Juan to help, she gave birth to a son on the dirt floor of the guard house. Toward morning, tired, she went to sleep just as the bugler on the parade ground sounded "reveille."

Soon the sergeant came around and unlocked the guard house. The east was just turning from white to pink. No wind blew. From edge to edge the sky was clear. No, not quite. To the south a puff of smoke crossed from the dark land to the white above. Another puff followed the first, then another. *Bilíį' Łání* had come back.

Behind the mess hall strips of beef for the soldiers' breakfast were frying over open fires. Nearby stood a barrel of lard. When the cook stepped inside, three quick chunks of lard sent three answering smokes drifting up over the buildings.

*Bilíį' Łání* came straight up to the fort. Juan said he was the baby's uncle, and the soldiers did not stop him. Years later *Bilíį' Łání* used to tell the story of that morning.

"I had expected the signal from *Tsé Naní'áhí*, but when I saw smoke over the fort, I knew Juan must be there. It was a warm day. Snow lay in patches on the ground. Juan came straight to meet me. 'Come, brother,' he said. 'Before we talk about anything else, I want you to meet our son.' He took me across to the guard house. A blanket hid one corner of the room. He pulled it back, and there I saw the mother and the baby. It had just come, and I was the first to see it."

"Henry Dodge we'll call him," said Juan.

"An English name?"

Juan smiled. "Why not? Dodge was a good man. Since he was born here, this place may always be a part of my son's life. He should have a name that both Navajos and whites can respect.

*As in the old days, when a baby comes they name it right away. To boys they give names beginning with* Hashké, *The Fierce One:* Hashké Yitah Deeyá, *Fierce One Who Walks Among Enemies;* Hashké Yił Deezdéél, *Fierce One Who Catches Them;* Hashké Ayííłt'e', *Fierce One Who Throws Down Their Bodies.*

*To the girls they give names with the word* Baa', *Goes to War:* Deezbaa', *She Goes Off to War;* Nánibaa', *She Came Back from War;* Naadlí Yitah Níbaa', *She Went to War Among the Warrior-girls.*

*These are the ceremonial names of Navajos, not what we are called every day. My grandfather gave me the name* Hashké Yibadooswod, *Fierce One Who Ran Them Down. In the old days when the Navajos went to war, they ran right over their enemies.*

—George Blueeyes

So that is one version of the story of the birth of Henry Dodge, much as it is told by his son Tom Dodge. The Navajos called him Chee as a boy for *Ashkii Lichíí'* (Red Boy). And Henry Chee Dodge did indeed win the respect of all who met him—Indian, white or Spaniard. He became a leader, a tribal chairman, a protector of Navajo land.

But all of that came much later. His youth was hard from the moment of his birth.

Major Shepherd soon let Juan and his wife leave the fort. He had gotten nothing by keeping them. War came again with the spring. Manuelito and a thousand riders attacked Fort Defiance in April and nearly took it before the better guns of the soldiers drove them back.

Soon after that, however, cavalry came back to Fort Defiance and began to march through Navajo Country. Utes, Mexicans and Zunis, sometimes paid and armed by the U.S. Government, joined them.

In June Navajos ambushed a band of slave raiders near Washington Pass and killed 35 of them. According to a few survivors who staggered into Fort Defiance, Juan had ridden with the Navajos and was wounded in the fight.

Not long after that, according to Tom Dodge, he left his home for Fort Wingate to interpret again, perhaps to talk peace. Somewhere east of the Chuska Mountains, night caught up with him and he hobbled his horses. The next morning as he was tracking his horses a band of soldiers saw him, and a lucky shot broke his leg.

There were Mexicans among the soldiers, and Juan called to them in Spanish. They recognized him as one of their own people, and they lifted him up, but he bled to death before sundown. They buried him there in Navajo Country, they say, on a hill near *Nahashch'idí* (Naschitti, New Mexico).

Chee and his mother stayed with her people near *Tsé Naní'áhí* until Kit Carson came in 1863. Then, with Manuelito, Ganado Mucho, Many Horses and others they ran west to the Grand Canyon. Near First Mesa in Hopi Country they ran out of food. Chee's mother climbed alone up the cliffs to Walpi to beg for corn. She never came back.

From then on Chee wandered with different aunts and relatives until he came to *Hwééldi* (Fort Sumner). Still later he lived at Fort Defiance and became an interpreter like his father.

But the old leaders, Ganado Mucho and Manuelito, made sure that he never forgot his Navajo blood. They found him and trained him. New dangers threatened Navajo Country when the Navajos came back to their old land. Only a person whom both Navajos and whites respected could speak for the people then.

There is more than one version of the birth of Chee Dodge. Many of the details have been lost in time, and it is possible that Chee Dodge himself did not know the whole story. Tom Dodge told his version on March 12, 1976, at his home in Scottsdale, Arizona. Additional descriptions have been added, based on historical facts documented by Frank McNitt in *Navajo Wars*, pp. 149, 215, 223, 319–23, and 347, and by J. Lee Correll in *Through White Men's Eyes*, vol. 2, pp. 131–32, 188–89, 198–99, 240, 340; and vol. 3, pp. 36–38, 46.

# WHY WAR?

As the stories tell, war filled Navajo Country with fear and hardship. But fear never killed people's love of the land. Many died fighting for their homeland. Chee Dodge's father, born Mexican, was one of them. And *Asdzą́ą́ Atsidí* prayed, "Even though there is nothing for me . . . I go back because I long for my land."

And why did so much blood and sadness flow over this land? Here three people give three reasons why the Navajo wars happened. Probably all three tell part of the truth. Who can say now what the whole truth really was?

In one way, however, the three reasons here are the same. Each speaker talks of one group treating others as if they weren't people at all.

What would the people in the stories have said? *Asdzą́ą́ Atsidí*? Juan Anaya? The Ute woman whose brother was killed by Navajos? Do people treat each other better today?

### The Navajos

According to *Tł'ááshchí'í Sání* of Lukachukai, Navajo thieves started the wars.

*There was a time when our ancestors hid like the deer in rocks and canyons because they were afraid of being captured, but it was their own fault.*

*There were Navajos then who had nothing. No livestock of any kind. Building a hogan, planting a crop, hoeing — they never thought of it. Like coyotes or wolves that steal in the night, they raided the Utes.*

*They sneaked up on the Utes and took their livestock and killed them. So the Ute wars began. The Ute leader Gray Hair (Tsiiba' Łigai) came down against the Navajos. My own grandfather traded bow shots with him.*

*Then there were the Mexicans who lived along* rivers east of Huerfano Mountain. *They had stock in their corrals too. From as far as Black Mesa Navajos traveled over there like mice in the night and took it.*

*So also with the whites. North of Fort Defiance my father and grandfather once met a white man looking for his horses. As he talked to my father, my grandfather bashed in his head. They killed his horse too and threw everything in the wash.*

*It was robbery! They told fine stories about "going to war", but they were just saying that. They were stealing. Soon everyone turned against the Navajos, and the word got back to Washington.*

*"If the Navajos stay out there, things will only get worse," they said. "Let's just round them up and get them off their land." That's when the army came looking for us.*

## The Mexicans

Louis Kennon, a U.S. Army doctor who lived in New Mexico many years before the Long Walk to Fort Sumner, blamed Mexican slave raiders for the wars. He wrote:

*. . .in all fights the Mexicans have always (started the trouble.) . . .If you asked them any reason for making war, they would only say that the Navajos had a great many sheep and a great many children.*

*. . .I know of no family which can raise $150 but what buys a Navajo slave, and many own four or five. (They were bought and sold) like pigs or sheep.*

*. . .Fortunately for the Navajos, they generally (beat) the Mexicans in their warfare until the Americans came. . . .*

## The Americans

Kit Carson's commanding officer, Gen. James Carleton, attacked the Navajos because he hoped to find gold and saw nothing wrong with killing people who got in his way. These quotes come from his letters:

*. . .A country as rich, if not richer in mineral wealth than California, extends from the Rio Grande northwestwardly. . . . If I could have but one first-rate regiment of infantry, I could brush the Indians away from all that part of it east of the Colorado River. The troops for the fight against the Navajos take the field next month.*

\* \* \*

*. . .The Indians will not themselves work the mines; they should not be allowed to wait to murder (those) who come to explore their country for its hidden wealth. This they will surely do unless they are exterminated or placed on reservations.*

*Colonel, . . .tell (the Navajos) that the troops cannot tell good (Indians) from bad. They have until the 20th day of July of this year (1863) to come in: after that every Navajo that is seen will be considered as hostile and treated accordingly.*

\* \* \*

*Captain, . . .send a company of infantry from your post to scour the eastern slope of the Sandia Mountain country. . .with instructions to kill every male Navajo or Apache Indian who is large enough to bear arms.*

\* \* \*

*. . .In all that I have had to do in this command, so far as the Indians are concerned, I have (tried) to treat them justly, and I point to this record of over three years of anxiety and toil, mostly on their account, as one of which I do not feel ashamed.*

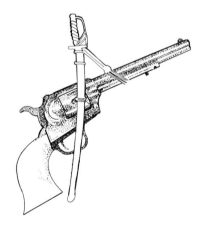

Statements by Carleton and Kennon are recorded in a special report to the U.S. Congress, *Condition of the Indian Tribes*, March 3, 1865. Statements by 80-year-old *Tł'ááshchi'í Sání* were made in a personal interview July 7, 1980.

143

# RESERVATION: The Old Paper

Keeping the Navajos at Fort Sumner, far from their own land, did not work. The tribe was bigger than anyone expected. New Mexico had barely enough food for the U.S. Army. Crops for the Navajos at Fort Sumner failed. Food for 8,000 people had to come by wagon from the East. It couldn't be done.

Plans for mining and cattle raising on Navajo land didn't work either. There was no gold or silver, and New Mexico didn't have enough people or stock to use land taken from the Navajos.

Also, many, like *Asdzą́ą́ Atsidí,* didn't go to Fort Sumner. The U.S. Army wasn't strong enough to guard the fort, track down the rest of the Navajos and fight other tribes that were still free.

So the government offered to let the Navajos go back to a piece of their old land, if they would sign a "peace treaty".

This treaty, called the *Old Paper (Naaltsoos Sání)* in Navajo, said which land would belong to the tribe, what power the government would have on that land, and what it would do for the People.

The treaty brought both good and bad to the People, and even today many things in Navajo country are decided by what is written in the Old Paper.

Here are some of the most important parts of it:

## Law and Order

The first part of the treaty says that even on Navajo land, the laws of the United States must be obeyed and that a U.S. court can handle crimes on the reservation.

*From this day forward all war between the parties to this agreement shall for ever cease. The government of the United States desires peace, and its honor is hereby pledged to keep it. The Indians desire peace, and they now pledge their honor to keep it.*

*If bad men among whites, or among other people. . .shall commit any wrong upon the person or property of the Indians, the United States will. . .at once cause the offender to be arrested and punished according to the laws of the United States.*

*If bad men among the Indians shall commit a wrong or depredation upon the person or property of any one, white, black, or Indian . . . the Navajo tribe agree that they will . . . deliver up the wrongdoer to the United States, to be tried and punished according to its laws . . .*

This seems to take all power away from the tribe to make laws and govern its own people. Does it really? Even though the treaty takes power from the tribe, it talks about the tribe as a nation. Because of this the Navajos have kept the right to have their own government, and over the years they have won back many of the powers they lost at Fort Sumner.

## Land

The most important parts of the treaty give the boundaries of the reservation and say what they mean.

*. . .the tribes (give up) all right to occupy any territory outside their reservation...but (still have) the right to hunt on any unoccupied lands (near) their reservation.*

By this did Navajos lose the right to live off the reservation? The treaty says so, but in fact it was never enforced, and in time Navajos gained both land and power outside the original reservation.

*(The Navajos) will not in the future oppose the construction of railroads, wagon roads, mail stations, or other works of utility or necessity which may be ordered or permitted by the laws of the United States....*

Does this mean that the Navajo Tribe cannot keep outsiders from building roads, powerlines, mines and other things on the reservation? Many have tried to argue that it does. So far, however, the tribe has stopped them by arguing that the U.S. Congress must pass a law "ordering" something to be built. Until then, the tribal government has power to say yes or no.

*No future treaty for the cession of any portion or part of the reservation. . .shall be of any validity. . .unless agreed to by at least three-fourths of all the adult male Indians....*

Does this mean that Navajo land is safe forever? Not quite. The U.S. government made the treaty. If the U.S. Congress passed a law to change it, who could stop them?

## Water

The Old Paper says nothing about the water found on Navajo land. Recently this has become an important question. People in all southwestern states have made plans to use water from rivers that run through Navajo Country. Mines pump huge amounts of water from the ground. The land would become useless without water.

The treaty does say Navajos should farm:

*When the head of a family shall have selected lands. . .he shall. . .receive seeds and agricultural implements. . . .*

To keep its water rights, the Navajo Tribe has said, "The Old Paper promises to help Navajos become farmers. But this can't be done if others take our irrigation water. That means the government must also protect our water and not let others take it."

By this argument the tribe will surely keep some of its water. However, the exact amount may be a question for many years.

## Education

The Old Paper promised free schools:

*. . .The United States agrees that for every thirty children between the ages of six and sixteen who can be induced or compelled to attend school, a house shall be provided and a teacher competent to teach the elementary branches of an English education shall be furnished. . . .*

For a hundred years after Fort Sumner Washington hardly tried to keep this promise, but Navajos soon saw that unless they could read the treaties and laws themselves, they would quickly lose everything.

# WINNING THE PEACE

The map here shows in dark gray the original reservation made by the treaty at Fort Sumner, the Old Paper. The other areas around it are pieces of land that Washington added to the reservation later, making it by far the largest piece of Indian land in the United States today.

How did the Navajos win back in peacetime land that they lost in war? They won it with livestock. Sheep and cattle held land that guns and arrows could not.

In the chapters about plants and animals it was said that each kind of animal has a "niche". It is "specialized" in what it eats and how it lives, and other animals depend on it. The Navajos survived because they found a niche for themselves as stock raisers.

Long before Mexican or Texan ranchers could move herds into Navajo Country, the Navajos themselves filled it again with their own sheep and cattle. The ranchers took land from tribes that had no livestock, but only a few cared to go where Navajo herds had already eaten the grass.

People who came through Arizona and New Mexico to build railroads, cut timber, or buy supplies for the growing state of California wanted meat, wool and blankets more than they wanted Navajo land. Nobody in Navajo Country could supply these better than the Navajos.

Because of this, people like Chee Dodge and friends he made among traders, missionaries and government officials could persuade Washington to give land back to the Navajos.

In earlier times the tribe had managed to take from their Spanish enemies the very things that could make them strong. Now, also, the years

at Fort Sumner did not destroy them, and they turned defeat into victory.

Other tribes were not so lucky. Those that depended on hunting and those that had no way to defend their land from the miners, ranchers and farmers who wanted it were all nearly wiped out.

The dates on the map show the year when an area was added to the reservation. Notice that some areas were added and later taken away.

Land added before 1918 was added by "executive order". That means the president alone did it, and he could also take it away by simply signing his name to a piece of paper.

In 1919 the U.S. Congress took this power from the president. Now only an act of Congress can change Indian land, and there is no difference between land given by the Treaty of 1868 and land added later.

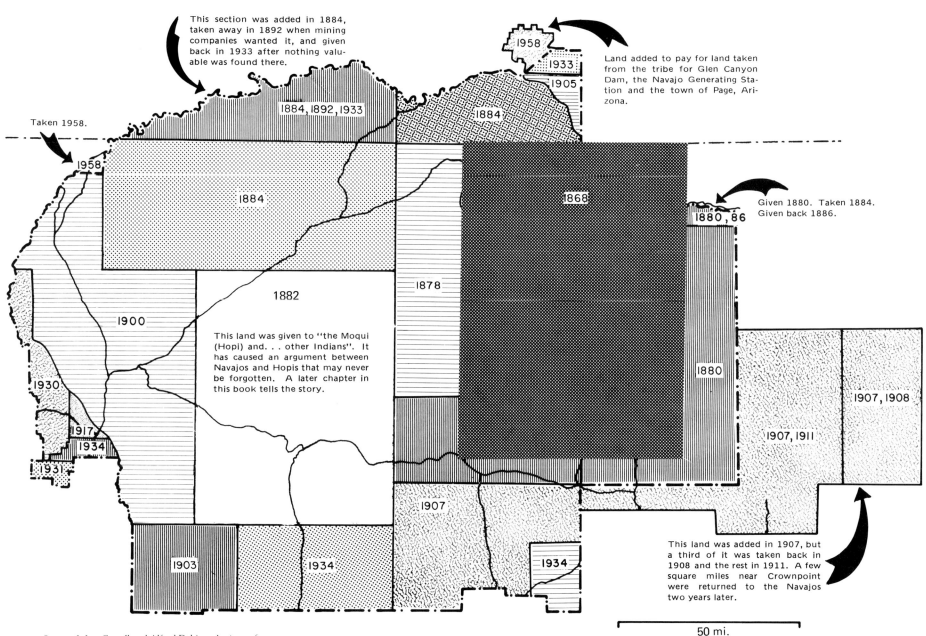

This section was added in 1884, taken away in 1892 when mining companies wanted it, and given back in 1933 after nothing valuable was found there.

Land added to pay for land taken from the tribe for Glen Canyon Dam, the Navajo Generating Station and the town of Page, Arizona.

Taken 1958.

1958

1884, 1892, 1933

1933

1905

1884

1884

1958

Given 1880. Taken 1884. Given back 1886.

1868

1880, 86

1878

1900

1882

This land was given to "the Moqui (Hopi) and. . . other Indians". It has caused an argument between Navajos and Hopis that may never be forgotten. A later chapter in this book tells the story.

1880

1907, 1908

1930

1917

1934

1931

1907, 1911

1903

1934

1907

1934

This land was added in 1907, but a third of it was taken back in 1908 and the rest in 1911. A few square miles near Crownpoint were returned to the Navajos two years later.

50 mi.

Source: J. Lee Correll and Alfred Dehiya, *Anatomy of the Navajo Indian Reservation: How It Grew.*

147

# CUTTING UP NAVAJO COUNTRY

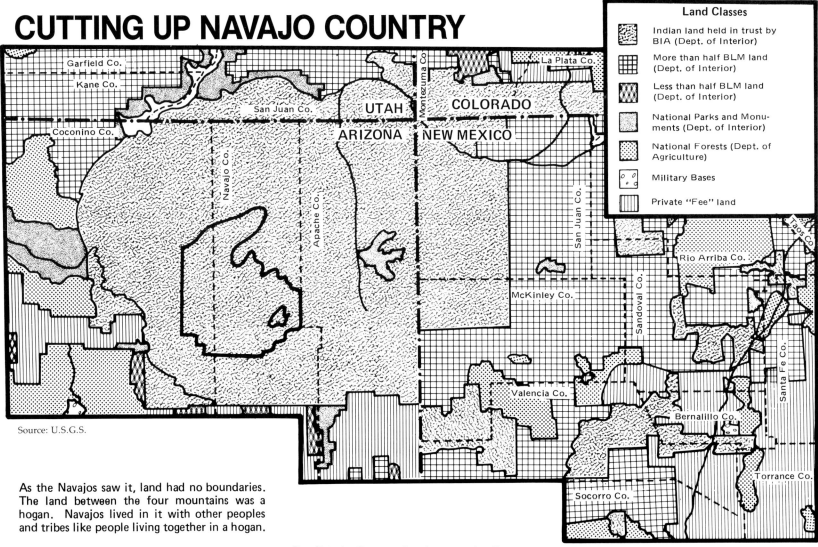

**Land Classes**

- Indian land held in trust by BIA (Dept. of Interior)
- More than half BLM land (Dept. of Interior)
- Less than half BLM land (Dept. of Interior)
- National Parks and Monuments (Dept. of Interior)
- National Forests (Dept. of Agriculture)
- Military Bases
- Private "Fee" land

Source: U.S.G.S.

As the Navajos saw it, land had no boundaries. The land between the four mountains was a hogan. Navajos lived in it with other peoples and tribes like people living together in a hogan.

People sharing a hogan may fight each other for many reasons, but they do not end the fighting by cutting the hogan to pieces. A hogan cut by walls is no longer a hogan. The fire place, the cooking place, the doorway, the smoke hole cannot be cut. So it was with land in the old way. It was all one piece like air or sunlight.

But Navajo Country has been cut by lines, reservation lines, state lines, county lines and property lines of many kinds. When the Navajos signed the treaty at Fort Sumner they gave Washington the power to divide the land and make laws for how it would be used. The tribe has lived with these laws ever since.

This map shows the ownership of land in Navajo Country today as well as county and state lines. For each line and patch there are different sets of laws and rules. Even the people who wrote the Old Paper at Fort Sumner in 1868 surely never thought their work could lead to such a complicated situation.

## The Reservation

Reservation land belongs to the Navajo Tribe, but Washington "holds it in trust" for them. That means it is up to Washington to decide what is best for Navajo land, and the Navajos must trust Washington.

In fact Washington has allowed the Navajo Tribal Council to keep some power over the reservation. The council can make laws for Navajos on Navajo land, and very little can be done on tribal land without council approval.

However, Washington must approve all council decisions, and the tribe depends on Washington for so much that sometimes it is very hard to go against Washington's wishes.

In Washington the secretary of the interior is in charge of land. He is chosen by the president, and the Bureau of Indian Affairs is his responsibility.

## States and Counties

The United States is divided by state lines and the states by county lines. Both states and Indian tribes are under the federal government in Washington and have similar powers over the land.

As the map shows, Navajo land (counting the Alamo, Canyoncito and Ramah reservations) lies in three states and nine counties. This has caused great confusion, and this book can't begin to explain all the problems that have come up.

In general, however, county and state lines mean little to reservation Navajos except for the public schools. They are organized by county. Most of the unanswered questions have to do with non-Navajos.

What taxes can states collect on Navajo land? From whom?   Can the tribe tax non-Navajos? Can a non-Navajo criminal be sent to a reservation jail?   Can reservation Navajos run in county elections?

## Federal Land

When the Navajos were told to live inside the small square boundaries of their reservation, what happened to the rest of their land?

In fact the U.S. government kept nearly all of it and allowed no one to live there permanently.

Over the years some of this land was given back to the Navajos, some was given to railroad companies to pay for laying the tracks, some was given or sold to ranchers and some given to state governments. Much, however, was kept. Today there are three kinds of federal land in Navajo Country.

*National Forests:*  These are controlled by the secretary of agriculture. The U.S. Forest Service takes care of them and sells the timber that is ready to cut. Ranchers, including many Navajos, also rent grazing land in national forests.

*BLM Land:*  This is controlled by the secretary of the interior and is taken care of by the Bureau of Land Management.  The interior secretary can give it away or sell it. Usually, however, only minerals under the land are sold. The land itself is rented to people who wish to use it.

*National Parks and Monuments:*  This land is cared for by the U.S. Park Service to protect its natural beauty or ancient ruins. Usually it can only be used for recreation. On the reservation, however, Navajos can use park land in the traditional way.

## Fee Land

Fee land is usually called "private" land. It can be bought and sold and passed on from parents to children.  Many Navajos have bought fee land outside the reservation. The Navajo Tribe itself has bought a lot of land. Tribal fee land is NOT part of the reservation. The council can sell it, rent it or build on it without permission from Congress or the Bureau of Indian Affairs.

Owners of fee land cannot do anything they wish with it, however. They must pay taxes to the states.  And state and federal governments can pass laws that say how any land may or may not be used. They can also force landowners to sell land needed for roads, railways, etc.

## Land Grants

In New Mexico many patches of land were "given" to Spanish settlers by their king. Some, including the Cebolleta and Cubero grants near Mount Taylor are still owned by the descendants of the original settlers. Land grants are taxed like fee land but often controlled by elected trustees who work much like a tribal council.

Spanish kings also "gave" land to the Pueblo tribes. These grants at least protected some of their land from settlers and later became part of the Pueblo reservations.

# THE CHECKERBOARD

Even though new land was added to the Navajo Reservation many times, people and their herds spilled over the official lines. Except for the Spanish land grants, the U.S. government now claimed all of this land.

The United States was still a poor country, however, and Washington wanted railroads built and empty land used. So land was marked off in one mile squares called "sections" and given away by the section and quarter section as "homesteads" for farms or ranches. Many sections also went to railroad companies and were sold or rented out to raise money for laying track.

Much land went to non-Indians. Even so, Navajos got more than other tribes. The government wanted the land ranched, and Navajos had stock. Although Navajo and non-Navajo ranchers argued and even killed each other for land outside the reservation, the government finally gave everyone the same rights.

Nearly 5,000 Navajos got homesteads. These "allotments" however are not "fee land". The Bureau of Indian Affairs (BIA) controls them like small reservations. Navajo "allottees" can use them or rent them out, but not sell them.

At Alamo, Ramah, and Canyoncito, allotments have been grouped together into three "satellite" reservations. Elsewhere they are mixed in with squares of other land in a "checkerboard".

Life in the Checkerboard Area is complicated because there are at least 14 different kinds of land, each controlled by different laws. The map on the right is an example.

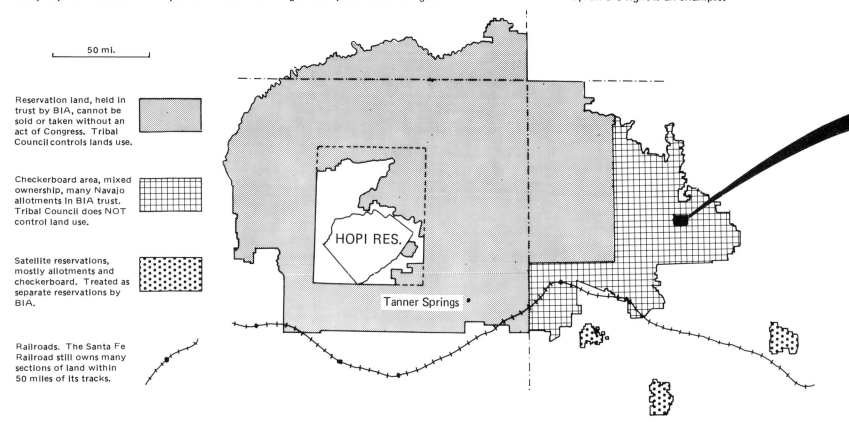

50 mi.

Reservation land, held in trust by BIA, cannot be sold or taken without an act of Congress. Tribal Council controls lands use.

Checkerboard area, mixed ownership, many Navajo allotments in BIA trust. Tribal Council does NOT control land use.

Satellite reservations, mostly allotments and checkerboard. Treated as separate reservations by BIA.

Railroads. The Santa Fe Railroad still owns many sections of land within 50 miles of its tracks.

HOPI RES.

Tanner Springs

## The Fight Goes On

The story of *K'ai' Si'ání* (Tanner Springs) shows how land was taken after Fort Sumner. Tanner Springs, on the wash 20 miles southwest of Wide Ruins, is not in the Checkerboard Area, but its history is similar.

In 1883 a relative of Ganado Mucho drove his sheep to water at Tanner Springs, and a cowboy hiding behind the tank shot him dead. By the new land laws, he owned the water. Miles and miles of good grazing land were useless without that water, and the rancher meant to keep it all for himself.

Ganado Mucho's people at once prepared for war, and soldiers marched out from Fort Defiance to stop them. Chee Dodge was interpreter, and like his father Juan Anaya, he stood between the two sides.

Chee's words, and fear of the soldiers, finally made the dead man's relatives put down their weapons, but the fight for Tanner Springs did not stop there. A few years later, Chee Dodge borrowed $900 from a white friend in Gallup and bought the land himself. He paid back the money in less than a year with the cattle he raised there, and the land is now part of the Navajo Reservation. It was a small battle in a new kind of war, and Chee Dodge won it.

Other little fights happened over minerals. At least four people looking for silver in Monument Valley and one in the Carrizo Mountains were killed by Navajos. In 1890 Chee Dodge and some soldiers arrested 15 gold-seekers who had been stopped and surrounded by angry Navajos in the Carrizos. (No gold was ever found there.)

Nobody won anything in all the shooting. In time people on both sides learned, like Chee, that money, politics, and law had more power than guns. But the fight goes on. Valuable minerals have been found, especially in the Checkerboard Area, and many people stand ready to take them.

Source: Bureau of Land Management.

## LAND OWNERSHIP AT PUEBLO PINTADO

Navajo allotments. May not be sold.

BLM land "withdrawn for Indian use". May be taken.

BLM land. May be rented to anyone.

State land. Belongs to New Mexico State Government.

National Park land. Pueblo Pintado Ruins.

Private "fee land".

Pueblo Pintado School (BIA)

U.S. Government owns all minerals. May be sold separately from land.

U.S. Government owns coal only.

Other government mineral ownership situations.

# PEACE AND LIVESTOCK

# PEACE AND LIVESTOCK

In the treaty made at Fort Sumner in 1868, the U.S. government and the Navajos promised to end all war in Navajo Country. Peace did not come at once of course, and even today the Navajo Tribe must struggle to hold onto its land. Nevertheless, the shooting and fear did pass away, and a new chapter in Navajo history began.

When they left Fort Sumner, the Navajos had nothing. Washington gave out two or three sheep and a few supplies for each person, but from then on the People had little help. Twenty years later, however, many families had over a thousand sheep and cattle. Forty years later Navajo herds were over a million head. Navajo rugs and silverwork had become famous across the country. The tribe grew quickly. The 10,000 Navajos who spread out over the land in 1869 were at least 20,000 in 1900 and 40,000 by 1930.

Nothing came easily, however. Modern people can hardly imagine how hard their ancestors worked at planting, herding and gathering food. But the old people had the strength. They survived. They did not ask for help. And from year to year life grew better. The land had not seen so many people since Anasazi times 600 years before.

The stories in this section are pictures of Navajo Country as it was between 1863 and 1933 when the People were making a new life for themselves and their livestock. Those are the times that old people remember now when they talk of the "traditional life." They were times when the land and the seasons told people how to live. When the land said, "Take your stock to better grass," the people moved. When the weather said, "It's time to go to winter camp," the people went. When the trees said, "Now you will pick pinon nuts," it was done.

That chapter of Navajo history ended in 1933 when Washington became worried that too much livestock might ruin the land. All over the western United States, ranchers who used land held by the U.S. government had to cut their herds and obey new grazing laws. Because Washington also held Navajo land "in trust," Navajo herds were also cut down, and grazing laws were made for them too.

The cutting down of livestock is known as *Stock Reduction*, and people remember it with sadness the way they remember Fort Sumner. But the good years before Stock Reduction gave them strength to face the future. Even today, stories from those years are told to show how people should live together on the land.

Clan: *Bit'ahnii*
Born for: *Tł'ízí Łání*

## SON OF OLD MAN HAT

*This is a story of how one Navajo family moved around looking for grass in a dry year in the 1880s. It was told by Son of Old Man Hat. He was of the Bit'ahnii Clan, and was born on the way back from Fort Sumner. Old Man Hat himself was Tł'ízí Łání—Many Goats Clan—and did not go to Fort Sumner. He lived on Black Mesa without livestock during those years and only found his wife and her new son when they came back.*

*They started their livestock herd with seven sheep. Old Man Hat traded a Paiute slave to buy them. When he died 25 years later, he and his wife and son had 1,400 sheep and many cattle and horses. The story here is from a book written in 1934 called* Son of Old Man Hat.

(We were living in a canyon north of *Dziłijiin* [Black Mesa], and my father was worried.) . . . "There isn't any feed from the top of Black Mesa all the way to Black Mountain Sitting Up," he said. "The winter before, they say, it didn't snow, and last summer it never did rain, and now, this last winter, it didn't snow either. So everything is dried up. There isn't a green thing sticking up all the way down to Black Mountain Sitting Up. Nothing at all but dust and dirt. I don't know what we'll do about our stock. The only place it snowed was where we lived last winter, and from the foot of the mountain down into this flat there's quite a bit of grazing. But after they eat it up I don't know what to do."

We lived at that place a long time. Then we heard a number of people had moved down from Black Mesa, and some were still coming down. My mother said, "They'll soon be out here where we're living. And they'll be moving into this canyon too. We'll move closer to the mouth of the canyon, so that when they come here we won't let them in. We can't let them use it. There's lots of grazing in the canyon, but it's just enough for our own stock. So if they move here we'll tell them to stay out."

My father said, "Everyone thinks like us. We moved to many different places for grazing, and now, all those people are that way; they're moving to different places to find grazing for their stock. That's the way we were too. It's no use for us to turn the people down. Let them go wherever they want to."

Several days later some people moved into the canyon with a big herd of sheep. Five days later another outfit moved in and located a little above the others. They had a big herd too. It wasn't long after these people moved into the canyon that there was no more grazing.

My father said, "I guess it's no use for us to live here any longer. The horses are looking pretty bad because they haven't any feed, and the sheep are just the same. In this canyon there's nothing. Even under the cliffs there's no grazing. So we'd better move to *Nídeesk'id* (Hill Across). I think it rained some there. It looks like it's been raining a lot up there. So we'd better move. . . ."

The sun was pretty well up when we started. We camped that night on the way, and the next morning we moved again and got to a spring up high in the rocks where the horses and sheep had water. We stayed two days, and my father said, "I'd like to ride around to see where there's some grazing and water." He was gone all day. When he returned in the evening he said, "There's nothing. I've been to *Tsé Ani'įįhí* (Thief Rock) and around *Ma'ii Łání* (Many Coyotes), and way down in the valley to Hill Across. The other side of Hill Across is the only place where I could find a little feed. The grass is just about an inch high. That's the only green spot." The next day we moved to that place. There were some trees coming out from the foot of the mountain, and a little lake, and a little grass just getting to be an inch high.

Every evening and morning my father and mother talked about the grazing, water and stock, about different places and about moving. My father and I herded every day.

One day as we were herding, a man came riding out in the flat on the trail going to the northeast. When he'd almost passed by he looked up and saw us and so started riding over. My father recognized him and greeted him saying, "Where are you from? I haven't seen you for a long time, cousin."

He answered, "I'm from below *Oozéí* (Oraibi). I'm going to my brother's place. They say he lives around here somewhere."

Then my father said to him, "Tell me how the places are towards your home. Tell me how the weather is and what the land is like, the grazing, the water, the feed for the stock. Get down off your horse and tell me about those things."

As he got off his horse he said, "I've got nothing to tell." But when he sat down beside my father he said, "There's nothing from here on all the way down to *Tsé Dildǫ́'ii* ("popping rock point": Hard Rocks). A little beyond there is good feed. From there on this way there's nothing, but from there on over towards *Gad Íí'áhí* (Cedar Standing), down in that flat, there's plenty of grazing and water. Lake Oraibi (toward Tolani Lakes) has lots of water, about a mile across. So there's plenty of water and large areas for grazing, too, and not much stock."

My father said, "Tell me just how much feed and how high the grass is, my baby."

He pointed to a bush about two feet high. "The shortest grass," he said, "is about that tall, and the highest is about three feet. And it's mixed with all kinds of weeds. The weeds begin at about the same height as the grass and are up to five feet high. So there's not much feed to tell about." He was riding a nice, big, fat horse.

"Is that right, my baby?" said my father. "And how is the corn and other food, melons and peaches?"

"They're about ripe now at the Oraibi and Hopi places," he replied.

The next day we started moving. On the third day we came to the foot of *Dził Nitsaa* (Big Mountain). When it got cool we went on up the west side towards the east. We went over the mountain and as we got out in the flat the sun was going down. A long distance off towards the south were the Oraibis (Hopis). We kept on going along until after midnight, and then we stopped and camped. We started again the next day before sunrise and got to *Gad Íí'áhí* a little after noon. Long ago two cedar trees stood there, they said, but they were dead. The two stumps were there by the water, and they still called it Cedar Standing.

We unpacked our horses and my mother started cooking. The sheep and horses were lying around, they didn't know what to eat they had so much to feed upon.

Everything was ripe. Peaches, corn, watermelons and other crops were all ripe at the Hopi village of Oraibi. Two days after we camped at Cedar Standing, my mother and father decided to go there. They killed two goats, butchered them and cut them up and took over the meat and skins. They were gone all day and stayed one night. The next day they came back with two big sacks full of peaches, and some corn and a few watermelons. They said, "The Pueblo people we visited were kind. They want us to visit them every once in a while. They'd like us to come again soon."

Late in the fall we moved back to the foot of Black Mountain Sitting Up, where we found a hogan and lived in it.

Reprinted with permission of Mrs. Ruth Dyk from *Son of Old Man Hat*, recorded by Walter Dyk, 1938. (Lincoln: University of Nebraska Press, 1966) pp. 129–37, 150.

Clan: *Tábąąhí*
Born for: *Tł'ízí Łání*

## GEORGE BLUEEYES

*George Blueeyes, also known as* Tábąąhí Ts'ósí, *is a medicine man living at Rock Point, Arizona. He was born about 1900 and is* Tábąąhí *Clan, born for* Tł'ízí Łání. *His grandmother, Red Woman, was also* Tł'ízí Łání—*The Many Goats Clan—and was a close relative of Old Man Hat. In this next story he tells of his youth and life around Rock Point before Stock Reduction.*

I was born just north of Rock Point not far from *Tséch'iltsoh* (Big Oak). It was summer. The wheat was knee-high and the *chiiłchin* (sumac berries) had just ripened. That was about 16 years before a fever swept over the reservation and killed so many people.

Babies then weren't born in hospitals. When the baby started to kick and was ready to be born, his mother held onto a rope hanging down in the hogan. Another lady sat behind her and held her around the stomach and helped push the baby down. A medicine man sat nearby chanting and singing.

After one or two songs the baby would come out, and a lady sitting in front of the mother would catch it. "A BOY! *K'é bidiní!*" she would shout, which means, "Speak to him as a relative!" So the mother would say, "MY SON!"—or "MY DAUGHTER!" if it was a girl.

And so it was that I was born. The minute I was born my mother told me, "MY SON!" That is how babies begin to know their mothers. Today babies are born in a hospital. How can they know their kinship in a place like that?

They gave me a name and they ran outside and washed me and then they carried me back in and placed me with my head toward the fire.

Later I was put in a cradleboard made from *nídíshchíí'* (ponderosa pine). The bow was made from *Tséch'il* (oak), and the straps and tie were made of buckskin.

And so I passed the first year. I didn't notice anything. I sucked milk from my mother. Today children drink from bottles, so the bottle is their mother. When they put down the milk bottle, they pick up the wine bottle. A child that drinks from his mother sucks up the spirit of her heart. She talks as he drinks, and he listens to her.

My grandmother was *Asdzą́ą́łchíí'* (Red Woman). She lived at Cove after coming back from *Hwééldi* (Fort Sumner), and my father was born there. They called him *Bináá' Łibáii* (Blueeyes). That's why my English name is Blueeyes. His father was a white man, maybe a soldier, so I call white people "grandfather" or "cousin."

While living at Cove, Red Woman met a man from Chilchinbito known as *Dibélchíí'* (Red Sheep). He took her and my father back there with him, but finally moved down to Big Oak.

My mother's people lived at *Dził Giizh* (Mountain Pass), northeast of Round Rock. She and her sister moved up to Big Oak to live with my father.

My grandparents and several other families planted along the Chinle Wash. The men from all the families around used to dam the wash each spring and irrigate. I remember my grandmother sending me with meat and cornbread for the workers when I was seven or eight.

There were only a few houses around in those days. There weren't as many people. We ourselves had only enough things so you could call our place a home. We had only about 30 sheep. We had so little that I went over to my grandmother Red Woman. She had enough livestock and she raised me.

About that time some men from our area married into a family from the San Juan River near Aneth and brought their wives back. The women belonged to a part of the *Kin Łichíí'nii* Clan that we call *Kin Łichíí'nii Diné Doo Bééhózinii* (Red House of the Unknown People). They are related to the *Kiis'áanii*, the Pueblos. These people had nothing when they came.

Food was scarce everywhere, and we were living mostly on wild plants, but Red Woman fed them and gave them livestock. From that start, those *Kin Łichíí'nii* people's herds grew until they had enough to live on. In return my relatives asked for a wife for me. And so it was decided that I should marry one of their daughters. I was 16 and she was 12 when our parents brought us together. We were still like children. We just played!

From then on I herded and herded and herded, and all of a sudden there were so many cattle—cattle, horses and sheep. I had to look after them all the time, sometimes on horseback, sometimes on foot.

At age 20 I started training as a medicine man. My mother's brother, *Naat'áanii Yázhí* (Little Leader), and a man called *Hastiin Ohodiiteel* (Mr. Wide Valley) were my teachers. The ceremonies and songs and stories I know now I learned from them.

In those days people would travel great distances to learn and tell stories. Often they wouldn't sleep at all at night. They just smoked mountain tobacco and told each other stories. Those stories made us strong and protected us.

All during the warm weather when the corn was growing, we stayed around Rock Point near our fields. But as winter came on we moved over to the foot of Black Mesa and sometimes up on top. We went there to be near trees for firewood. The ruins of our hogans there can still be seen.

While we spent the winter up there, the really big herds from Crystal, Tsaile, and Sonsela came down the Chinle Valley. From way over there the big herds came down from the deep snow on the mountains. They were owned by *Tsin Łizhin Íí'áhí* (Black Pole), *Tsiishch'ilí Ts'ósí* (Slim Curly), *Tsé Naatł'iní* (Rock Steps), and *Hastiin Adiits'a'ii* (Chee Dodge). Those men did not come themselves. They paid herders to do the work.

Yes, the herders came with their sheep and their donkeys carrying things. And we welcomed them. There were so many sheep! Each herd filled three corrals at least. They covered all the ground from Sonsela past Rock Point and often spent the winter on those mesas behind Dennehotso.

The herders stayed in the hogans we left behind for the winter. We did not mind. No one ever said, "Go away!" in those days. Nobody ever thought of stealing. When the snow melted on the mountains, the big herds went back.

Then it all stopped. Stock Reduction came and the horses were taken away. There was nothing to travel with then, and no reason to travel. The land was divided up. "This is my land!! Not yours!! Go away, back where you came from!!!" Everybody began to say that. Now you hear people saying that wherever you go.

Clan: *Kin Łichíi'nii*
Born for: *Kin Yaa'áanii*

## AMOS COGGESHALL

*Before Stock Reduction, people like Old Man Hat moved far and wide looking for grass for their live-stock. This story, however, shows that people also went long distances to gather wild foods, attend ceremonies and visit relatives. But they did have one place they called home, and there they always returned.*

*The storyteller here is Amos Coggeshall of Rock Point community. He was born in 1919. His clan is* Kin Łichíi'nii, *and he was born for* Kin Yaa'áanii. *His father was one of George Blueeyes' teachers.*

My father and the rest of my family lived at *Ohodiiteel*—the wide valley that comes down from Black Mesa to the Chinle Wash near where the Rock Point Trading Post now stands. There we did our planting, and there I was born.

My father was called *Hastiin Ohodiiteel*, Mr. Wide Valley, and members of my clan live there still. But even though we called Wide Valley home, we were always on the move, to Rough Rock, to Tsaile, Black Mesa and other places. Even when the family did stay for a while in one place, the ones who herded hardly stopped. My uncle covered most of the land from Rock Point to Rough Rock—*Ligai Deez'áhí* (White Point), *Dibé Bichaan Bii' Tó* (Sheep Manure Spring), *Jádí Hádét'įįh* (Antelope Lookout). With a small pack he went wherever the grass grew, camping each night in a different place. His wife stayed at the hogan, but he moved with the sheep, alone.

161

When we finished the planting at Wide Valley and summer was coming on, my father would say, "Let's move up to Tsaile and live there for a while." He had relatives up there and some cattle he liked to check on. In those days no one ever said, "This is my land! Get your stock out of the way!" We just lived among each other with our sheep and cows.

So when my father talked of leaving we just packed the wagon and the donkey. The water barrel, food, snacks and bedding all had to go, and the stock had to be gathered together.

From Wide Valley we went up past places whose names are forgotten by young people today: *Tsé Názwodí* (Winding Rocks), *Tsélchííť'aa* (Close to the Red Rock), *Tsé Bii' Hodiits'a'í* (Echo Rocks), *Ni' Hodiits'a'í* (Ground Echoes), and on to *Bis Dootł'izh Deez'áhí* (Blue Clay Point), where the Round Rock Trading Post is. There we camped.

In the evening we would milk the goats. Goat milk and corn bread cooked in the ashes made our supper. The next day we went up *Tsékooh Hootsoii* (Yellowstone Canyon) and on to Greasewood Spring and the Greasewood Trading Post. The third morning we would come to our relatives' camp at *Nídíshchíí' Ch'íhiníkaad* (Pine Growing Out). That's near where Navajo Community College is today.

That was a three-day trip, but often it took longer because we stopped to hunt rabbits or prairie dogs or to pick *chiiłchin* (sumac berries) or *tł'ohdeii* (goosefoot). People did not have big herds then, and we depended on wild plants whenever we could find them.

We might stay near Tsaile for a few months if the pinon trees had nuts. Some might stay and others come back for the corn harvest. Then half the family might winter at Wide Valley while the others spent the winter at Tsaile with the livestock. Then we would all get together again in the spring for lambing and shearing. And all the time our livestock stayed over there in Tsaile, our grass here would be growing back.

I herded sheep. Everyday I took the sheep to graze until sunset. Corn bread thrown in a sack—that's all I had to eat. At noon,

when the sheep stopped to cool off, I boiled milk from one of the goats and ate.

When three or four of us boys got together we chased chipmunks and squirrels through the oak thickets and young pines. We had no guns or even bows, so we used clubs. You could butcher those little animals and sell the skins to the trader for high prices. So we killed a lot and sometimes forgot about the sheep.

That's how it was all summer, but when the pinons ripened, we picked nuts all day long. Our pants had holes in the knees, but we crawled around under the trees until dark. Our fingers split, but at night we melted sap from trees and put it on the sores so we could go on picking the next day.

We moved from place to place, living in *il názt'i'*—brush shelters made by dragging big branches together in a circle. They had a door to the east, but no roof. Late in the fall it got cold and even snowed for two days at a time, but as long as we could sweep away the snow under the trees, we kept on picking. The goat skins we had for bedding kept us warm enough even in the rain.

When the snow got really deep we moved back to the hogans, but the pinons stayed under the snow, and in spring you could go back and pick for another month.

That's how we lived and shared the work. Old people who grew up like that are never lazy.

At harvest time, of course, some of us had to gather the corn at Wide Valley. We spread the ears around on greasewood bushes to dry and then beat off the grain. That took about a month.

After the harvest we could travel again. I remember once when part of the family had gone to Black Mesa in the summer and stayed to pick pinons near *Kits' iilí* (Ruins). The rest of us were herding and looking after the camp at Wide Valley. But when we heard of a *Na'akai* (*Yé'ii Bicheii* dance) over near Pinon, my brother Harvey said, "Let's go."

In the morning we brought in the horses and packed them, then set off up Wide Valley past *Dibé Bichaan Bii' Tó* and on to the

Rough Rock Trading Post. From there a trail climbs to the top of the mesa. Around sunset we got to *Kits'iilí*. A lot of Rock Point people were there picking pinon nuts.

That night it snowed heavily, so some of them started saying, "The snow is too deep for picking. Let's go to the ceremony!" Six of us went on down the valley past *Kin Náazhoozhí* (Ruin Sliding Down) to Pinon. The ceremony was about two miles north of the Pinon Trading Post, and we spent two days there. Back then the *Yé'ii Bicheii* dances were truly respected. You never saw a drunk, and no one went near the house of the *Yé'iis* except the dancers.

It snowed another foot before the Rock Point people started down off the mesa. The wagons were loaded with pinons and firewood. We tied wood behind the wagons to slow them down as they rolled down the steep trail to Rough Rock, and we held back the wheels with ropes. From Rough Rock on to Wide Valley we had no trouble.

We traveled so much in those days. We did not worry about our hogans and blankets and valuable things. When we came back they would all be there. If you were traveling and night caught up with you, you could spend the night in any house you might be near. My uncle and I once traveled like that all the way to *Bá'azhchini* (Born for Him)—a place in Paiute Canyon by Navajo Mountain where his father was living.

All of that ended when Stock Reduction came and they counted and branded the livestock and set up grazing districts. We settled down at Wide Valley near Rock Point in District Nine because that's where we had always planted, and that's where the children were born.

We have relatives who settled in other districts.

Amos Coggeshall and George Blueeyes told their stories during the summer of 1979 to Rex Lee Jim, the grandson of *Hastiin Ohodiiteel*.

# THE GOOD LIFE

Story tellers have happy memories of the old days before grazing regulations, pickup trucks, electricity and boarding schools. Were those times better than the present?

Many died back then from foreign diseases like influenza and tuberculosis. Many went painfully hungry when rain didn't come or grasshoppers ate the corn. They got no food stamps to help them through. Few ever saw a town, and the towns they saw then were even rougher than now.

People do enjoy better health, eat better and know more about the world now than they did once. Those who remember don't deny it. "Yes, yes," they say, "Life was hard, but we lived it gloriously."

The pictures here show what a Navajo family in 1900 might have needed for daily life. Except for the wagon, much has not changed. However, in 1900 people got everything they needed from the land itself or from trade. Today it seems impossible to get along without money.

It was glorious to live from the land itself without worry about jobs, bosses, car payments and foreign languages. But the real glories of the past are not in the picture at all — the ceremonies, philosophy, storytelling, singing, and dancing.

The ancient arts of Navajo culture probably bloomed brightest in the years between the Long Walk back from Fort Sumner and Stock Reduction in the 1930's. Navajo Country had peace, livestock and little interference from the outside world. That had never happened before and might never happen again.

How hard is it today to find a teacher like Mr. Wide Valley who taught George Blueeyes his sacred chants? Are there *Yé'ii Bicheii* dances yet like the one Amos Coggeshall saw at Pinon? What have we gained that takes their place?

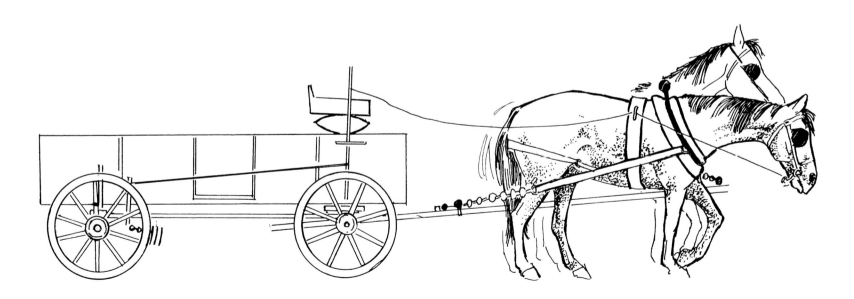

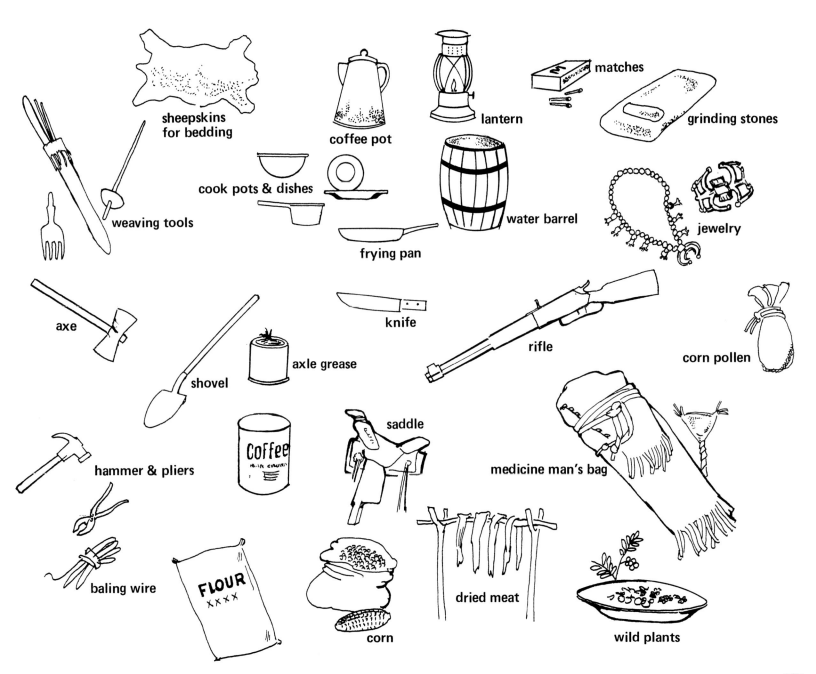

sheepskins for bedding

coffee pot

lantern

matches

grinding stones

cook pots & dishes

water barrel

jewelry

weaving tools

frying pan

axe

knife

rifle

corn pollen

shovel

axle grease

hammer & pliers

Coffee

saddle

medicine man's bag

baling wire

FLOUR
XXXX

corn

dried meat

wild plants

# LIVESTOCK AND LAND

In the stories of this chapter Son of Old Man Hat, George Blueeyes, and Amos Coggeshall all tell how they and others moved with their stock. None of them, however, wandered without plan or reason.

Most families then (some still do) had summer and winter areas where they went every year. Sometimes they moved only a short distance, sometimes fifty miles or more. In real emergencies they might wander to new areas, as Old Man Hat did in the story.

Moving livestock is natural. Wild animals move. So do stock-raising people of other countries.

There are many reasons. The people in the stories mention a few: to find better grass in dry seasons, to give plants a chance to grow, to escape deep snow, to be near firewood. There are other reasons. Before wells were drilled, many areas had to be used in winter because they had no water except from snow. People without farms might spend time near the Hopi towns to trade for corn.

People moved in different ways in different places. "How did you care for your stock in summer and winter?" is a good question to ask any older person.

The sketch on these pages shows an especially interesting way many people still move their herds on the east slope of the Chuska Mountains. Here is how they explained it to researchers from Navajo Community College who were looking for ways to improve grazing land:

*Winter camps are usually on the plain (halgai) at the foot of the mountain. Snow doesn't stay on the ground all winter, and water running off the mountain irrigates fields. We live here until planting is done.*

*The plants of the plain are mostly grasses and small bushes. Sunflowers and taller plants grow in damp places where mountain washes meet the plain. Other plants take over as soon as the mountain starts rising.*

*Sage brush and scattered junipers and pinons give this land the name halbatah (gray land). It is too steep for much grazing, but people from camps on the plain get firewood here; when deep snow covers the plain, stock can survive on the taller plants here.*

*Above the gray land the mountain rises less steeply and the pines and taller trees begin. Many families make a halfway stop here on their way to the top, and some stay all summer. There is enough flat land and water for squash and cool-climate crops like potatoes. Meadows once grew enough grass for hay cutting too.*

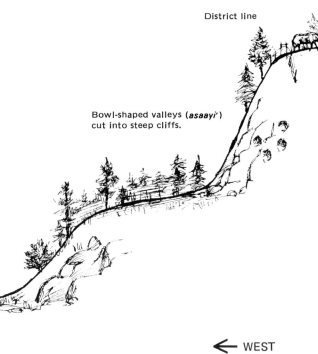

District line

Bowl-shaped valleys (*asaayi'*) cut into steep cliffs.

DEFIANCE PLATEAU

← WEST

*From this level area the mountain rises steeply again to the top. Until recently few people used this area because it is so steep, so deer and bear made it their home. Now, however, roads built to get logs for the sawmill at Navajo bring in people all summer, so the wildlife is being pushed out.*

*On top the mountain becomes flat again. Tall trees, meadows and lakes make it the best grazing land in Navajo Country. Many families stay here from June through October.*

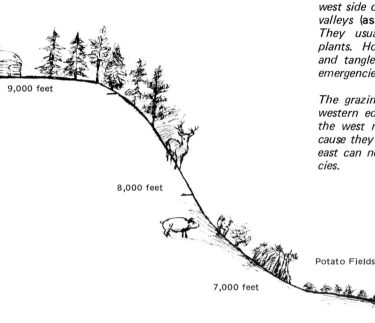

9,000 feet

8,000 feet

7,000 feet

Potato Fields

EAST →

6,000 feet

HALBATAH (Gray Land)

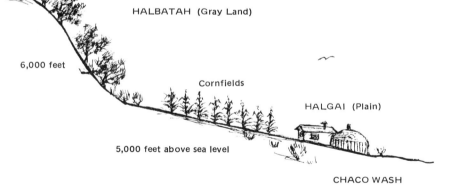

Cornfields

HALGAI (Plain)

5,000 feet above sea level

CHACO WASH

In very dry years, even the mountain plants dry out. Then people used to move over to the west side of the mountain into the bowl-shaped valleys (asaayi') just below the mountain top. They usually had more water and greener plants. However, before roads were cut, bushes and tangle made them hard to use except in emergencies.

The grazing district lines now run down the western edge of the mountains. People from the west now use the asaayi' all summer, because they can't come on top; people from the east can no longer use the asaayi' in emergencies.

In October people start moving down the mountain again. Some go ahead to start harvesting crops planted lower down. Others follow with the herds.

Herds moving up and down the mountain by this pattern waste very little of the food that grows over a wide area, but do not kill plants by overgrazing.

Today, however, more people with smaller herds and less time to move them properly have hurt the land. District boundaries have not helped. Neither have large numbers of horses and cattle that in recent times have been allowed to roam freely in the same area for months at a time.

According to the traditional way, herders take sheep out in the same direction every day for a week or two. Then the direction is changed to rest that land and let plants grow back. Rams and ewes graze separately.

Mountain plants have very little salt because rain washes it out of the soil. Without salt sheep weaken and start eating poisonous plants. Before the days of salt blocks, sheep had to be driven back down to the gray land about once a month to find salt bush and sage.

167

# OPEN LAND

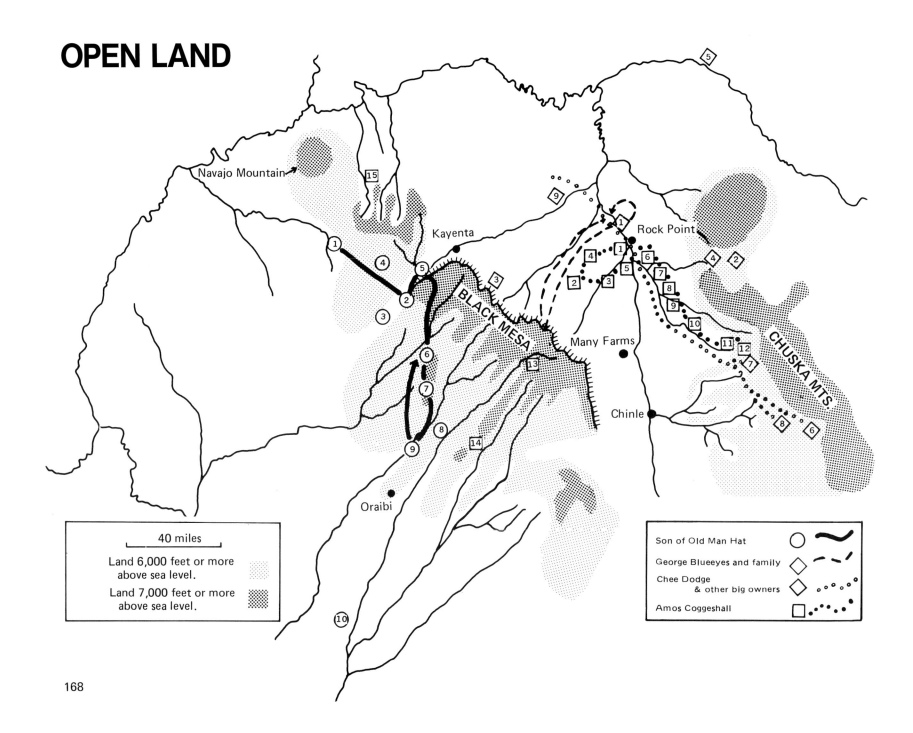

Navajo Mountain

Kayenta

BLACK MESA

Many Farms

Rock Point

CHUSKA MTS.

Chinle

Oraibi

40 miles

Land 6,000 feet or more
above sea level.

Land 7,000 feet or more
above sea level.

Son of Old Man Hat

George Blueeyes and family

Chee Dodge
    & other big owners

Amos Coggeshall

168

## WHERE THEY ROAMED

### Son of Old Man Hat

1. Start
2. *Bidáá' Tóhi* — Water High Up
3. *Tsé Ani'jíhí* — Thief Rock
4. *Ma'ii Łání* — Many Coyotes
5. *Nídeesk'id* — Hill Across
6. *Dził Dashzhinii* — Black Mountain Sitting Up
7. *Dził Nitsaa* — Big Mountain
8. *Tsé Dildǫ'ii* — Hard Rocks
9. *Gad Íí'áhí* — Cedar Standing
10. *Tó Łání* — Tolani Lakes

### George Blueeyes

1. *Tséch'iltsoh* — Big Oak
2. *K'aabizhii* — Cove
3. *Chiiłchin Bii' Tó* — Chilchinbito
4. *Dził Giizh* — Mountain Pass
5. *T'áá Bíích'íjdii* — Aneth
6. *Tó Niłts'íli* — Crystal
7. *Tsééhílí* — Tsaile
8. *Sǫ' Silá* — Sonsela (Lying Stars)
9. *Deinihootso* — Dennehotso

### Amos Coggeshall

1. *Ohodiiteel* — Wide Valley
2. *Łigai Deez'áhí* — White Point
3. *Dibé Bichaan Bii' Tó* — Sheep Manure Spring
4. *Jádí Hádét'jjh* — Antelope Lookout
5. *Tsé Názwodí* — Winding Rocks
6. *Tsélchíít'aa* — Close to Red Rock
7. *Tsé Bii' Hodiits'a'í* — Echo Rocks
8. *Ní' Hodiits'a'í* — Ground Echoes
9. *Bis Dootł'izh Deez'áhí* — Round Rock Trading Post
10. *Tsékooh Hootsoii* — Yellowstone Canyon
11. *Díwózhii Bii' Tó* — Greasewood Trading Post
12. *Nídíshchíí' Ch'íhiníkaad* — Pine Growing Out
13. *Kits'iilí* — Kitsili (Ruins)
14. *Be'ek'id Baa Ahoodzání* — Pinon
15. *Bá'azhchíní* — Paiute Canyon

## FENCES

Both George Blueeyes and Amos Coggeshall say that the old life ended with Stock Reduction. Stock Reduction began in the 1930's when the U.S. government forced Navajos to give up much of their livestock and set up grazing districts in Navajo Country.

The next chapter gives more details about what happened and the reasons. The two maps here, however, show what grazing districts did to the kind of wandering life described by Son of Old Man Hat and the others.

At left are the trails they followed and many of the places they mention. Below are the same trails on a grazing district map. It is illegal now to take livestock across district lines. They would have crossed many. Fences made people live differently.

Some say the wandering life had to end anyway as the land became more and more crowded. But the district lines made the end quick and certain. One family on the way from Navajo Mountain to their land near Lukachukai happened to be near Many Farms when the districts were set up and have been stuck there ever since. Many families have such stories.

Now however, grazing districts are part of Navajo life, and it is hard to imagine the reservation without them.

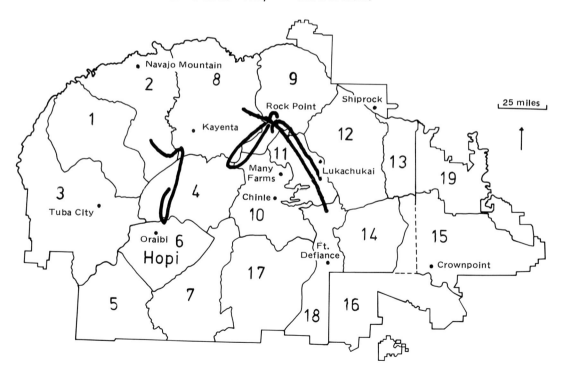

# STOCK REDUCTION

In the last chapter both George Blueeyes and Amos Coggeshall said that the old style of life came to an end when Washington forced the Navajos to cut down the number of livestock they owned. This was Stock Reduction.

The head of the Bureau of Indian affairs in Washington at the time was John Collier. To this day older Navajos remember him as the man who took their animals and destroyed their way of life.

Charlie Yellow, a medicine man of the Many Goats Clan from Kayenta, remembers Stock Reduction like many others who saw it:

> The sheep, the horses, and the cattle grew to great numbers, and the ground became bare like the floor. Now people speak of that time as "The Time the Horses Died of Starvation." What was left grew again and grew again to great numbers. Then John Collier came running with his Stock Reduction.
>
> Our animals! He ate them up!
>
> We were herding some distance from here when Collier's men caught up with us. Right there all the goats were killed, about a hundred of them. The sheep that survived grew and grew for several years. Then along came Collier again.
>
> I took my sheep all the way down to a place called Teel Ch'ínít'i', Cat Tails Come Out, and hid them. All the horses and goats and many sheep around here were killed. Their bones still lie around. We live among their bones.
>
> When they reduced the stock, many men, women, boys and girls died. They died of what we call ch'ééná, which is sadness for something that will never come back. Because of Stock Reduction, many people passed away.

Clan: *Tł'ízí Łání*

173

John Collier did not mean evil for the Navajo People. There were at that time nearly 1,500,000 head of livestock in Navajo Country. Many of them were horses that nobody seemed to use. Several times, thousands of horses and other animals did die because they could find nothing to eat, as Charlie Yellow said.

Collier believed that dry years killed so much livestock because there were too many animals to begin with. Scientists from Washington told him that the limit for reservation land was only 500,000 sheep. They told Navajo livestock owners that 500,000 well-fed animals would probably grow more meat and wool than a million starving ones. The Tribal Council even agreed that this might be true.

Most livestock owners, however, did not believe Collier or his experts from Washington. When they refused to cut down the size of their herds, Collier decided to use force. Livestock owners first had to sell off horses, then goats, and finally ewe sheep. Thousands of animals were shot and left to rot.

Some people like Charlie Yellow managed to hide their sheep, but others who disobeyed the orders were caught and sent to jail.

Grazing laws were made for Navajo Country:

- Navajo land was divided into "grazing districts."
- Livestock could not be taken across district lines.
- No one could own livestock without a permit, and no one could hold permits for more than 350 sheep or goats (1 horse = 5 sheep; 1 cow = 4 sheep).
- No one could move livestock onto land traditionally used by someone else.

Washington hoped that the plant life of Navajo Country would become richer than before. To help people along until that happened they hired Navajos to build dams, schools and bridges, dig irrigation ditches and drill wells, so people who lost livestock could earn a living some other way.

Unfortunately nothing turned out right.

Because of the grazing laws, people stopped moving around to look for grass. Each family settled in one place and tried to hold onto as much land as possible. As George Blueeyes said, "Everybody began to say, 'This is my land! Not yours! Go away where you came from!' "

The jobs that Washington paid for in Navajo Country did not make up for the lost livestock. After Stock Reduction many people had to leave home to find work or go on welfare.

Worst of all, Stock Reduction did not help the land itself. Grasses and plants that used to grow died away completely. Tumbleweed and snakeweed covered places where they never grew before. The sunflowers that turned the land yellow for miles in the old stories bloomed only by the roadsides and irrigation ditches. Medicine men, herders, scientists, and government officials all agree that something went wrong.

Even without Stock Reduction there might have been problems as more and more people filled the land. In South America, Africa, Australia and Asia, miles and miles of grazing land turn into desert every year. The problems of Navajo land are also problems of the world. Something must be done before Navajo herds disappear like the Anasazi.

- The land is unhappy. Both the scientist who studies the land and the medicine man who prays for it agree. But they do not speak the same language or think in the same way, and only the land itself can answer them.

- The fighting over land that began at the time of Stock Reduction has gotten worse. The 40,000 Navajos alive at the time of Stock Reduction are now 160,000, and they need land for homes, for towns, for livestock.

These two problems are really one problem of course, because people and land belong together.

# SCIENTISTS AND OFFICIALS

Government officials began stock reduction because they thought they knew what was best for the land. Their reasons were scientific. But did they know enough?

A habitat is limited, they said. The plants will only feed a certain number of animals. Too much stock eating too many plants will kill the plants and then starve themselves.

If plant life is dying, they said, then there must be too many animals. Reduce the stock and the plants will come back.

To be sure there isn't too much stock, all of it should be counted and branded, and the land divided. Then it would be easy to see who is responsible for each piece of land and how many animals graze there.

# MEDICINE MEN AND HERDERS

Herders like Old Man Hat and George Blueeyes also knew that habitats are limited. (Too many sheep in one canyon eat the grass and have to move on.) But they did not believe that you can balance plants and animals just by killing off the right amount of stock.

They talked more about interdependence, how plants, animals, rain *and people* help each other. "They are all sacred," said Amos Coggeshall's uncle who used to camp alone with his sheep. "There were ceremonies and medicine men who knew the Rain Way. They would say, 'It will rain,' and our plants would come back."

The older herders did not call themselves scientists. Science, however, comes from watching things carefully, and they had seen a lot. How good was their knowledge?

"They said to reduce the sheep so the plants would come back. It was all for nothing! The plants didn't come back. Plants come only from the rain, and the sheep and horses are dressed in rain. They were put on Earth with rain. So when sheep and horses were reduced, dryness came over us, and we settled down into dryness."

Yellowman's Brother
(Amos Coggeshall's uncle)

"Plants come up only where there are sheep and horses. Those are the places where it rains. If the ground is hard, when it rains the water just flows. It doesn't soak in. It soaks in only when the sheep walk on it. They walk over their dried manure and mix it with the earth. When it rains, it soaks into the ground with the seed."

George Blueeyes

# WHAT CAN WE DO?

The years after Stock Reduction showed that neither the herders nor the officials knew the whole truth.

The officials saw only the bad. Too much stock killed plants and should be cut down.

The medicine men saw only the good. Animals helped plants, and people with prayers and ceremonies could bring rain.

The officials could not completely explain why plant life got worse instead of better after Stock Reduction, or why many plants like sunflowers and goosefoot were killed by dryness, not livestock.

On the other hand, even George Blueeyes had to admit more plants grow by highways where fences keep off most of the stock.

Because Stock Reduction by itself did not work, many plans to make the land feed more stock have been tried. They are all "scientific". Some, however, come more from the thinking of the old stock reduction officials. Others are closer to the science of the herders. Here are two:

## BRUSH CLEARANCE

When killing off stock didn't bring back "good" plants, many people decided to try killing off "bad" plants.

Around Pinon and on the Defiance Plateau, especially near Crystal, bushes and trees were broken down, piled up and burned. All other plants were plowed under and killed.

A new grass from Europe called crested wheatgrass* was planted like a farm crop, and more livestock feed grew in two years than ever before. It looked good, BUT:

*Clearing, plowing and seeding cost a lot, and the land couldn't be used for two years.*

*Crested wheatgrass was a "good" plant, but wasn't enough by itself. It became so hard in mid summer that only starving stock ate it. It didn't keep soil from blowing away. And in seven years so many "bad" plants came back that the land needed plowing again.*

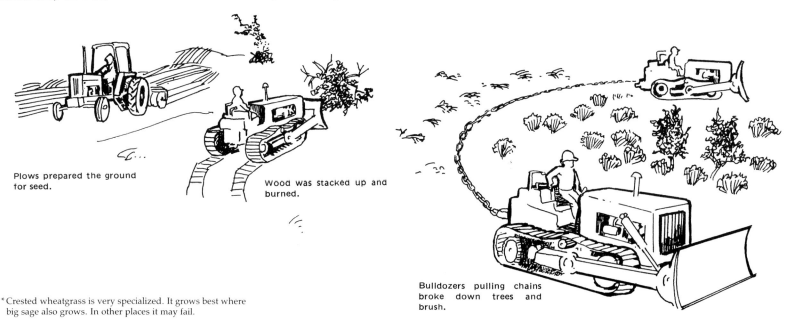

Plows prepared the ground for seed.

Wood was stacked up and burned.

Bulldozers pulling chains broke down trees and brush.

*Crested wheatgrass is very specialized. It grows best where big sage also grows. In other places it may fail.

178

Allan Savory agrees with Navajo medicine men who say people, not animals, cause most problems. Most of all, land needs careful planning, cooperation among neighbors, and daily attention.

On well-managed land, grass will return without help from tractors. Good plants will increase and poor plants decrease unitl the land looks as it did when only wild animals lived on it. That is natural succession.

How long do most people graze stock in the same place? How often does stock cross the same land going to water and back to the corral? How often do neighbors use the same land without planning? These things hurt land more than herds that are too big.

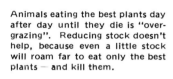

Animals eating the best plants day after day until they die is "overgrazing". Reducing stock doesn't help, because even a little stock will roam far to eat only the best plants — and kill them.

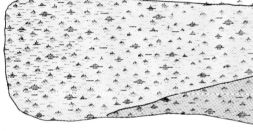

BUT if stock moves in a tight herd from one area to another and doesn't spread over the land, plants have time to grow before they are bitten again. All the land is used equally. Careful herding or cheap, smooth-wire fences can make a herd graze in this way, as wild herds do.

Urine, manure, and trampling feet of a tightly packed herd fertilize soil, help seeds start, and open the ground for rain.

A rancher must notice how the plants grow. In spring, fall, and wet times, he can move a herd faster because plants grow quickly and need less rest. In dry times plants must rest more between grazing, so stock must move slower. In winter stock moves through all areas to use all the grass left standing.

## SAVORY GRAZING

This idea comes from Africa. In the country of Zimbabwe, people noticed that ranch land was poorer than "wild" land. Where buffalo, antelope and zebras grazed freely, grass was better and more animals grew fat than where people kept horses, cattle and sheep.

Elk, antelope, deer and wild sheep once roamed Navajo Country too, and the land fed them well. Wild animals and plants belong together. Why not livestock?

The African scientists Allan Savory and Stanley Parsons discovered that:

*Wild herds moved often. After a few days in one place, they didn't return for a month or more. Ranch stock didn't move and bit off the best plants again and again until they died. The old Navajo herders did well to camp each night in a different place, traveling far to find grass.*

*Wild herds were big like the old Navajo herds. Their manure fertilized the land.*

*As George Blueeyes said, the feet of big herds did plant seeds and open the soil so rain soaked in. Where few animals grazed, plants dried out faster and fewer seeds grew. Stock truly was "dressed in rain".*

Savory Grazing makes stock graze like wild herds. Animals spend only a short time in one place. Herds move together over the whole land, eating the best food everywhere. When they return to the start, new, tender food is ready. Plants have time to grow but never become old and tough. Nothing is wasted.

After a few years on this plan, some range land has been able to feed three times the number of animals it once did. A ranch the size of the Navajo Reservation maybe could feed 1,500,000 sheep — about what Navajos had before Stock Reduction.

# THE PEOPLE PROBLEM

*In the next story one man says, "Can't people see that because of their bad thoughts the Earth herself, the air, and the sunshine are taking the livestock away!" And he is right. The problems of the land almost always come from people.*

*There might be hundreds of ways to make Navajo Country bloom again with sunflowers and grass. Unfortunately none of them can work as long as people fight over land.*

*People fight over land for different reasons, but this story from a district grazing committee meeting shows how people think about their land.*

*Navajo grazing committees work on many land problems, plan sheep dipping and branding, handle emergency livestock feed, water supplies, etc. The committee members are elected from each community in a grazing district. They take their work very seriously, but there are problems that they cannot solve.*

*In this story of course the names of people and places have been changed.*

The Navajo flag flew over the Slippery Rock chapter house, and pickup trucks filled the yard. Small children and dogs chased each other in the dust. A dozen young cowboys sat in the shade talking and spitting tobacco out into the sun. But inside, the chapter house was full to the last row of folding chairs, and everyone was quiet.

Elmer Becenti, grazing committee president, stood before the microphone dressed in his best silver and turquoise.

"Welcome friends, brothers, grandparents, cousins, and all who have come to this meeting. I hope we are all here with good thoughts about the work we have to do. Some are here for grazing permits, some have their thoughts on a land argument. Some are only here to listen. Among you there are some who wish to keep things holy and others who only want to argue. For all of you I want to begin this meeting with a prayer so our work will be done in the right way.

> *You who are Holy before all things were made,*
> *You who are Nílch'i Diyinii, the Holy Spirit,*
> *We live by you.*
> *With your breath we breathe.*
> *Make things beautiful for us.*
> *You who are Holy,*
> *We call on you every day and night.*
> *You cover us at night so we sleep.*
> *At dawn you give light, so we work.*
> *Because of this people have come together*
> *To make things beautiful for each other.*
> *You who made us from our toes to our heads*
>   *and our voices,*
> *Make things beautiful for us.*
> *Today make things beautiful for us.*
> *In time to come make things beautiful for us.*
> *Make things beautiful for us.*
> *Let it be so! Amen.*

And so the meeting began. The committee took care of old business first. A man in the chapter had died, and his daughters were dividing his grazing permit. An animal doctor from Window Rock gave a speech about vaccinating sheep. Someone wanted a report on plans for a new well.

When that was over, Hoskie Smith, the committeeman elected from Slippery Rock, took the microphone, and all talking in the room stopped.

"Welcome friends," he said. "Welcome to all of you who have come and to you on the committee, my cousins, brothers and in-laws. I am told there are two ladies here who have an argument. I am hoping they will come to the front of the room and tell us their thoughts."

Two ladies about 45 years old came from the back of the room. Both walked proudly in their best jewelry, but they did not look at each other. Committeeman Smith asked one of them to speak first.

"Welcome and thank you, grandfather," she said, "and also to the others who sit in front of us, my uncle, my brother, and my brother-in-law. I am called Clara Sandoval. I am Yucca Fruit Clan. My father was Water's Edge. You on the committee have already heard what I am going to say. That one over there has stolen our land. She has taken it away. I ask you to do something about it. She says the land is hers, but she cannot show any papers that say it is hers. We have papers. You could have decided this argument long ago, but you didn't. Now our cattle have been chased off, and some of them are lost!"

"Hmmm," said Committee President Becenti, "I understand, my sister, but you should not blame us for your problems. There must be respect among us. We are here to listen to everyone."

Now the second woman spoke in a very small, shy voice. She was Lucy Platero of the Mud Clan, born for Bitter Water. "Welcome, uncle," she said. "This is truly an argument about land, and we need your help. As you know, my father, Old Man Bitter Water, used to hold all this land, and his palomino horses were known everywhere. But soon after I was born, John Collier and his Stock Reduction took most of our livestock. It killed my father. He lost interest in living. We gave everything we had for medicines and ceremonies, but it was no use. When he passed away, we had nothing left. So my older sister and I were raised by an aunt at Leupp. My sister soon married and came back, but I stayed in Leupp and then worked in Flagstaff until a few years ago. But all this time I longed for my land. When I finally came back I found that these people had taken my land. They even got angry when I built a small house for my old age.

Now I live quietly alone. I have my own livestock. I have no reason to bother theirs. I don't tell them to get off the land. Land is just land. Everyone has a place on it. You can't drag it away and move it somewhere else."

Right then, Clara's husband, John Sandoval, jumped to his feet. His great-great-grandfather was a famous warrior, and he himself looked very tall and fierce beside the two ladies.

"How many times do we have to say it!" he boomed. "The land really is ours. My wife was living on it thirty years ago when I married her. No one heard of this other lady for twenty-five years after that. Then she comes along and tries to chase us off. I am Bitter Water Clan like her father. We should call each other "father" and "daughter," but she speaks to me like an enemy. How can we settle anything when she won't treat me like a relative?

"She even lies to you! She does run off our livestock. Her sons run it off with their motorcycles. Her dogs run it off. She chases it with her pickup. Whenever I come near, she picks up rocks. She tells you she is poor and alone, but she has children and grandchildren. She has social security checks and pension checks from working in Flagstaff. We have nothing but our livestock and our land. That's all I'm going to say."

As John Sandoval spoke, a rushing sound like wind in a cornfield filled the room. The people now began to argue among themselves in low voice. Then suddenly Lucy's aunt, Old Lady Mud, stood up and began shouting from the back of the room. She was tiny and wrinkled like a raisin, but she banged her cane loudly on the floor between words.

"You there!" BANG "My in-law that they call John!" BANG "Don't you know that the land you live on belongs to the Mud Clan!" BANG. "Everybody knows that. But I don't blame you. I don't blame you even though your horses and cows run everywhere and we have nothing. I don't blame you, even though you have built houses all over our land. I'm sure this all happened because your wife is jealous of my niece. Maybe that's where it all began. I think that could happen.

"But, my children, do not say you are arguing over the land. The land is something that should be respected and kept holy. It gives us our life. We use its plants and soil in our ceremonies and living. We MUST NOT ARGUE ABOUT LAND, because our

Mother Earth holds us all. Wherever we go, we are still together on this earth. When we die, we become part of the earth. If this hatred is still there when we go back, it will come up with the plants, which livestock will eat, which our children will eat. Therefore this must be settled so our children will grow up with holy thoughts."

For a moment the room was silent again, but everyone could hear John Sandoval grumble, "How can she talk about jealousy! If she brings that up, we'll never agree. She knows too much about jealousy from her own life."

Then President Becenti stepped to the microphone and waited until the cornfield wind sound stopped.

"Friends," he said, "I am sad to see the way younger people argue with each other. Things happened between the older people too, but this is much worse.

"You ask this committee to decide everything, but we can't. We can only bring you together and give you advice. You yourselves should settle this argument the way your grandparents did, by talking with respect as relatives and listening to the advice of your elders.

"If you cannot settle the argument that way, you can take it to court, but that is difficult and will leave some of you angry. I want you to listen to a story that was told by the old people from a long time ago. I want you to think about what can happen if you ask a court to solve your problems:

*Once upon a time, they say, a snake lay all curled up under a bank, when a rock fell on top of it. It couldn't move, so it waited until a rabbit came along. "Help! Help!" called the snake, and the cottontail lifted the rock at once.*

*Shoooo YA! That snake grabbed the rabbit and raised back to strike.*

*"NO! WAIT! I HELPED YOU!" cried the rabbit.*

*"Tough luck," said the snake. "No law says I can't eat a rabbit whenever I catch one."*

*But the rabbit cried out again, "Wait, there's a horse over there. Let him be the judge." But the horse backed off and said, "I can't say anything about your problem. I only work with humans. I work and they feed me, and besides that I don't think about what's going on."*

*The snake got ready to strike again, when a donkey came along. But the donkey also would not judge. "I never saw anything like this," he said. "All I know how to do is eat. Then I find some mud or ashes and roll in it. That's my life. But that fellow over there might help you."*

*That fellow of course was Coyote. He listened to both the rabbit and the snake. "I almost starved under that rock," said the snake, feeling a little guilty. Then Coyote scratched himself a long time and said, "I want to see how this all happened. Snake, go curl up where you were before." And the snake did.*

*"Now rabbit," said Coyote. "You put the rock back so I will know just how much work you had to do." And the rabbit did.*

*"All right, rabbit," said Coyote, "just run over there a little way like you were when you heard the snake."*

*As the rabbit trotted away, Coyote himself took off, saying to Horse and Donkey, "You see, that's all there is to it."*

"That's how it may be, if you ask a court to solve your problems instead of working things out yourselves."

The people in the room all laughed, but not too loudly. No one wanted to be thought of as snake, rabbit, horse or donkey.

After that several people from the two families spoke, but none of them would agree to anything the other side said. Both Lucy Platero and Clara Sandoval cried real salt tears more than once. Finally Hoskie Smith, the grazing committee member who came from that chapter, asked to speak one more time. Everyone could see that he was tired of listening to the same things over and over again.

"Friends," he said, "my cousin, the committee chairman, told you a story that was full of wisdom. Why don't you listen to him. Children! Grandparents! Cousins! Uncles! Everyone from old to young, listen! When I was elected to this committee these people had already started arguing. Why can't they settle it? They blame

184

each other for missing livestock. Can't they see that because of their bad thoughts the Earth itself, the air, and the sunshine are taking the livestock away?

"The argument will not be settled until the two families say to each other, 'Let's make peace. Our grandparents lived here with the same prayers and songs we live by today. Let us find a way to live together.'

"But you do not say that. You go on fighting with words and papers and arguments. It is true that Old Man Bitter Water roamed over this land. It is true that he passed away. It is true that a boundary was made and permits were given out. Now it seems that the permits and the boundaries have become holier than the land itself. Remember, it's the land that's holy, not a piece of paper. Look back to your ancestors. Now they ARE the land.

"If you decide to go to court, the court will look only at the permits and the maps, nothing else. The court will ask questions. 'Where did the permits come from? Was it written down when your parents divided them among you? Do you have more stock than the permit allows? Did you buy the permits? Was THAT written down?' If the court finds anything wrong, all of you could lose something. But I will say it again, if you can't agree among yourselves, the court is the only way."

At that moment a young Navajo woman asked to speak. She sat with the committee but was not one of them. She said that she worked for the Bureau of Indian Affairs in Tuba City in the Branch of Land Operations. The committee had asked her to give her opinion.

"We have checked the land boundaries," she said, "and I can tell you that according to the old maps, Lucy Platero's house is on the Sandoval's land. Lucy herself does not have a grazing permit. Her older sister does. The court will probably tell her to put a fence around her house and move her stock away. She will either have to get rid of the stock or get her sister to split her permit. Either way, one of the sisters will have to get rid of some stock.

"The court will not listen to anything about Old Man Bitter Water and where he used to herd, because the map and the permits ARE clear in this case."

And so the meeting ended. The snake was back under the rock. The Sandovals and Plateros could still settle the problem themselves. The Sandovals now knew that they could win something if they took the argument to court. But they also knew that the Plateros would always be their neighbors. The land itself held them together and would not forget any hatred between them.

As people left the meeting, a very old man with ragged clothes and tangled hair began shouting in a loud voice, "My children! My children! Many years ago our ancestors went to Fort Sumner. They came back because they longed for their land! Their songs and prayers were heard! We must keep those songs and prayers! We must not argue! Let us live happily and joyfully on the land from birth to old age!"

But the old man was blind and deaf. He did not notice that the room was empty except for the echo of his own voice.

# YOU ARE THE JUDGE

## Justice and the Law

Laws are written to help settle arguments and make sure that everyone is treated in the same way. As the characters in the coyote story discovered, however, laws and judges can't always satisfy everyone.

The BIA official at the grazing committee meeting said the Sandovals had a right to use the land because their name was on the grazing map and they had a grazing permit. But in fact they did not "own" the land.

According to tribal law people do not "own" reservation land. They may own grazing permits and live in "customary use areas" shown on grazing maps. They may rent land from the tribe. But land really "belongs" to the whole tribe, and the Tribal Council can decide what to do with it.

Navajos cannot sell, trade or pawn reservation land. Usually the Tribal Council will not even allow someone to rent land unless the people of that community agree.

These are the laws, but they do not answer all the questions that come up, and these are left for the grazing committees, the tribal courts and the people themselves to work out. Here are a few hard ones that come up all the time:

Often the maps are not clear. Anyone who wants to build a fence must get his neighbors to agree where it will run. How can this be done?

Because most of the land has no fences, horses and cattle may wander freely onto other people's land. This is illegal, but almost impossible to stop unless people decide to build fences. What should be done?

Most old grazing permits have been split into dozens of small ones by the grandchildren of the original owners. What happens when two small-permit owners from different communities marry?

Adopted children and children who live with their father's parents may grow up on land that "belongs" to another clan. Should they have any rights to that land when they start their own families?

By law the tribe may take someone's land, build houses, start an irrigation project on it or rent it to a mining company. In the past the Tribal Council has said, "This is good for the whole tribe, so we will do it even if the people on the land disagree." Is this fair? How much should people be paid? Where can they go?

# WHO OWNS THE LAND?

### The Sandoval-Platero Case:

In the old days before Stock Reduction and grazing regulations, people like Old Man Hat and George Blueeyes called certain places home, but they did not say, "We own this land." As Amos Coggeshall told it, "No one ever said, 'This is my land' . . . We just lived among each other with our sheep and cows."

Stock Reduction changed that. Each family group was assigned a "customary use area", just big enough for the livestock allowed by their grazing permit. These use areas were sketched roughly on maps but not marked on the land. From that time on "Who owns land?" has been an important question.

By tradition a man moved in with his wife's clan. So the Plateros say Old Man Bitter Water's territory belongs to members of his wife's clan, the Mud Clan.

The Sandovals say the land is theirs because they have legal permits to use it, and they HAVE used it for nearly 30 years while Lucy Platero worked in Flagstaff. Every community on the Navajo Reservation has problems like this. Can they be solved by clan elders, courts, grazing committees — or Coyote?

What if someone else proved that his family had lived on the land and used it before Old Man Bitter Water? Would he have the right to push off both the Sandovals and the Plateros?

Since Clara Sandoval's husband is the same clan as Old Man Bitter Water, should the Plateros feel differently about sharing the land with him?

Does it matter that the Sandovals have used the land? How long should people have to use the land before it becomes their land?

What will happen to the children and grandchildren of the two families? Will they carry on the argument?

Will either family care properly for the land while they are fighting, or will the land itself suffer as they chase each other's stock back and forth across it?

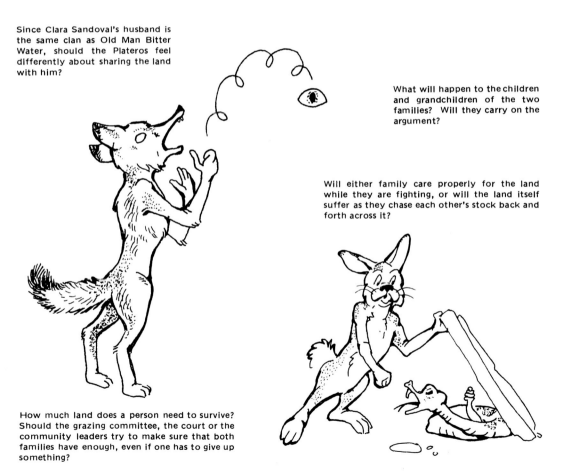

How much land does a person need to survive? Should the grazing committee, the court or the community leaders try to make sure that both families have enough, even if one has to give up something?

# PEOPLE WITHOUT LAND

In the story Lucy Platero said, "Land is just land. Everyone has a place on it. You can't drag it away and move it somewhere else." Unfortunately, the laws of the United States and the Navajo Tribe do NOT say that everyone has a place on the land. Many people now have no land and no way to get land.

This can happen for many reasons:

*The Tribal Council or the U.S. Congress can take land. This has happened, as the next chapter will show.*

*Orphans who grow up on land belonging to another family may have no land.*

*The children of men who marry outside the Navajo Tribe may have no land.*

*Children who leave Navajo Country for a long time may find no room to settle on if they return.*

*In the Checkerboard Area especially, a family may not own much land. After grandchildren and great grandchildren have divided it, the pieces are too small to live on.*

Navajo tradition cannot easily take care of landless people because land never ran out in the old days. No one even imagined life without land.

Elsewhere a person might at least buy land, but on the reservation that is impossible. A landless person has a hard time renting even a small patch.

Because of this:

*People will do almost anything to hold onto the land they have. This can lead to arguments like the one in the story. It means that people don't dare leave their land. They keep as much livestock on it as possible so no one else can move in on them.*

*People who cannot live from livestock must leave their land to find work, but they look for jobs like construction, railroad labor and fighting forest fires that don't take them away from the land for years at a time like some jobs do.*

*Those who have no land often buy land or rent land around the edges of the reservation or try to find work in reservation towns where they can rent housing. Others crowd into mobile home towns like Kayenta.*

*But many also leave Navajo Country altogether, and a few never come back.*

What does it mean to have land? Does a person hold onto land because he loves it or just because he wants to use it? What does it mean to leave your land?

# POPULATION

This page shows the crowding of Navajo Country. It was nearly empty in 1868 when a young man returned to Rock Point from Fort Sumner. He is remembered as Tsin Sikaadnii Tsoh for the tree he camped under with his two wives — a Ta'neeszahnii woman from Canyon de Chelly and her daughter.

From them came over 250 people whose mothers or fathers are Ta'neeszahnii. Fannie Begay, granddaughter of Tsin Sikaadnii Tsoh and clanship instructor at Rock Point School, has listed here those still at Rock Point or close to people there. But the family is so large and grows so fast that she asks Tsin Skiaadnii's other relatives to forgive any mistakes.

Try doing this for your own family, and you will appreciate her work and learn much about yourself.

Many families growing like this have caused the population of Navajo Country to jump from about 10,000 in 1868 to about 160,000 in 1980.

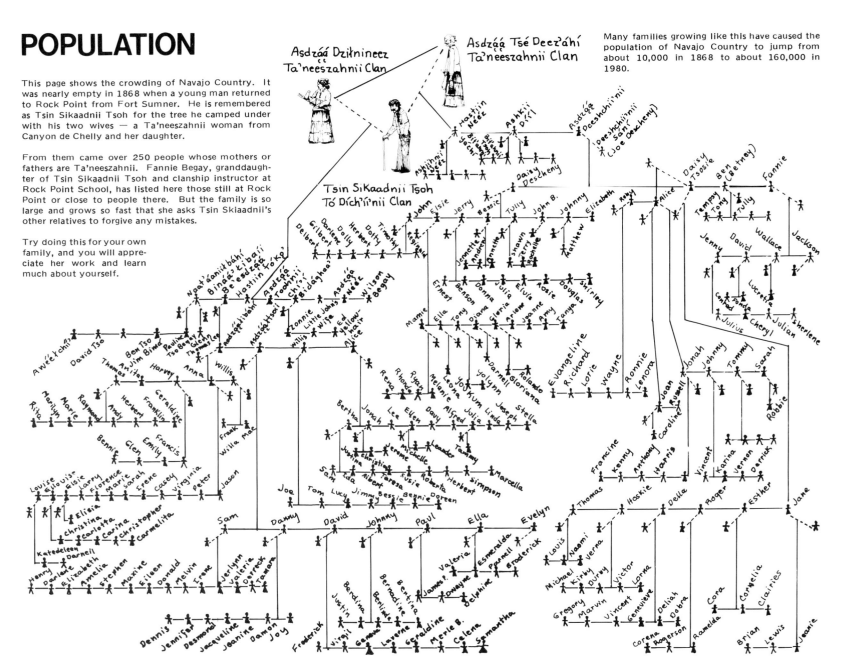

# NAVAJOS AND HOPIS

# NEIGHBORS

As earlier chapters have shown, life in Navajo Country changes as the land fills up with people and new ideas. The old ways Navajos and Pueblos shared the land is changing too. Just as neighbors in turn share land and argue over it, so do tribes and nations.

Hopis and Navajos have lived in the same country for centuries, sometimes helping each other, sometimes fighting. The Hopis lived together in their villages. The Navajos spread out over the land. But on the land itself no clear line ever divided them. They have learned from each other. Many of their clans are related. And they face the same future because they live on the same land.

In 1958, however, the Hopi and Navajo Tribal Councils asked a U.S. court to decide what land would be all Hopi and what land would be all Navajo. And so a long argument between the two tribes came to a climax. This chapter tells about that argument, the Navajo-Hopi Land Dispute.

The roots of the Land Dispute go back many years. The U.S. government drew the first lines on maps in 1868 to mark the Navajo Reservation. That first reservation area was much smaller than the land where Navajos had roamed in the past. No fences marked the reservation, however. The Navajos moved east and west, and no one stopped them. From time to time more land was added to the reservation, but most Navajos did not notice any changes. At that time they could travel quite far in all directions without meeting other people.

In 1882, 14 years after the Navajo Reservation was made, the president of the United States created a reservation for the Hopis. This land, he said, is for the "Moqui (Hopi) and such other Indians as the secretary of the interior may see fit to settle thereon." The secretary of the interior is the person in the U.S. government in charge of land.

On the land itself, however, no lines were drawn. No fences were built. The people living on the land could not know where one reservation ended and the other began. The secretary of the interior did nothing to stop Navajos or Hopis from living wherever they wished. Most of the Hopis at that time lived in villages at the south end of Black Mesa and farmed. Few herded livestock. Navajos, however, had big herds that had always moved across the land all around the Hopi villages.

Fifty years after the Hopi Reservation line was drawn, Washingon noticed that more Navajos than Hopis lived there. When grazing permits were handed out, Navajos got most of them. Only Grazing District Six was Hopi.

Many Hopis thought they should be allowed to use the rest of the land on their own reservation, even though Navajos had lived there for a long time. However, nothing happened until the 1950s. The U.S. government decided then to settle all questions about Indian land in the United States, especially where valuable minerals were found. Soon after tests showed coal *and* oil might be under Black Mesa, the Navajo and Hopi Tribal Councils agreed to let a United States court decide what the reservation lines really meant.

Three judges heard the case in Prescott, Arizona, and in 1962 they announced their decision: District Six would be all Hopi land. The rest would be called a "Joint Use Area" (JUA), and Hopis and Navajos would share it 50–50.

The Navajos living on this land, however, did not share it. No Hopis were given grazing permits or room to build homes. Because of this, the Hopi Council again turned to Washington and asked the government to divide the land clearly between Hopis and Navajos. They wanted to split the land, and they wanted the Navajos to move off half of it.

## A HOPI RANCHER—JULY, 1972

Hopi kachinas are dancing at New Oraibi. A great drum is booming. On all the housetops the people stand watching as the dancers come, bells and turtle shells on their legs, a turquoise-painted rattle in each right hand.

Clowns leap around the dancers, making jokes. One of them wears a sign that says "Hopi-Navajo Joint Use Area."

Thirty-three-year-old Leroy Kaye and two of his small sons watch the ceremony from the back of a white pickup. He does construction work in the border towns to the south but comes home on weekends to see his family and take care of his live-stock. He owns 75 head of white-faced beef cattle.

In the past most Hopis have farmed, tending fields below villages perched on high mesas. But Kaye says that many younger men like himself are no longer interested in farming.

"Most of these older men—they're farmers. But it's not guaranteed to give you so much each year. In a dry year you get nothing, you know. A lot of younger people would rather be making money than doing farm work."

He is not happy with his construction job because it means leaving early Monday morning for a nearby border town and not coming back until Friday. "I'm working for someone else and I'm not getting ahead no matter how much money I make."

"Long ago all this land on Black Mesa belonged to the Hopis," he says. "Then the Navajos moved in on us. The Hopi, you know, like to live close together because of things like these kachina ceremonies. But that is changing. If we could get our land back, more Hopis would get cattle—maybe even move up there. Maybe I'd move up there myself. Right now there are too many Navajos up there. The grass is so poor. I wouldn't take my cattle out there. Even though it's supposed to be shared 50-50 with the Hopis, there is no law up there. I would lose my herd."

Leroy Kaye's brother-in-law is Abbott Sekaquaptewa. The Sekaquaptewas and their in-laws are among the most important ranching families on the Hopi Reservation. Abbott has been elected tribal chairman several times and has probably worked harder than anyone else for a law to claim the Hopi share of the JUA.

Is Mr. Sekaquaptewa interested only in getting more land for his family's livestock? He says that is not the case, and that he is asking for land the Hopis have always used—for gathering wood, hunting, visiting shrines. The Hopis have always had their own traditional way of using land, he explains, and that should not be judged by the standards of the whites or Navajos.

"The Hopi people are close to their land," he says. "The land not only lets us make a living. It is part of our religion. As I learned from my clan elders, it is marked for us by our eagle shrines."

While he agrees it would be better not to fight over land, he feels there is no choice. "The leaders have said we should not fight with others, but the Navajos are a fighting people. They have pushed us back with violence and fear. Hopis have been run down and beaten and their houses burned many times. I know

this from my own father. He spoke Navajo very well. He had good Navajo friends, but he had to earn their respect with his fists more than once."

Many older Hopis agree with Sekaquaptewa. Silver-haired Viets Lomahaftewa, 85, told congressmen that he would compare the Navajos to the Spaniards. Centuries ago the Spaniards came to the Hopi mesas and made slaves of us, he explained. Finally the Hopis got rid of the Spaniards, but then "the Navajos came. Their raids and plundering equaled that" of the Spaniards, he said. "For more than a century" the Navajos have run over us and paid no attention to "our rights as a people." Lomahaftewa and others begged the congressmen to "remove the Navajo from our midst."

## A NAVAJO RANCHER—JULY, 1972

It is dawn. Pinon and juniper stand out black against the white in the eastern sky.

Avery Luna, his hair tied back in a traditional *tsiiyééł*, hair bun, is already at work splitting juniper logs into stove wood. His neighbors know him as *Hastiin Dah Násk'id Biye' Aláąji'ígíí*, Eldest Son of the Man of the Mesa.

Inside the hogan his wife is at her cooking, boiling coffee and heating last night's mutton and potatoes for breakfast. Down in the corral, bells tinkle as the sheep and goats move restlessly against the great twisted logs that fence them in.

The herd is the life-blood of the family. Even before breakfast Luna's 18-year-old grandson Eugene is out loading three bawling goats into the pickup. His mother will trade them to a neighbor for a bundle of cloth. She is paying for the truck with rugs. She weaves one rug a month with wool from her own sheep.

In an hour or two Luna himself will saddle his horse and take his sheep to graze. He has done that almost every day of his 74 years. The family's herd is older than memory. A hundred years ago and more, the ancestors of the people and the ancestors of the sheep rode out together on the same land in the same way.

The Luna's camp is on Black Mesa, just north of Big Mountain between the Dinnebito and Moenkopi washes. Avery Luna married a granddaughter of *Dzaanééz Hólóonii*, Many Mules, and *Asdzáá K'ai' Deezt'i'*, Willow Line Woman, who lived on that part of Black Mesa about the time of Fort Sumner. Willow Line Woman's clan, the *Tó'áhaní*, claim the land still. Many Mules himself belonged to the *Tł'ízí Łání* Clan, who according to Luna are blood relatives of the Hopi Pumpkin Clan.

The land has seen many people come and go. Anasazi pottery turns up in the Luna's corral. "When I was little," says Luna's daughter Alice, "we used to find whole bowls while herding sheep. My grandmother used to scold us and make us take them back."

Clan: *Tó Dích'ii'nii*
Born for: *Lók'aa'Dine'é*

196

"In later times," says Florence Luna, "Navajos from here would butcher sheep and take them down to Hopi towns to trade. The wagons would follow one another and be gone two weeks. I can remember far enough back to know, because I heard and saw them. The Hopis and Navajos valued each other's friendship. One of our sisters is married to a Hopi. There were no problems until something was found under our land that you could get money from—coal."

The year is 1972. Changes bigger than any in the past are about to happen. To the north the Lunas can see the dust and machines of a huge coal mine that will one day swallow the ground they stand on. And on maps in far-away offices, lines are being drawn around their land.

These lines go from the Lunas' camp on south past the homes of thousands of other Navajos. The lines say that the land those Navajos live on in fact belongs to the Hopi Tribe. In the next ten years, as many Navajos as once limped into Fort Sumner may face the loss of their land forever.

For Luna, a medicine man, the land has sacred importance. Sorrow chokes Luna's words when he speaks about it. "When the Navajos came into this world, they were assigned a place to live," he says. "They were given animal life and plant life. They received language and livestock and knowledge to assure that they and all they had would live well and grow. The places where our clans began are known.

"The Hopis also were given a place to live by their creator. They, too, were given knowledge of how to live and their own legends. They are not completely different from ours. This knowledge has not been forgotten and put away. It is still alive. It is something you can put your hands on.

"This land tells us that other people did live here. We now belong here, because our forefathers are buried here.

"Our way of life is defined in our myths, legends, and prayers. We were given our own set of teachings to abide by. We were given our language. Our livestock. Our land. Our own way of handling problems. Those things are what make us who we are.

"If we have to leave our land, if we have to give up our livestock, if we have to go away from the things that make us what we are, we will no longer be the same people.

"I have heard it said that the Navajos would only exist for twelve lifetimes. Maybe that time is coming to an end."

Luna's daughter Alice dropped out of college to fight against the coal mine digging up the mesa to the north. However, she found that wherever she went on Black Mesa people wanted to know about the Land Dispute as well. So she traveled here and there trying to find out all she could and telling people the news. She went down to the Hopi Mesas and talked to Hopis. She organized bus trips to Washington for Black Mesa people to visit congressmen and officials. She found out all she could about the history of the mine and the mining company.

"No one ever said to me, 'We want to split the land to open it up for mines,' " said Alice, "but don't tell me the fence and the mine came together by chance. When I looked behind the scenes of both issues I found the same people and heard the same names. The lawyers for the Hopi Tribe, congressmen, Interior Department and mining company officials were all connected by business deals, long friendships, the Mormon Church, or shared interests."

Alice learned more than she could explain to the people who most needed to know. "Who are these judges?" James Begay, a Navajo from east of Big Mountain, wanted to know. "Who are these people, these judges, these senators and leaders who decide these things? Why don't we see them? Did they spend time, months, years, visiting the Hopi people, finding out about their culture? Did they visit the Navajos, go to the hogans, go to the places where they brand their livestock and feed their herds? Will they do that before they make people move?"

Others just said, "We will fight before we will leave our land."

## LAND OPERATIONS—JULY, 1972

In the Hopi Agency headquarters of the Bureau of Indian Affairs (BIA) at Keams Canyon, the Land Dispute seems quite simple.

Behind a door marked "Land Operations" is a clean bright room like the operating room of a hospital. Albert Purchase works there for the BIA and does what the BIA superintendent tells him to do.

The superintendent gets his orders from the area director in Phoenix, who gets his orders from the commissioner of Indian affairs in Washington, who gets his orders from the assistant secretary of the interior for land management, who gets his orders from the secretary of the interior, who gets his orders from the president, who must listen to Congress and the judges of the federal courts.

Except for Purchase himself and his superintendent, none of these people has ever lived in Hopi or Navajo Country.

Maps of the Navajo-Hopi Joint Use Area and pictures taken from airplanes cover the walls of the Land Operations office. Purchase points to them and scratches his gray hair. "This had to be done," he says. "I've been in this country 35 years. I never could see how you could have two farmers on one farm."

He stops and looks around to see who might be listening. "But, you know it's funny," he goes on. "Many Hopis can't stand this work. That's because they're Hopi. They don't believe land can be divided.

"They ask me, 'What are you doing?', and I tell them I'm dividing the land the way the government said. They just shake their heads and say, 'Which half is mine? How does your government know that?'

"A lot of Hopis think that way. Others know that this dispute is going to be settled the white man's way by the white man's law. They know they'd better take their half while they can. It won't be done in the Hopi way."

Purchase shakes his head again and turns back to his maps. The land is rolled out in front of him all white and clean. He sharpens his pencil and looks for the wash or the hill or spring where he made his last mark, brings down the pencil, and moves on.

## MINA LANSA —JULY, 1972

The land looks different from the top of Third Mesa. When the leader of Old Oraibi goes out to feed her golden eagles, she and the birds look out over a thousand miles of mesas, plains, and deserts, all changing colors in the shadows of a thunder cloud. Fences hardly show at all. Mina Lansa, an elder of the oldest living town in the United States, keeps her eagles for ceremonies as ancient as the eagle shrines that mark the land. Who can say how long ago her own people, the Parrot Clan, wandered into that land?

She and the chiefs, the *kikmongwis,* of some other villages have never agreed that the Hopi Tribal Council should speak for the Hopi people. For her, the laws of the land were given at the time of creation, and there are no others. No council organized by the Bureau of Indian Affairs can change them. No BIA map-maker can bend them. Her small body shakes with anger when she talks about the new line.

"The line will destroy our very land and life," she says. "It will divide us and the Navajo people, so that there will be more problems for both of us. As a leader of my people I look on all land as our land. All things on it and all people that are on it are in our care. Our songs and ceremonies call us caretakers of this land for ALL people. We should not keep anyone from using it.

"We have been taught to take care of the land in this way so that ALL people will benefit and ALL living things. The white people also came among us. I do not say that they cannot live on the land. We are the keepers and caretakers of this land for ALL PEOPLE!"

When the U.S. Congress began discussing what would be done with the JUA, Mina Lansa left her cornfield, her grandchildren and her ancient village on the mesa and traveled to Washington. She entered the high halls of Congress itself, stood in front of the microphones, and explained the wisdom of her ancestors as clearly as she could.

The lawyers and congressmen asked her questions. The tape recorders rolled. The official reporters and secretaries took notes. When she finished they shook her hand, and some of them said that her words had been very interesting. Then she went home.

She never stopped praying for the Earth and its people—all of them, but she did not live to see the end of the Land Dispute.

## TEN YEARS LATER—JULY, 1982

By the white man's law, the U.S. Congress had the power to split the JUA and throw the Navajos off half of it. In 1974 Congress decided to do that. Three more years passed, and the line Albert Purchase drew became official with few changes.

According to the new law, all Navajos except the very old would have to be off the Hopi side of the line by 1986. They would get a house and, if they moved quickly, some money. But there was no room for so many families and their livestock elsewhere on the Navajo Reservation, where people were already arguing over grazing land.

Congress gave the Navajo Tribe the right to buy land, but as of 1980, no land had been found. Some people were given homes in towns near the reservation, but those who spoke no English and knew only the herder's life suffered terribly.

Congress created an official relocation commission to solve the problem, but the commissioners soon discovered that the job was bigger than anyone had guessed. By 1981 they had a list of 109 Hopis and 9525 Navajos caught on the wrong side of the line. The BIA counted only 8400 people in the entire Hopi Tribe. Never since the end of the Indian wars a hundred years before had the U.S. government tried to move so many Native Americans off the land where they were born. It could not be done without tremendous pain and difficulty and would cost hundreds of millions of dollars.

The question of minerals and the wealth of the land itself was easier to solve. When the court created the JUA, it said that minerals under the ground belonged equally to both tribes. The new law did not change that. Only "surface rights" were split. But Navajo families watching the coal mines advancing from the north knew that people must be cleared off land before mining begins. They charged bitterly that the real reason for moving them was to save mining companies that trouble and expense.

Staying on the land became more difficult every year. Even before Congress split the land, the court ordered all JUA Navajos to reduce livestock and forbade them to build any new houses or corrals until the Land Dispute was settled. That forced many younger people to leave, even though their land later ended up on the Navajo side.

In 1977 construction crews brought barbed wire to Big Mountain not far from the Lunas' land. Pauline Whitesinger, a 43-year-old woman, asked why they were building a fence. They insulted her. She knocked down one of the men and ran off the rest. It was a sign that many Navajos meant to fight for the land. Two years later another Big Mountain woman, Katherine Smith, went to court for welcoming a fence crew with a bullet, but the law was not changed.

In 1981 the Hopis officially took control of their side of the JUA, and police had orders to take Navajo livestock. Horses tied outside some Navajo hogans had rifles slung from the saddle horns. Angry Navajos marched outside the BIA offices in Flagstaff and Phoenix. And even in Washington some congressmen began to wonder if they had made a terrible mistake. Some even talked of changing the law, redrawing the line, or allowing Navajos to buy land from the Hopis. Few, however, thought to say what Avery Luna had said when he first heard of the Land Dispute years before—

"Bless your animals. Bless your earth. Live in spiritual harmony. Perform the ceremonies. And you will be given the rain you need. You will be given whatever you need.

"If we do what is ordered by Creation, then the rains will come. We will live in harmony with the Holy People and ourselves. There will be no need to fight our neighbors over a little bit of land."

Independent

NAVAJOS SET UP
THEIR OWN WAY

Villie '80

# THE LAND BELONGS TO US!

Many people use the words "Our Land". Why do they say that? What do they mean? Listen again to the people in the story:

*"When the Navajos came into this world, they were assigned a place to live..."*

*"The Hopis also were given a place to live by their creator..."*

*"Long ago all this land belonged to the Hopis..."*

*"...it is marked for us by our eagle shrines."*

*"The land tells us that other people did live here. WE now belong here because our forefathers are buried here."*

*"If we could get our land back, more Hopis would get cattle — maybe even move up there."*

*"There is no law up there now."*

The way you think about these words will affect the way you think about your land, your neighbors, and even your religion. It will affect what you do with your land.

What does it mean when two people both say they were given the same land at the time of creation?

Why is the land of our forefathers important to us? How did our ancestors get the land they lived on? Who else might have used it far back in time?

If land is "Our Land", does it mean we can use it any way we like — to live on, to run livestock on, to farm, to hunt over, to collect sacred plants on, to mine? Do we have the right to destroy "Our Land" if we wish?

What does it mean to say, "There is no law up there now..." Does "Our Land" have to have "Our Law"? Is land only ours when we can make laws and punish people who break them? How is "Hopi Law" different from "Navajo Law"? What about the laws of Arizona or the United States?

Different people and different cultures will answer these questions differently, and traditions may change over time.

The land laws of the United States are mostly European. Navajos and Hopis do not always agree. However, every individual will use the words "Our Land" in his own way, and more than one tradition may guide him.

# WE BELONG TO THE LAND!

When people talk about land rights and boundaries, laws and grazing districts, they are thinking about what they can take from the land. To some people, however, the words "Our Land" mean giving:

*"I look on all land as our land. All things on it and all people that are on it are in our care. Our songs and ceremonies call us caretakers of this land for ALL people. We should not keep anyone from using it."*

*"We are keepers and caretakers of this land for ALL PEOPLE."*

*"Bless your animals. Bless your earth. Live in spiritual harmony. Perform the ceremonies. And you will be given the rain you need. You will be given whatever you need."*

*"If we do what is ordered by Creation, then the rains will come. We will live in harmony with the Holy People and ourselves. There will be no need to fight our neighbors over a little piece of land."*

When Avery Luna and Mina Lansa said these things they thought of the land itself, not of who should draw a boundary line on it. They asked very different questions:

*What is our responsibility to care for "Our Land"?*

*What do we owe the land that gives us life?*

In years to come when generations yet unborn call us "ancestors", will the land still feed its people?

Since all land is part of "Our World", what can we do to protect even the land that others say "belongs" to them?

These questions guided the prayers and songs of the Navajo medicine man and the Hopi village chief. The other questions seemed to them unimportant or even dangerous. They both died hoping that generations to come would not forget that the Earth is the true mother of all their children.

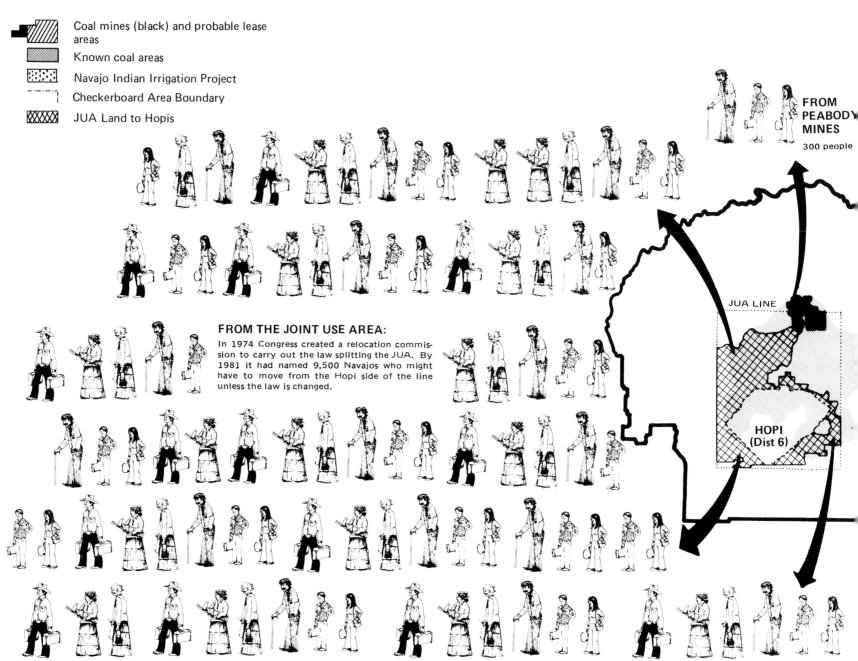

Coal mines (black) and probable lease areas

Known coal areas

Navajo Indian Irrigation Project

Checkerboard Area Boundary

JUA Land to Hopis

FROM PEABODY MINES

300 people

**FROM THE JOINT USE AREA:**

In 1974 Congress created a relocation commission to carry out the law splitting the JUA. By 1981 it had named 9,500 Navajos who might have to move from the Hopi side of the line unless the law is changed.

JUA LINE

HOPI (Dist 6)

# THE LONG WALK OF MODERN TIMES

Before the end of the century, thousands of people may have to change their way of life as they are forced off their land. The Navajo-Hopi Land Dispute affects many, but coal mines and a new tribal irrigation project else-where in Navajo Country will uproot many others. Gray shading on the map shows how much coal land there is. Black areas and stripes show existing mines and likely mining areas in 1981.

This great movement of people may change lives everywhere on the reservation as refugees flood towns, move in with relatives and search for homesites on land already claimed by other families and torn by grazing disputes.

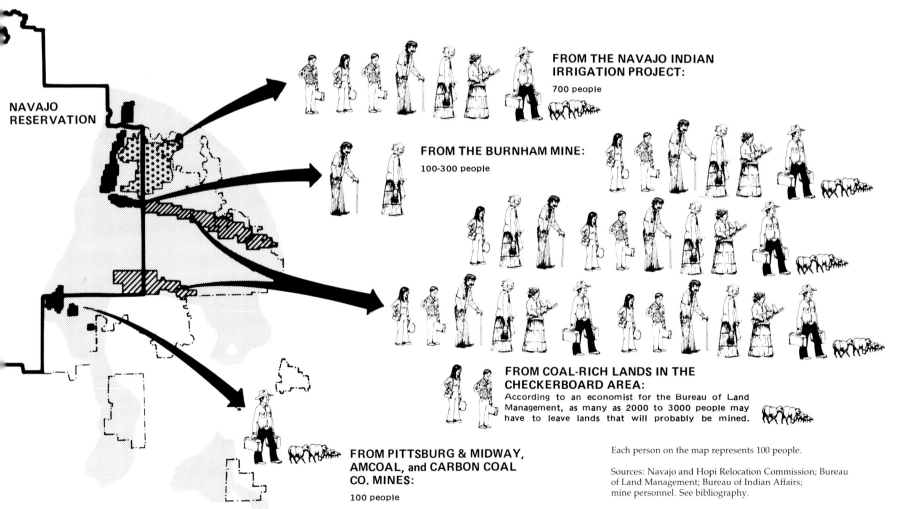

NAVAJO RESERVATION

FROM THE NAVAJO INDIAN IRRIGATION PROJECT:

700 people

FROM THE BURNHAM MINE:

100-300 people

FROM COAL-RICH LANDS IN THE CHECKERBOARD AREA:

According to an economist for the Bureau of Land Management, as many as 2000 to 3000 people may have to leave lands that will probably be mined.

FROM PITTSBURG & MIDWAY, AMCOAL, and CARBON COAL CO. MINES:

100 people

Each person on the map represents 100 people.

Sources: Navajo and Hopi Relocation Commission; Bureau of Land Management; Bureau of Indian Affairs; mine personnel. See bibliography.

# LAND: Who Gets to Use It?

Both Navajo and Hopi elders say, "People should not fight over land." However the Navajo-Hopi Land Dispute and speeches in every grazing committee meeting show that problems do come up when two people want to use the same land for the same thing. What happens when they cannot agree to share?

## Power

How much land in the history of the world has changed hands because one side was tougher than the other? How much land did Indian tribes lose to the U.S. Cavalry? Did Navajos ever take land?

Old records mention Hopis farming in Canyon de Chelly, Havasupais living along the Echo Cliffs north of Tuba City, and Paiutes around Navajo Mountain. Did they join the Navajos freely? Did any become slaves? Where did they go?

The old arguments for taking land have always been, "We should have more land because we have more people or more knowledge."

Should Europeans have Indian land because Europeans know how to mine it or plow it? Should Navajos have Paiute land because Navajos have bigger herds? Should Hopis have Navajo land because Hopi land is crowded?

Can such questions be answered without war?

## Money

According to Navajo and Hopi traditional belief, land has no price. It cannot be bought and sold because money comes and goes while land is there forever.

Nevertheless, some say it is better to settle land fights with money than war, if there is no other choice. Congress and the U.S. courts have decided both ways.

*The Navajo Tribal Council offered to buy the Hopi side of the Joint Use Area. They said it would cause great suffering to move the Navajos off land they had used for over a century. Congress, however, decided to move the Navajos (with force if necessary), paying only the cost of moving.*

*Five years after Congress divided the Joint Use Area, the Passamaquoddy and Penobscot Tribes proved that the State of Maine had illegally taken an area twice the size of the JUA. This time, however, the tribes had to accept money. According to Congress it would cause too much suffering to move people off land they had used for over a century.*

Which decision was fairer? Why would the two situations be decided differently? If you were a judge, would you force people to move or force them to sell? How would you set a price on the land?

## TIME: Important Events

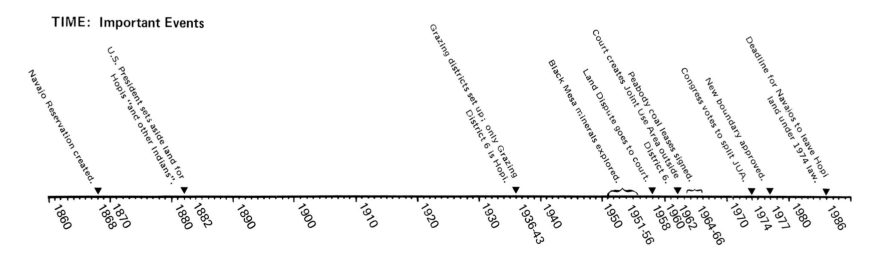

Navajo Reservation created.

U.S. President sets aside land for Hopis "and other Indians".

Grazing districts set up; only Grazing District 6 is Hopi.

Black Mesa minerals explored.

Land Dispute goes to court.

Court creates Joint Use Area outside District 6.

Peabody coal leases signed.

Congress votes to split JUA.

New boundary approved.

Deadline for Navajos to leave Hopi land under 1974 law.

1860  1868  1870  1880  1882  1890  1900  1910  1920  1930  1936-43  1940  1950  1951-56  1958  1960  1962  1964-66  1970  1974  1977  1980  1986

# WHO DECIDES?

When Alice Luna brought news of the Land Dispute and the coal mine to people on Black Mesa, they asked her one question — "Who decided to do these things to us?"

This question led to others. Were the coal mine and the Land Dispute connected? Were Hopi ranchers the only ones who wanted to split the land? Did coal company money push Congress and the tribal councils?

Within sight of the Lunas' camp is the Black Mesa headquarters of the Peabody Coal Company. For nearly 100 years only Hopis and Navajos cared about the land on Black Mesa. That changed when it was discovered that large amounts of coal, water, and perhaps also oil and uranium might be found there. Oil and uranium brought a good price world-wide, and every big city in the West wanted to see the coal turned to electricity.

## Mineral Wealth

Whoever could get these minerals quickly and cheaply could make a great deal of money. However, no minerals could be sold if no one agreed on who owned them. Both the Hopi and Navajo Tribal Councils hoped to get money from Black Mesa minerals, and both voted to ask a U.S. court to decide who owned the land. Each tribe thought it could win the larger share. The Navajo Tribal Council discussed the matter for about 15 minutes and voted 66 to 0 to take the question to court.

The court decided that the land should be shared (that is what "joint use" means) and that the money from minerals should be split 50–50.

Four years after the JUA was set up, both the Navajo and Hopi Councils gave a coal lease to Peabody Coal Company. The Hopi Council wasn't happy, however, because Navajos still lived on the land. The coal company wasn't happy because it had a hard time dealing with two tribal councils that were fighting each other. There are some who believe that the coal company also saw that only Navajos lived on the best coal land. If Congress gave that part of the land to Hopis only, the U.S. government would pay to clear Navajos off the land and make room for more mines.

The Hopi Tribal Council did not mind asking for help. Soon after the JUA was set up, the Hopi lawyer said publicly that mineral companies should push Congress to split the JUA if they ever hoped to work there. Later the council hired a public relations company in Salt Lake City to help tell the American people their side of the story. The company also did advertising and public relations for the same power companies that wanted Black Mesa coal.

The public relations company had such power, according to one newspaper reporter, that a TV crew could phone Salt Lake to get Hopi range riders to round up stray Navajo stock for their cameras. Suddenly stories about a "range war" turned up nation-wide. Congressmen who had never seen Arizona saw Navajos "stealing" Hopi land on TV and read about it in the papers.

The congressmen and government officials who worked hardest to split the land talked only about peace and justice. None mentioned helping energy companies. But energy companies did help some of them.

## Coal and Congress

Rep. Wayne Aspinall of Colorado asked Congress to cut the JUA as early as 1963. When Congress took up the question again in 1971, he worked to get it approved. He also fought hard against laws that would make coal companies fix up land they mined. Colorado voters turned against Aspinall, however, when they heard that much of the money he spent to get himself elected came from mining companies outside Colorado, including several thousand dollars from Kennecott Copper Company of New York. At that time Kennecott owned Peabody Coal. Soon after leaving Congress, Aspinall accepted a top job with a large mining company, AMAX.

The assistant secretary of interior then was Harrison Loesch. He worked hard to split the JUA, against the wishes of the BIA commissioner who worked under him. When people asked his office for information about Black Mesa, they got booklets printed by Peabody Coal.

In the end, Loesch worked so hard to help mining companies on Indian land that several Indian groups protested, and he was removed. However, he was immediately hired by the Senate Interior Committee, which handles laws concerning Indians and the land. There he continued telling senators to split the JUA. Two years later, Peabody hired Loesch as company vice-president with very good pay.

Alice now believes that mining and power companies have used the Land Dispute to get Indian coal land. The facts *do* show how events and people most Navajos never heard of have great power in Navajo Country. If so...

*Who decides the future of Navajo land?*

208

# THE TRAIL BACK

*Like the old wars and the Long Walk and Stock Reduction, the Navajo-Hopi Land Dispute will mark Navajo history forever. By 1981 it had already broken up homes and caused old people to die of grief. It forced people leaving the land to crowd in on relatives until they began to fight. Money that could have helped the land was spent to move people. Officials and experts who should have been thinking about the land and water that the mines on Black Mesa swallowed day by day spent all their time fighting over the land itself.*

*But old customs die hard. Two tribes that have survived side by side through peace and war and drought and invasion do not shut the door on a thousand years of shared history without letting some light shine through the cracks.*

In the old days, when pueblo towns brought in their harvest, the Navajos rode down from the steppes and mesas with horses, fresh meat and dried meat and buckskins from the hunt. In the towns they traded, gambled, raced and visited.

So in the legend they came to the Towering House, *Kin Yaa'á*, in ancient times. So they came to Jemez in the time of the Spaniards. And so they came to the Hopi towns as well. Son of Old Man Hat traded there in the years after Fort Sumner. And horses that won races at Oraibi became famous in all Navajo Country because people from everywhere saw them.

People alive today have not forgotten how it felt after three days of dusty trails to come up to the Hopi villages and see the people on the rooftops and hear the drums. And Hopis have not forgotten the visitors who sweetened their stew pots with mutton.

In 1979, while the barbed wire was reaching out along the new Hopi-Navajo boundary, a group of Navajo young people from Rock Point School set out on horseback to find the old trade route to First Mesa and see how much history still survived.

Elizabeth Blueeyes, an older lady who had been to the Hopi Mesas often in her youth, warned the riders, "You will be very sore," but the trip made her think of her own past.

"The Hopis are friendly people," she said, "We used to go down to Hotevilla. They always invited us in and fed us and asked us to stay for their dances. They dance with masks in long lines like our *Yé'ii Bicheii* dancers and have an enormous drum that goes slowly . . . tum . . . tum. The dancers have rattles made of turtle shells tied behind their knees. Ruk . . . ruk . . . ruk they go."

"In many ways the Hopis are like us. They have clans like we do. They use corn pollen and meal in their ceremonies, but they grind their corn differently—finer than we do. And they don't leave their houses when someone dies. They just keep right on living in the same place. You will see their prayer feathers tied in little bunches that they use. When I used to go, they had few horses, only donkeys."

Kee Pahe, vice-president of the Rock Point School Board, told how once he and his brother rode to Second Mesa to see a Hopi doctor they called *Dló'ii Yáázh*, Little Weasel. "We rode there by Chinle and Cottonwood. It's not so rough that way," he said. "We carried corn for the horses in sacks. We stayed there several weeks and worked for that medicine man. He showed us how to gather plants and gave us sweat baths. We used to go down to a holy spring where the Hopis put their prayer sticks."

The map showed the words "Horse Trail Canyon" on the mesa behind Rough Rock. Sally Woody, a lady of the *Honágháahnii* Clan who lives behind Rough Rock Trading Post, remembered Rock Point people who used to come that way in former times. "Go up this canyon, and you will find the trail," she said. "Navajos used to escape from Utes up there. When I was a girl I used to see people coming through with their pack horses. For a long time I didn't know where they were going or why they came. Later I found out that they went down to the Hopi Country to trade.

"My father often went there himself after the harvest. He took fresh mutton, because the Hopis are really meat hungry. They are that way even today. We took some sheep legs there just last week and sold them right away. My dad used to bring back corn, dried peaches, and those little chilies that they grow. I think he mostly went for the races, though. He had a pinto horse that people said had holy power. It never lost."

Time and change had hidden the trail in Horse Trail Canyon. It was goat country now. Horses and riders struggled until dark but never found the old trail up in the cliffs. Long after midnight the new truck road led them to the camp of Atsidi Benally on the top of Black Mesa.

Atsidi Benally is an old man now, but he laughed when he heard of the students' long ride. "I've ridden from one end of Navajo Country to the other in those chaps hanging there on the wall," he said. "You have to be tough to do that. You'll find out."

He pointed the way on to First Mesa. "It's the shortest way," he said. "We used to go there often until all the arguments about the land started. Now it seems that the Hopis have too many hard feelings against the Navajos, so we don't go any more."

The way south led over a few low hills into the narrow green valley of the Wepo Wash. Pinon and juniper trees covered the hills. Here and there a tall fir or ponderosa pine found water and shade enough to grow.

The road ran on and on past hogans and windmills and people working. Storm clouds crept up over the sides of the valley, and distant thunder warned of rain. Cattle grazed beside the road, and once a half wild stallion charged the riders until the boys chased it off with ropes.

An old man collected plants from the shade of juniper trees beside the road. He wore a medicine man's white scarf around his forehead and carried a small buckskin bag. He did not look up from his work as the riders passed. Later he went by them in his grandson's pickup. Bumper stickers on the truck said, "AIM— Indian Power!" and "Save Big Mountain."

Once where the riders stopped to rest there were pictures on the rocks. Some were old. Anasazi holy signs? Hopi clan marks? Some were newer—horses and riders, but who? Utes? Navajos? Spaniards?

Just north of Pinon the Wepo Wash leaves its narrow canyon and cuts across open country. There, where the pinon and juniper end and the steppe begins again, the riders took off at a gallop, covering mile after mile through a sea of flowers. They galloped on past a low rocky hill that was once an Anasazi town and past the new town of Pinon. They could see the trailer homes where fence crews lived. The fence crews were working along the new Hopi-Navajo line.

That night the riders camped southeast of Pinon. Rena Johnson, a woman of the *Ta'neeszahnii* Clan, welcomed them and invited them to sleep near her hogans.

"So you're going down the Hopi way," she said. "The grass is so beautiful that way. It's too bad we have to argue about it. That's all they talk about at chapter meetings now. They've hired Navajos to build the new fence between us and the Hopis, but the people don't want them to go ahead. Some of them have said angry things which should not be said."

The next day the riders crossed the Hopi fence. From then on they passed no more Navajo hogans, only a few stone houses built in the Hopi style.

At the farming village of Wepo, springs run out from the sand dunes on top of the mesa. Cottonwood trees grow there, and the Hopis grow chilies and vegetables in small gardens cut into the side of the mesa. Not far away it is said that the hearts of Ute warriors lie buried under a juniper tree. Three hundred years ago the Hopis of First Mesa asked Tewas from the Rio Grande to help them fight the Utes and Navajos. After a battle at that place the Tewas made their homes on First Mesa. They share it with the Hopis to this day.

In a house below the mesa the riders found old-style hospitality. The Koopee family invited everyone in to eat. It was a modern house, but the hominy and corn bread on the stove came from a long tradition. And in the pickup trucks parked outside, prayer feathers hung from the rear view mirrors.

When the meal was over, the riders were told, "You must go up to the village now. The kachinas are dancing."

So the trip ended. The great drum beat slowly . . . tum . . . tum . . . tum. The turtle shell rattles marked the time. Dressed now as bighorn sheep, the dancers came from their kiva.

As the sacred dance went on, rain swept over the plaza. It was the female rain, the soft rain that brings new life to the land. It

brought to mind the words Avery Luna had spoken on the other side of Black Mesa:

*"If we do what is ordered by Creation, then the rains will come. We will live in harmony with the Holy People and ourselves. There will be no need to fight our neighbors over a little piece of land."*

The following Rock Point students participated in the May, 1979, trail ride from Rough Rock to the Hopi villages on First Mesa: Earl Begay, Susie Begay, Lorraine Coggeshall, John Glen Dan, Roy Roger Descheny, Arlene Littleben, Russell Paul, and Lewis Tsosie. They were accompanied by Nada Woody, Reeder Descheny, Ralph and Elsie Descheny, Jones Lee, and Sam Bingham.

211

# MODERN TIMES

Now our Sacred Mountains are being abused.
People dig in them and drill in them.
They strip away the ornaments and jewels.
We say Nahasdzáán Shimá:
Earth, My Mother.
So it is in fact our Mother who is hurt.
Our Father Sky is jealous
Because the diggers and drillers rape her
    with cold steel.
As a man gives his wife beautiful things
    to wear,
So our Father Sky does the same.
He sends down rain on Mother Earth,
And because of the rain, plants grow.
Flowers appear of many colors.
She in turn gives him food.
But because our Father Sky is jealous,
The rain falls short.
Sickness surrounds us.

—George Blueeyes

Díí Dził ahééníniligíí k'ad nihits'ą́ą́' atídeiiłį́.
Yii' nida'ageed jó akǫ.
Yee hadadít'éhę́ę bą̨ah dajinizh.
Nahasdzáán Shimá dii'ní.
Áko díí nihimá atél'į́.
Yádiłhił Nihitaa' łe' nízin.
Kodi asdzání bits'ą́ą́' atél'į́igo,
Béésh da nidabiizǫ́ǫsgo biniinaa.
Díí asdzání yá'át'éehgo bił naash'aash doo
    jinízin łeh.
Nihitaa' t'áá ákwíinízin, ą́ąjí háidiil'į̨h.
Níłtsą́ ą́ą́dę́ę́' kojį' kóyiil'į̨h.
Ch'il bílátah hózhóón ałtah ą́ą́t'eełii
    haajah.
Kodóó yidinínáádóó yitsą́ á'ál'į̨h.
Nihitaa' łe' nízinígíí
Biniinaa doo hazhó'ó nahałtin da.
Ts'íįh niidóóh t'áá naaghá.

                                    -Tábą̨ąhí Ts'ósí

# MODERN TIMES

Four hundred years ago the Spaniards came to Navajo Country looking for gold. They found none, and the Navajos held their land and became stronger. Three hundred years later the American army attacked the Navajos because they also wanted gold. But they found none, and the tribe survived war and prison, held onto their land, and became stronger.

Now the world has changed again. Machines now do the work of the world that men and animals once did, and the minerals that feed the machines—coal, oil, gas, and uranium—have taken the place of gold in the eyes of modern treasure-seekers. The gold hunters of times past never dreamed of the riches that lie under the mountains and deserts of the west, and under Navajo Country first of all. No Navajo warrior of old ever imagined what this hidden wealth might mean for his land.

Whether this modern treasure will bring strength or sorrow is not yet known. Navajo Country has become crowded. People went hungry at the time of Stock Reduction, and the Navajo Tribe has more than doubled since then. Thousands would simply starve to death now if they had to live off the land without welfare, food stamps, government jobs, or money from off the reservation. Navajo mineral wealth might help.

But mineral wealth can also bring suffering. Today's treasure hunters will steal coal and oil as quickly as yesterday's stole gold and silver, and the mining itself can wreck land and destroy old ways of life. Before the end of this century, thousands of people all over the reservation will be forced to leave their land because of mines and other development projects.

In this chapter you will see what happened to the family of Avery Luna and some of their neighbors on Black Mesa. The land was split between the Navajo and Hopi Tribes, and part of it is now home to one of the biggest coal mining operations in the United States.

When Avery Luna first heard that he might lose his land because of the Navajo-Hopi Land Dispute and the mine, he said:

> If we have to move to a new place, if we have to give up our livestock, if we go away from the things that make us what we are, we will no longer be the same people.

Eight years after Avery Luna said that, he himself was gone. His family had lost their land, sold their livestock, and moved off Black Mesa. They could not hope to live their old life again because there was no open land left in all Navajo Country where they could go. For others, the mining and drilling, the moving and rebuilding, the living without land had just begun.

Coal, oil, gas, and uranium had been found all over Navajo Country, and Luna's words echoed everywhere. What could we lose? What could we gain? Will we always be the same people?

# FLORENCE LUNA—FEBRUARY, 1980

At the Golden Sands Cafe in Kayenta a juke-box blares. Dishes clatter. A horn honks. Truck motors roar. Smells of hamburger, french fries, barbecued beef and exhaust smoke mix in the darkened dining room where sun-burned tourists and dusty coal miners wait for lunch.

You can find Florence Luna at the back of the cafe in a steamy kitchen, a pan of hot grease in her hand. She works here now as a cook, far from the silence of the home where she once lived on Black Mesa with its smells of sheep, cedar smoke and pinon.

Ten years ago Florence, her son Eugene, and her father Avery Luna lived quietly there among their relatives, herding their 300 sheep and caring for their horses and cows. But the drag-lines of Peabody Coal Company moved toward their land from the north, and from the south came the barbed wire fence that now cuts their camp between the houses and the corral.

The mine came because of an agreement signed by the coal company and the Navajo Tribe. The fence was the U.S. government's way of settling the Navajo-Hopi Land Dispute.

One by one Florence's brothers and sisters left for school or jobs in distant places because they saw there was no room for them on the land. Her stepmother passed away. Her son married and went to work at the mine. She and her father held on for a while. Then they too left the mesa.

One of Florence's sisters married a Hopi, and he got a job at the mine. They had permission to use an acre of land near some relatives outside Kayenta. There was room for Florence and her father, but not for the livestock. The sheep were sold.

"My father tried to stop the mine, but he didn't stop it," says Florence. "Then at the end he seemed to say, 'Okay, let it happen, whatever is going to happen.' He saw the mine and he heard what the Hopis were saying. From then on he was different, as if he saw no reason to live. He died from his longing for the land. This is what we think. Many older people died almost the same day. It seems that only the young ones are left."

Florence, then in her 40s, changed her flowing Navajo skirts for slacks and jeans and found work as a cook at the Golden Sands in Kayenta. Like Florence herself, the cafe and the town are there because of the coal mine. Miners from the trailer court nearby stop at the Golden Sands for coffee or a meal before driving up to the mine. So do tourists heading for Monument Valley. The cafe tries to make them think of the "real wild west." Junked Navajo wagons lie by the front door. The wagon wheels now carry lights and hang from the ceiling inside. Dusty old saddles sit on the roof beams. Fried bread and stew made by Florence Luna sells for $2.75. Waylon Jennings will sing two songs from the juke box for a quarter.

Florence can remember when irrigated cornfields covered the land now taken by the cafe, streets and buildings. Her father used to come down from the mesa in the summers to tend his field and listen to the wind whispering through the corn stalks. No paved highway went through Kayenta then and no roaring pickups or diesel rigs.

Florence can remember when the first school was built in Kayenta. Then came another school and a chapter house. Now Kayenta is one of the only real towns on the reservation. There is a new housing project, two trailer courts built by Peabody Coal Company, two large motels, including a Holiday Inn with a heated swimming pool, several gas stations and restaurants, a post office, a laundromat, a TV repair shop, and a bank.

Driving home from the cafe after work, Florence points to the bank. "My father used to say that our sheep corral was like a bank. 'When you need money,' he would say, 'you can go to your corral, take out a sheep and sell it. That is like making a withdrawal from a bank. You walk away with money.' "

Florence finds it hard to save enough money to put in the bank, however. And she can no longer go to her corral. She misses her livestock. "If you have a job you can always get laid off or fired any day. Then you have nothing! You have nothing to fall back on. With livestock you always have something to come back to."

Florence lives with her eight-year-old niece Donna in a tiny hogan next door to her sister and a few miles from town. This land where they first lived after moving off the mesa is used by her father's relatives. Before Florence's sister built on it, all the relatives had to agree. She could not have made a home there if even one person had disagreed. The relatives have their own livestock, and Florence and her sisters know there isn't room for more.

"It's like bouncing up in the air and not knowing where you will land," she says. "It's like that here where I'm living now. I built this small hogan last summer, but in a way I stole the land. If we let sheep out to graze, someone would be over right away saying,

'What right do you have to graze livestock?' and I couldn't answer them. So I am living *anaashii*—as an outsider. I don't really belong.

"I would like to have sheep and maybe two cows because of my niece. You use livestock to teach your children. When you are a child you learn to think for the sheep. You have to think, 'Where are they going to drink? Where are they going to eat?'—just as you would for yourself. You think and you see that you will have to build a better house for them, just as you will have to plan a house for yourself. You learn to love them, just as you will one day love your own children. As you care for your sheep, so you will learn to care for your own children in the same way."

Florence worries about Donna growing up without learning these things. But she has no choice. "There is no land. So we just live here. Just live. No livestock. That's how it is."

Clan: *Tł'ízí Łání*
Born for: *Tó'áhání*

## FLORENCE'S SON EUGENE—FEBRUARY, 1980

At the new Peabody Trailer Court in Kayenta, most of the streets are named after trees. Ponderosa. Aspen. Juniper. Trees like those used to surround Eugene Leonard's hogan up on top of Black Mesa.

But from the window of his shiny new double-wide trailer in the town at the foot of the mesa, the only forest to be seen is a forest of telephone poles and TV antennas.

The Leonard family has two TVs sitting one on top of the other in the center of the living room. A large 8-track stereo sits in another corner. His children Darryl, 4, and Yolinda, 2, play in shirts and underpants on the carpeted living room floor. Eugene has just arrived home from work and is stretched out on the sofa, relaxed in white T-shirt, jeans, bare feet.

Eugene works at the Peabody mine. "I started out shoveling the coal that fell off the conveyor belt," he says. Then he became a high wall shooter, blasting the ground that covers the coal. Then he was a coal shooter, blasting the coal itself. He has driven haul trucks and done other jobs. Now he changes tires. The tires he changes are more than eight feet high and have to be lifted with a fork lift. A single tire can take two to six hours to change. They stand higher than a hogan, with hubcaps as high as a man's chest.

"Even an uneducated man can learn on the job if he tries. It's up to you. But sooner or later all the jobs get boring. You're doing the same thing hour after hour, and the same thing the next day and the day after that."

Last year he earned $29,000. The money disappeared fast. Living in town is expensive. Every month the bills come in. He pays rent on the space for his double-wide trailer. He makes payments every month on the trailer itself and on his two pickup trucks. He pays for electricity to light his trailer and gas to heat it. He drives 60 miles every day going back and forth from Kayenta to his job at the mine, which means filling up his tank four times a week. Then he has payments on his furniture, his stereo, and his two TVs.

"In some ways the mine has been good to me," he says. "We have electricity and running water. It makes life easier. Like if I was up on the mesa right now, I would have to be running outside to chop wood and haul in water. I'd have to be out there in the cold and the mud. And if I had livestock, I'd have to be out there worrying about them. These days you can't really earn enough to make it just from livestock, so you really have to take another job too. And then you come home tired and you still have to go outside and take care of your livestock. Down here when I come home after work I can sit down, relax, and watch TV."

Eugene looked around the trailer as he spoke. He looked at his wife fixing supper in the bright shiny kitchen, and at his kids and their shiny plastic toys. He sipped a cold pop fresh from the refrigerator and wriggled his bare toes in the thick warm carpet. Snow and freezing rain fell among the trailers crowded around outside. He remembered it was lambing season. Back on the mesa he would be out there shivering all night by a fire.

Then he thought a long time and said, "I miss having a horse. You can't keep a horse here in this little yard. And it's harder to raise kids down here. There are cars, and you have to worry about the kids running into the street. Up there on the mesa you can just let them loose to play wherever they want.

"Then too, down here you never know who their friends are. Up there on the mesa they'd just be playing with their own cousins and relatives, and you'd know they were brought up the same. Down here there are kids from different kinds of families, and you don't know how they've been raised or whether they've been raised the same. You have to worry more about who they're with.

"To have certain things, you have to give up other things," says Eugene. "After a while you forget about the things you miss. You put them out of your mind and don't think about them. Living down here, you start to think differently."

## MANY MULES' GRANDDAUGHTER AND HER HUSBAND—FEBRUARY, 1980

Most of the time these days, Many Mules' granddaughter and her husband, *K'ai' Bii' Tóonii*, just sit. They sit by the stove in their new cement block house in a room already blackened by coal smoke. They don't speak much now, even to each other. They just stare straight ahead lost in thought. On a nearby ridge giant coal shovels are biting away the land where they have lived and herded sheep most of their lives.

For more than 60 years they walked the hills and gullies of Black Mesa with their sheep. They knew where water ran all year, where grass grew best in certain seasons, and where to find shade from the sun or shelter from the wind. From their door sagebrush, pinon and juniper spread as far as they could see.

Now enormous drag-lines gulp up mouthfuls of earth and spit them into tall piles. The machines work tirelessly, day and night, digging for the treasure of coal beneath the land. They take the coal, spit back the dirt, and push it into shapes nothing like the canyons and washes the old couple once knew.

Clan: *Tó'áhaní*
Born for: *Áshįįhí*

Their four corrals stand empty. They have not herded since the day 20 sheep drank water near the mine. Chemicals from the blasting had poisoned it, and the two old people watched their animals die one by one. The heavy trucks that roar past their house had already killed enough of their stock. They gave up, sent the rest of their herd to a daughter who lived farther away, and now they just sit.

"There is no way the mining company can ever pay us for what we have lost," says *K'ai' Bii' Tóonii* in a low voice. "They are making money from our land while we have nothing. They have cut down the trees we used to build our hogans. Our livestock can no longer drink the water. Once we made a living out of livestock. Now we are poor."

Clan: *Tł'ízí Łání*
Born for: *Tó Dích'íi'nii*

This is not the life that *K'ai' Bii' Tóonii* saw ahead fifteen years ago when word first came that coal might be mined in their area. They had never seen a coal mine. They had no idea what a dragline does to land, and never dreamed their world could change so much and so fast.

"There was a meeting, and we were asked to agree to the mine. One of my wife's older relatives got up and spoke. He said, 'This mine will provide jobs. These new jobs will provide us with money and our children with money. So let us agree.' He was the first to agree with this, and we all followed with no questions asked. But even then I wondered what would become of this land. I wondered what it would look like. Maybe people should have asked questions back then."

*K'ai' Bii' Tóonii's* wife nods her head. "My grandfather Many Mules roamed this part of Black Mesa over 100 years ago. He used to tell stories of how he ran away from Fort Sumner and came all the way back because he missed it here," she remembers. Her family had used the land for so long that they thought they would at least be paid when the mining company took it.

They soon learned, however, that they did not own the land. According to the Navajo Tribal Code, the land belonged to the tribe. The Tribal Council had agreed to let the coal company mine it. The company paid the tribal government. People living on the land would not even get enough to replace homes and corrals eaten by the coal shovels.

The old people's son Cecil protested. Other families joined him. But they got no help at mine headquarters or tribal offices. Finally Cecil's son Tommy called in friends from the American Indian Movement (AIM). The young people sat down in front of the machinery and said, "Pay for the land or kill us." The coal company called the tribal police to haul off the protesters, but Tribal Chairman Peter MacDonald ordered the police to stay away.

Two weeks later Peabody Coal Company agreed to give families $50 an acre for land being mined. *K'ai' Bii' Tóonii* and his wife split their share among seven married children and numerous grandchildren. They ended up with materials for a two-room block house and $3,000. And they found out what a mine does to land.

*K'ai' Bii' Tóonii* goes outside. He points toward distant piles of broken gray rock that stretch to the horizon like the waves of an ocean. "You just look over there," he says. "You look at it and you think, 'They're doing just as they please with our land. They tear it up. They move it around. They make big holes in it.' "

Every bite of the shovel tears into a memory. He was married on the torn-up ridge across the way. His wife grew up on the ridge beyond, and there her brother broke horses for Many Mules.

His wife seems surprised that the mining company pays no attention to their wishes. "I told them I didn't want my waterhole disturbed," she says. "I told them to leave that alone. I kept saying NO. But they tore it up. There were some old hogans around here. They were ours. They tore them up too. Then there was a windmill. I told them I didn't want that touched either, but they took it away and tore up the water.

"We wanted them to make the land beautiful again. We wanted them to plant trees and saltbush and greasewood and cliffrose. They told us we could use the land again in two or three years, after it was mined. . . ."

Mining began in 1970. Ten years later the company still had not allowed livestock back on any land. Tumbleweed and crested wheatgrass grew in some areas. Others were bare. The company planted very few of the plants that grew there before and no trees at all. Mining officials now say it will be ten years at least before sheep can return to the land. In 1980 *K'ai' Bii' Tóonii* was 82 years old, and his wife was 76.

And so they sit inside their darkened room waiting as their lives are shoveled away. They have no place to go. All reservation land is divided up with invisible lines by other families and clans.

The granddaughter of Many Mules speaks softly from her place by the stove. "My grandfather a long time ago used to say, 'Rule this land! Hold it to yourself. Be stingy with it! Other clans keep coming on to it. Never let them take it!'

"But look at it now."

Clan: *Tó'áhaní*
Born for: *Tł'ízí Łání*

## NED YAZZIE—FEBRUARY, 1980

Not far away from Many Mules' granddaughter and her husband, one of their sons lives in another small house just off the main road through the mine.

Ned Yazzie grew up on hard work, and it shows. Sun and wind have worn his face, but his light strong body looks like it might last forever. He works so many hours at the mine that it fills his whole life. He almost never sees his parents anymore, but he thinks about them often.

He grew up on the land. He knows it and loves it. It is his. But he is a high wall shooter. Every day the coal company pays him to drill holes in his own land and blow it up. He mixes the chemicals that killed his parents' sheep. But he can't stop. He cannot stay on Black Mesa and live any other way.

"Yes, I am a person who works at the mine," he says. "In the beginning we agreed to everything without knowing what a mine is like. In the future, if it happens in another place, the people should say, 'No.' Here we are just shoved around. We can say No, but we can't stop anything. We just work.

"I argue with the bosses. They tell me I have no right to talk about what they're doing. But I argue because of the land. A long time ago, before the first bulldozer put its head in the ground, the mine people promised, 'The land will be put back the way you want it. We will plant everything you want on that land.' They said, 'If you want trees, we will plant trees.' They told us that we could use the land again three years after it was mined.

"We've been working here about ten years now. At last, two years ago, they started to fix up the land. For eight years they did almost nothing. Now they bulldoze the rock into rolling hills and put a few inches of dirt back on top. Plants with short roots grow there in the spring, but they die off. Nothing grows on into the fall. The plants that once grew there, like gramma grass and greasewood, they die, because the rock underneath the good soil holds no water. I'm afraid the plants will never grow back and it will look like the badlands around Tuba City."

Yet, even as he talks, Ned Yazzie knows that before the sun comes up in the morning he will be back out on the land in hard hat and boots. He will watch the drill rig tear into the ground. He will fill the holes with oil and nitrate. And he himself will strike the spark that blasts another chunk of his land into lifeless rock. He will keep it up ten hours a day for ten days straight before he rests.

In small bits of time away from the mine, Yazzie and his neighbors built a church near his house. He prays there for the land, for his parents, and for his own soul.

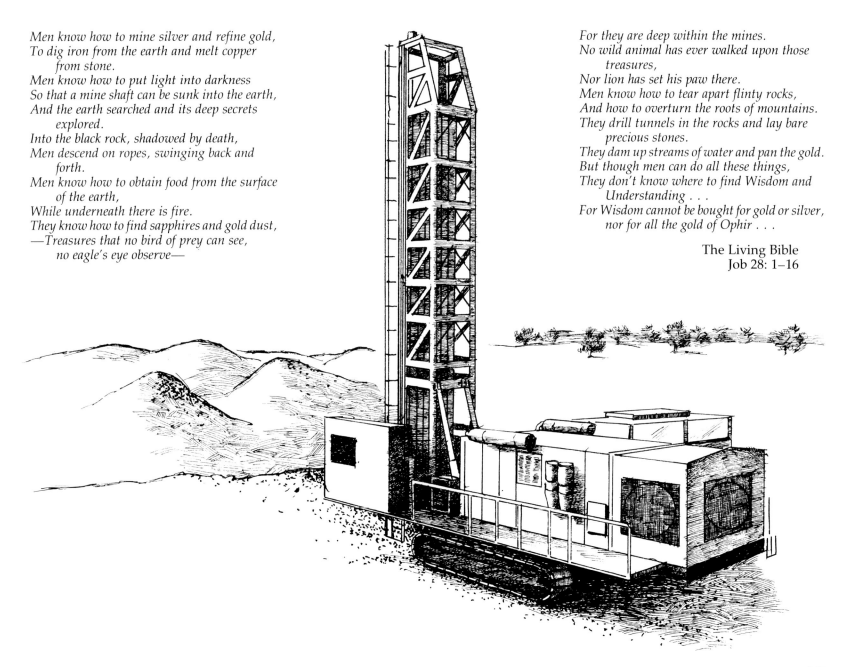

Men know how to mine silver and refine gold,
To dig iron from the earth and melt copper
    from stone.
Men know how to put light into darkness
So that a mine shaft can be sunk into the earth,
And the earth searched and its deep secrets
    explored.
Into the black rock, shadowed by death,
Men descend on ropes, swinging back and
    forth.
Men know how to obtain food from the surface
    of the earth,
While underneath there is fire.
They know how to find sapphires and gold dust,
—Treasures that no bird of prey can see,
    no eagle's eye observe—

For they are deep within the mines.
No wild animal has ever walked upon those
    treasures,
Nor lion has set his paw there.
Men know how to tear apart flinty rocks,
And how to overturn the roots of mountains.
They drill tunnels in the rocks and lay bare
    precious stones.
They dam up streams of water and pan the gold.
But though men can do all these things,
They don't know where to find Wisdom and
    Understanding . . .
For Wisdom cannot be bought for gold or silver,
    nor for all the gold of Ophir . . .

The Living Bible
Job 28: 1–16

225

## KEE Y. CHIEF—FEBRUARY, 1980

The mining on Black Mesa brought jobs. Eight hundred jobs. But people who didn't get hired found life harder than before. Their land and livestock were gone, and there was nothing to fall back on.

Kee Y. Chief is a short, wiry 26-year-old with sparkling eyes and a ready smile. He was a boy when people first talked about mining on Black Mesa, and he was 16 when the first coal shovels started to work. He remembers looking forward to working at the mine someday. He planned to join the armed services, then work at the mine when he got out.

He went ahead with his plan—but when he got back from his years in the service, it was too late. The jobs were already taken.

"They told us local residents would have first choice. And for about three or four years they were doing pretty good hiring local people. But when I came back after the service I found out that had changed. The hiring slowed down, I guess. People around here who weren't around at the height of the hiring are out of luck. Now there are hundreds and hundreds of people trying to get a job over there, and there's just one opening every little while."

So Kee Y. Chief is unemployed and looking for a job. If there were no mine, he probably wouldn't have found work near home either. But if there were no mine, he could have always come back to the family land between jobs. He might have looked for construction work in Farmington to help out his family. Between jobs he would have come home, helped with the livestock, and eaten fresh mutton until another job turned up.

"Raising livestock up here, you can't get very much out of it. But one reason people raise it is for security. As a back-up. And the older people pretty much depend on it. I myself would like to have a few cattle as a back-up if you get into a little financial difficulty."

But that will be impossible. The blasting at the mine is now so close that his house shakes. His parents have cut down their herd from 100 sheep to 40. Soon the grazing land will go to the coal shovels. And Kee Y. Chief must worry not only about himself, but also about his parents, who will soon have no way to live.

Most of the people in this chapter were interviewed by Judy Apachee, of Wide Ruins, Arizona. Ms. Apachee once worked in a uranium mine.

*"This is just the beginning. There's coal here we didn't even know about when we started mining. Coal underlies all of Black Mesa. Black Mesa is practically made of coal. There's enough coal here in this area to be mining coal on this reservation for the next 100 years. Coal will change the lifestyle of people more than you can know, and that's what I predict—that after we've left, they'll be mining coal just a few miles away."*

—Gary Melvin
Manager, Environmental Quality
Peabody Coal Co.
February, 1980

# MODERN TIMES AND...

## Energy

In Avery Luna's youth, all things in Navajo Country moved at the speed of nature. No one traveled faster than the fastest horse. Nothing flew higher than the strongest eagle. Wild plants and animals, cornfields and herds gave food according to the seasons.

Modern Times began the day fire did the work of people and animals. The power of engines run by heat has given us almost everything made of metal, glass, plastic, or rubber, most things run by electricity, all crops tended by tractors and grown in fertilizer, and most of our transportation.

The coming of Modern Times to other countries is called the Industrial Revolution. It began over 150 years ago in Europe and only touched Navajo Country recently. What changes did it bring?

Have you used five things during a single day that were NOT made, fed, or carried with the help of some kind of engine?

The first trains steamed through Navajo Country in 1882 along the cross-country route through Albuquerque, Gallup, and Flagstaff.

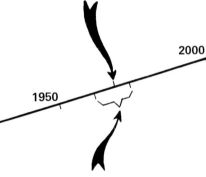

In 1966 the Four Corners Power Plant near Shiprock started making electricity from Navajo coal. The plant's turbines do the work of 2,780,000 horses.

2000

1950

1900

1850

1800

1750

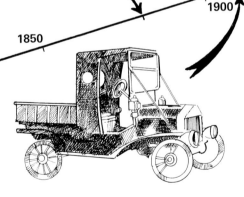

The first useful steam engine was built by James Watt in Scotland in 1769, starting the Industrial Revolution. The first good gasoline engine was made in Germany in 1876. Electricity made with steam power lit streets in San Francisco in 1879.

The first trucks were seen in Navajo Country about 1910. The first paved road for Navajo and Hopi traffic between Tuba City and Window Rock was not started until 1951 and not finished for over ten years.

Between 1960 and 1970, horse-drawn wagons and plows almost completely disappeared from Navajo Country. The wheels became decorations for fences and restaurants. The bones of the wagons rot in every camp.

# ...THE HERDER'S LIFE

## Wealth

As a young man Avery Luna hardly ever saw money. A family then measured wealth in livestock, jewelry, goods, and knowledge, but not money. Most of what they needed came from the land itself. They paid for anything else with sheep, rugs, or crops that the land gave them.

Even in 1972 Florence Luna bought a truck with rugs woven from the wool of her own sheep. Her father used to say, "The corral is our bank."

He was right. Bank and corral do the same thing. However, Modern Times and its factories, mines, highways, and machines force people like Florence to use banks. Because of the mine she no longer fills her needs from the land itself. She earns money cooking for miners and saves it in a bank.

She says about her new life, *"I can support myself and live the way I want to live, and there is nobody to argue with me."* Later she adds, *"If you have a job, you can always get laid off or fired any day. Then you have nothing."*

What has she gained? ... or lost?

## Comfort

Modern Times brought conveniences that money can buy, but often you must live in a certain way to enjoy them.

Eugene Leonard says, *"... the mine has been good to me. We have electricity and running water... Down here when I come home after work I can sit down, relax, and watch TV."*

Later he adds, *"... you can't keep a horse here in this little yard. And it's harder to raise kids down here."*

What has he gained? ... and lost?

## Time

Once, only Nature measured time and work. Lambing season meant staying up all night by the fire. Spring meant shearing. Fall meant stacking wood. On the land, people work, rest, eat, and work until a job is done.

Modern machinery, however, goes by its own time. It will run day and night in all seasons, and the people who run it must do the same. Eugene and Florence and Ned Yazzie work and rest by the clock. Their vacation and sick leave days are counted out.

*"Sooner or later all the jobs get boring,"* says Eugene. *"You're doing the same thing hour after hour."* And yet the old life was tough too. *"On the Mesa, especially if you have livestock, you have to think about them all the time. You have to think about how you're going to live...,"* says Eugene.

## Thinking

*"Living down here, you start to think differently,"* Eugene says. Is he right?

# ENERGY WEBS

When Spaniards invaded Navajo Country in 1540, they pulled the land and its people into a web of Empire. In that web Navajo history became part of world history, and world events echoed in Navajo Country.

That web was built on gold and silver that paid soldiers, built ships, and bought and sold goods around the world. The modern world, however, spins its webs by machines, and the old hunger for gold was turned into a hunger for fire to feed them.

Navajo Country is rich in fire — coal, oil, gas, and uranium. Perhaps no other place on earth holds such supplies of all four minerals that power the modern world. They are now worth more than all the gold and silver treasure hunters of the past could imagine.

The power of energy minerals dug out of Navajo land is huge. If everything taken in 1980 were turned into electricity, it would do the work of 24,658,000 horses working eight hours a day every day of the year.

| Production | Horsepower years[*] |
|---|---|
| Coal: 20,300,000 tons | 18,600,000 |
| Oil: 7,200,000 barrels | 1,780,000 |
| Gas: 4,700,000,000 cu. ft. | 252,000 |
| Uranium ($U_3O_8$): 1,490,000 lbs.[†] | 1,700,000 |

The companies, such as Peabody Coal Company, that mine and sell the minerals are among the most powerful organizations in the world. Many handle more money in a year than all but the richest nations and may employ hundreds of thousands of people world-wide.

They are not owned by one person. Anyone can buy shares. Companies may even buy each other. Many thousands of shareholders around the world may care nothing for Navajo Country. Most think only about the money their shares will earn when they elect company officials, and officials who succeed are paid well. The top two officers of Mobil Oil Co., which mines uranium near Crownpoint, together received $6,539,415 in 1979 — more than the tribe got from all coal mines.

Large energy companies can do things that the Navajo Tribe can't afford. But they can also try to push the tribe into agreements it doesn't need. Tribal leaders must understand both the opportunity and the threat.

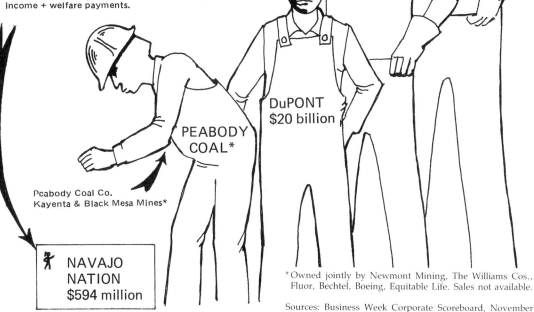
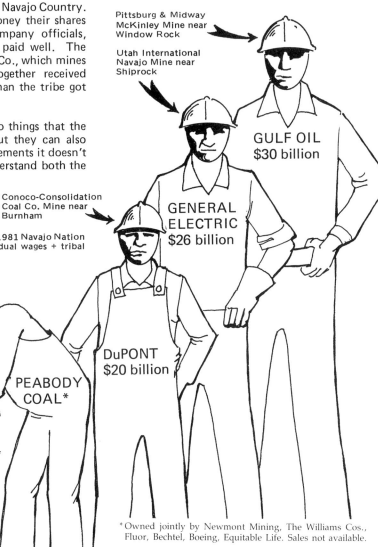

## 1981 YEARLY SALES OF COMPANIES OWNING COAL MINES ON THE RESERVATION

Pittsburg & Midway McKinley Mine near Window Rock

Utah International Navajo Mine near Shiprock

GULF OIL $30 billion

GENERAL ELECTRIC $26 billion

Conoco-Consolidation Coal Co. Mine near Burnham

Compared to major company sales 1981 Navajo Nation income was $594,000,000 = individual wages + tribal income + welfare payments.

DuPONT $20 billion

PEABODY COAL*

Peabody Coal Co. Kayenta & Black Mesa Mines*

NAVAJO NATION $594 million

*Owned jointly by Newmont Mining, The Williams Cos., Fluor, Bechtel, Boeing, Equitable Life. Sales not available.

Sources: Business Week Corporate Scoreboard, November 16, 1981, and 1980 Navajo Nation Progress Report.

* Horses required to do the same work in a year.
†Estimate without accident that closed one mine.

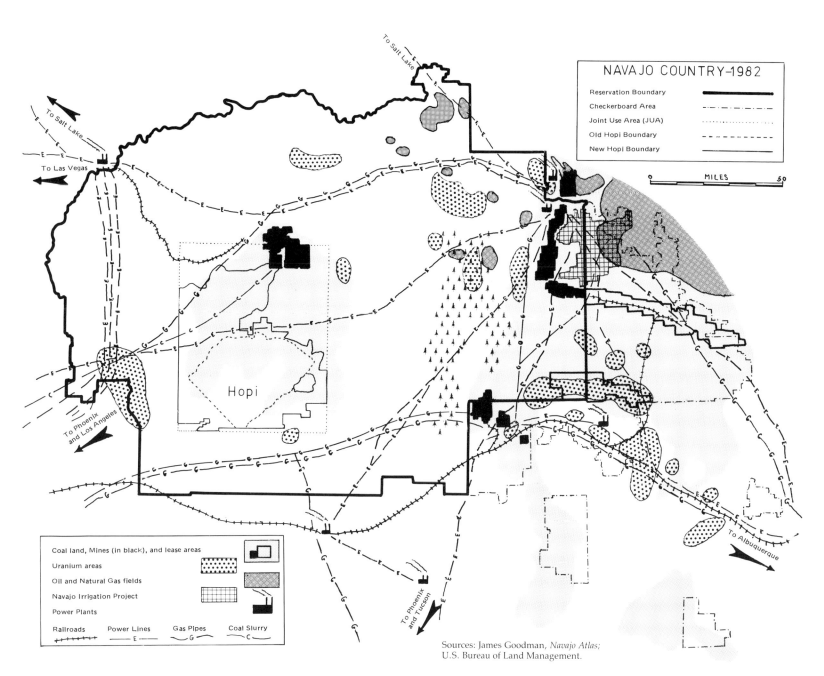

NAVAJO COUNTRY-1982

| | |
|---|---|
| Reservation Boundary | |
| Checkerboard Area | |
| Joint Use Area (JUA) | |
| Old Hopi Boundary | |
| New Hopi Boundary | |

MILES
0       50

To Salt Lake

To Salt Lake

To Las Vegas

To Phoenix
and Los Angeles

Hopi

To Phoenix
and Tucson

To Albuquerque

Coal land, Mines (in black), and lease areas

Uranium areas

Oil and Natural Gas fields

Navajo Irrigation Project

Power Plants

Railroads    Power Lines    Gas Pipes    Coal Slurry
              E            G          C

Sources: James Goodman, *Navajo Atlas;*
U.S. Bureau of Land Management.

231

# WHY MINES?

Eugene Leonard said it. *". . . you can't really earn enough to make it just from livestock."*

When they first heard of the mine, even the elders said, *"These jobs will provide us with money and our children with money. So let us agree!"*

Too many people live in Navajo Country now to live well on sheep and small corn patches. A huge number of people depend on government money, either from welfare or government jobs. Other jobs are scarce, and most young people sooner or later think about leaving the reservation because they can't make a living at home. Mines pay well.

The Navajo Tribe also needs money. Without money of its own, tribal government would be helpless. It could not even hire lawyers to help defend tribal land. There would be no tribal scholarships, Navajo police, general assistance, etc.

Most of the tribe's income has always come from mining and oil. The Navajo people cannot do without it, unless other income can be found, and that may take years.

Because people badly want jobs, and tribal government needs money, tribal leaders have leased land to mining companies. And in fact the mines did bring in all the jobs and income they promised.

Unfortunately, however, a good deal of poverty and misery came along with the wealth. Future leaders should understand why.

## Hidden Costs and Benefits

Something is usually said to be good if the benefits are greater than the costs. However, something is wrong when one group benefits while another pays. In the story, when Kee Chief lost his land but did not get hired, he paid for someone else's benefit.

When the company said the tribe had responsibility for moving people off the land, the company took the benefit and wanted the tribe to pay the cost.

Protesters forced the company to pay at least some of that cost, but the tribe and the U.S. government were left with others: the loss of land and water, the cost of roads, sewers, police, fire protection, and schools for the mining community, and the problems of people who did leave their land. These hidden costs took up much of the money that came from the mine in the first place.

## Personal Income

This graph shows where people living on the reservation got their money in 1979. The big share from mining, power plants, etc., shows why many welcomed mines on Black Mesa.

Three-fourths of all income came from outside the reservation through government programs that come and go. School jobs, construction projects, chapter work programs, etc., could end at any time.

Most of those on welfare, pensions, and food stamps wanted to make their own living but might have starved without help.

Farming and livestock brought in little, and other jobs like the sawmill, railroad, or fire-fighting, brought in even less.

How the money was shared is also important, however. Most people get a little bit from livestock. A few people get a lot from mining.

Source: Navajo Tribe.

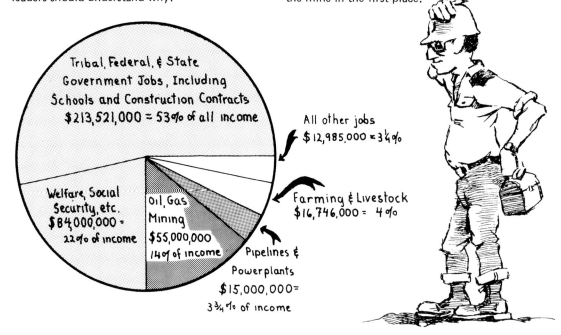

Tribal, Federal, & State Government Jobs, Including Schools and Construction Contracts $213,521,000 = 53% of all income

All other jobs $12,985,000 = 3¼%

Welfare, Social Security, etc. $84,000,000 = 22% of income

Oil, Gas Mining $55,000,000 14% of income

Farming & Livestock $16,746,000 = 4%

Pipelines & Powerplants $15,000,000 = 3¾% of income

## Taxes and Royalties

A *royalty* is money a company pays a landowner for minerals — usually a certain amount per ton, or a share of the selling price. The amount is agreed upon in the lease.

A *tax* is money collected to pay for hidden costs, so costs and benefits will fall equally on all. Most companies pay taxes to the government that controls the land. The government can use the tax money for roads, sewers, job training, welfare, etc., to spread the benefits to people who don't get jobs at the mine but suffer the costs.

Unfortunately, when coal mining began on Navajo land, leases set very low royalties, and tribes could not collect taxes. If tribes win the right to tax in court, and if they can force companies to pay higher royalties, more people will benefit from minerals.

## True Wealth

The coal, oil, gas, and uranium of Navajo Country became part of the land when the land itself was made. Nothing takes the place of all that we burn to run the lights and engines of the world.

Navajo oil wells that pumped record amounts in 1967 may go dry by 1997. Even coal mining, which now seems to have no end, must stop some day. These things that are destroyed forever the minute they are used are **non-renewable resources.**

They have great value, but turning them into money only takes from one hand and gives to the other. The money is more, but the land is less. In the eyes of history, nothing changes unless the money goes to strengthen living things.

Living things — people, plants, animals — are **renewable resources.** If they are cared for through generation after generation, they can exist until the end of time. Long after Navajo coal has gone up in smoke, the mountain forests should still give firewood and lumber. Corn and livestock should still grow. People should still have strength of mind and body.

These things are the *true* wealth of Navajo Country, and what happens to the earth, water, sunlight, and air can affect them far into the future.

The money that comes from mines and wells must be measured by what happens to living things, renewable resources. Can it help trees grow better on the mountains? Can it make fields and herds better than before? Can it help people find more ways to live, so life will go on when the mineral money stops coming in?

## Tribal Income

The Navajo Tribe received $25,410,000 in mineral royalties in 1980. That was only 4% of the value of the minerals at world prices. Companies do not always receive world prices because of agreements and regulations, but the minerals were worth that to the world that used them.

The drawings show world price values compared to the share received by the tribe in royalties. Royalties are represented by the black areas. Note that the tribe gets a bigger share of oil than of coal.

Sources: Navajo Tribe; American Petroleum Institute; Bureau of Mines.

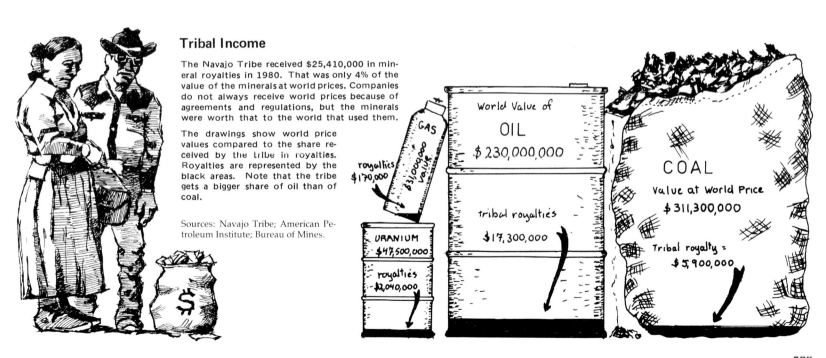

GAS royalties $170,000 / $31,000,000 value

World Value of OIL $230,000,000 / tribal royalties $17,300,000

URANIUM $47,500,000 / royalties $2,040,000

COAL Value at World Price $311,300,000 / Tribal royalty = $5,900,000

# IF WE HAD ONLY KNOWN

In the story, Ned Yazzie, his parents, and Kee Chief all say they once wanted to see a mine on Black Mesa. They don't say it now. *"Maybe people should have asked questions back then,"* says *K'ai' Bii' Toonii.*

They were told the mine would bring jobs and that they could use the land after three years. They didn't expect their lives to change much. In fact, they got exactly what the tribe's lease with Peabody Coal Company said they would.

At the time of the Long Walk the government said, "Since the Indians will not mine their land, we should take it." And they did. Congress still has that power, but on Black Mesa the company made a *lease agreement* instead. The company pays money while they use the land and will give it back when they finish.

By the Treaty of 1868, "Three-fourths of all adult male Indians" must approve leases. But the BIA created the Tribal Council in 1923 to get around this. A council majority can now lease land.

The lease said Peabody could mine for 35 years, paying the tribe no more than 37½ cents a ton. The company agreed to fix torn-up land, *"except for the normal wear, tear, and depletion incident to mining"*. The lease allowed Peabody to build roads and buildings and required that Navajos and Hopis be hired first.

When coal prices went way up, the tribe still got 37½ cents. Blasted rock piled up for four years; Peabody called it "normal wear and tear". They made no serious effort to make mined land useful for grazing until a federal law forced them to start trying in 1977.

When they began bulldozing houses, they said the tribe should care for people living in them. They told Kee Chief to wait in line for work. It didn't matter that they were mining his land.

The lease was a "standard form" used by the BIA. Tribal leaders were told they could not get a better deal. Leases will come up in the future; today's students will be the leaders asked to judge them. Will they know the game?

## How the Game is Played

Company officials who write leases know what they want and try to win the best deal for themselves. To get it they may use the same language a dealer uses to sell pickups. Tribal officials must recognize the traps.

1. *"I'm losing money, but you're my friend."* Don't believe this without driving the pickup. The BIA said 37½ cents a ton for 35 years was a good deal, but the tribe didn't know exactly how much coal Black Mesa had or what profit Peabody could make.

The tribe could have said, "Since we don't know what coal is worth now or in 35 years, you will pay us a share of your selling price, whatever it is." Coal companies elsewhere have agreed to pay 12% or more. Coal prices went up so much that 37½ cents was less than 3% of Peabody's price after ten years.

2. *"If you have trouble, we'll check it."* Promises mean nothing when your pickup blows an engine. Peabody likewise said nothing by promising to fix up the land *"except for normal wear, tear, etc."* Total destruction is normal in strip mining. A good lease might have said, "Ten years after mining, the land will feed 10 sheep per 100 acres according to expert judgement, or the company will pay..."

3. *"Buy now, or you'll lose your chance."* This might have been true. There is coal north of Navajo Country, but the location was worse for Peabody and the price probably higher. Peabody wanted Black Mesa coal.

4. *"Buy now or else...!"* A car dealer can't hurt you if you don't buy, but the U.S. government can tell the tribe, "Sign the lease or we'll cut your money for schools, etc." That hurts because the tribe depends too much on government money. A few companies have persuaded government officials to use that kind of power. Paying officials and congressmen for help is illegal, but it happens. The tribe must make its own friends in Washington.

5. *"We'll talk about details later."* After a car dealer has his money, he may not talk about details, ever. Leases must cover all details at the start: land damage, hiring, payments, caring for people on the land, and penalties if agreements aren't kept. Later is usually too late.

## Bitter Lessons

Besides the people near the Peabody mines, many have suffered from the carelessness or selfishness of companies working in Navajo Country. Here are some examples. None would have happened if regulations had been made and enforced.

**1950's:** More than 150 small uranium mines were opened in the Chuska Mountains, Monument Valley, and the Tuba City area. *No safety regulations were enforced.* Accidents crippled many. Blasting dust caused permanent lung damage, and by 1978 at least 25 miners had died of a kind of lung cancer rarely seen among Navajos.

Cancer from radiation in European mines had been known for years, but the companies weren't required to install blowers and filters or measure radiation. The companies paid nothing to the dead miners' families. When the mines closed, pits and tunnels were left open and are still dangerous.

**1960's:** Uranium mills at Shiprock, Monument Valley, and Tuba City closed, leaving behind several million tons of dangerously radioactive sand that 20 years later children still played on, home-builders mixed in cement, and wind storms spread over a wide area. The companies weren't required to clean up.

**1960's:** The Four Corners Power Plant near Shiprock, then the world's largest coal-fired power plant, was built without air pollution controls because the lease didn't require them. It pumped 252 tons of soot and 445 tons of smog-causing gasses ($SO_2$, NOx) a DAY into the sky. The smoke was one of the only man-made things the first astronauts saw from space. New Mexico passed a pollution law in 1970, but in 1980 the plant still broke it.

**1978:** Navajos in Aneth, Utah, oil fields took over wells and company buildings to protest oil spills, livestock losses, and insulting behavior by company workers. The leases were changed to handle the complaints.

**1979:** At Church Rock, northeast of Gallup, a carelessly-built dam at the United Nuclear Corp. mill broke, sending 95 million gallons of water and 1100 tons of mud, all dangerously radioactive, through several Navajo communities. That mill was not on Navajo land, but mills are planned for the reservation, and state laws may not give protection.

## Looking Ahead

Years ago Many Mules told his grandaughter, *"Rule this land! Hold it to yourself. Be stingy with it! Other clans keep coming on to it. Never let them take it!"*

In many communities neighbors fight each other so much over land that they can do nothing about real dangers facing all of them from outside.

Mining leases affect everybody in a community and the future of the whole tribe. They bring changes that can never be undone. The pressure from Washington and elsewhere to sign harmful agreements may be great. Some may seem to offer so much that they will be hard to turn down.

The strength to decide what is best and fight to get it comes only from working together. Certain questions must be discussed and answered for the benefit of everyone:

-*Can we satisfy our needs any other way?*

-*What will happen if we do not sign?*

-*Who will benefit?*

-*Who will lose?*

-*How much land will we lose, and whose land will it be?*

-*How much money does the tribe need?*

-*What does the tribe need the money for?*

-*Are there any benefits besides money?*

-*What new ideas and ways of life do we wish to encourage?*

-*Will old ideas and ways of life be made stronger or weaker?*

-*Are we willing to take responsibility for what happens?*

If questions like these can be answered clearly, no one will cry tomorrow over mistakes made today.

# WATER

*"I told them I didn't want my waterhole disturbed. I told them to leave that alone. I kept saying NO. But they tore it up . . . Then there was a windmill. I told them I didn't want that touched either, but they took it away and tore up the water."*

Many Mules' Granddaughter

She knew well the first rule of dry country: without water, land is useless. Without her spring it hardly mattered what else the mine did to her land. In fact, water is worth more to the Navajo Nation than any mineral wealth. It must be protected and cared for if the tribe hopes to survive.

The Treaty of 1868 says that Navajo land cannot be sold, taken, or given away without an act of Congress. Nothing protects Navajo water so clearly, but losing water in the end means losing the value of land.

## Rivers

Only two rivers on the Navajo Reservation flow all year long: the Colorado and the San Juan. They also carry a big share of all water used in seven western states and northwestern Mexico. Years ago these states and Mexico agreed on how much water each could use.

These agreements, however, did not include Indian tribes. They say that Indian tribes do have a right to some water, but in fact, the shares given to each state add up to more water than the rivers usually carry. Growing cities like Phoenix and Los Angeles, new irrigation projects, and power plants that need cooling water are now using up these shares. Nothing may be left for Indian tribes to claim.

Tribes should be able to claim a great deal of water. In 1908 the U.S. Supreme Court ruled that a Montana rancher named Winters could not take water from the Milk River because Indians on the Fort Belknap Reservation had a right to it. The Court said the U.S. government had clearly wanted Indians to farm when the reservation was made. That included the right to irrigation water. This *"Winters Doctrine"* also gives Navajos and other tribes a legal claim to water.

The *Winters Doctrine* doesn't say exactly *how much* water a tribe can claim, however. Several tribes, including the Navajos, have lost water rights before they ever knew how much they really had. Here are two examples:

*In 1962 the Navajo Tribe agreed to claim only enough water from the San Juan River to irrigate the 110,000-acre Navajo Indian Irrigation Project south of Farmington. In return the U.S. government agreed to put in the dam, ditches, and pipes to get the water to the land. The agreement also allowed San Juan water to be piped over the mountains to the Chama River, so the city of Albuquerque and New Mexican farmers could use it. The Chama pipe was quickly built, but 20 years later, the Navajo Irrigation Project was less than half finished, and New Mexico politicians were trying hard to cut the Navajo water share in half.*

*In 1968 the power plant built to burn Black Mesa coal at Page, Arizona, needed cooling water. The Navajo Tribal Council was persuaded (some say forced) to make only a very small claim to Colorado River water and then give two-thirds of it away to the power company and the town of Page. The water that the tribe might have claimed and the water they actually gave away is worth millions to the people who use it now. The tribe may never get any of it back.*

## Ground Water

Ground water supplies wells and springs. Traditionally the Navajo tribe has not used all they could, but ground water also has great value in modern times. It, too, can be lost, poisoned, wasted, or stolen.

Ground water comes from rain that soaks down into the earth until it reaches layers of rock that stop it. Some of the water in these underground lakes is thousands of years old. Wells and springs go dry if it is pumped out faster than rainfall replaces it.

Mining and drilling that breaks through rock layers may damage ground water. Layers of good water may mix with layers of bad water. Dangerous minerals from the crushed rock may poison it.

Deep mines like the uranium mines in the eastern part of Navajo Country waste enormous amounts of ground water. They must pump out millions of gallons to keep miles of tunnels dry. But dirty mine water is almost useless for drinking or irrigation. The mine pumping can affect wells over wide areas.

Black Mesa is another place where ground water has been taken and its true value forgotten.

# COAL AND WATER

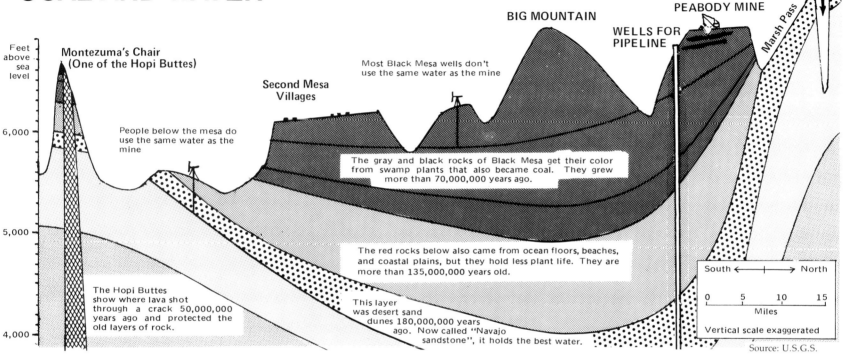

Tsegi Canyon

BIG MOUNTAIN

PEABODY MINE

WELLS FOR
PIPELINE

Marsh Pass

Feet above sea level

Montezuma's Chair
(One of the Hopi Buttes)

Second Mesa
Villages

Most Black Mesa wells don't
use the same water as the mine

6,000

People below the mesa do
use the same water as the
mine

The gray and black rocks of Black Mesa get their color
from swamp plants that also became coal. They grew
more than 70,000,000 years ago.

5,000

The red rocks below also came from ocean floors, beaches,
and coastal plains, but they hold less plant life. They are
more than 135,000,000 years old.

South ←——→ North

The Hopi Buttes
show where lava shot
through a crack 50,000,000
years ago and protected the
old layers of rock.

This layer
was desert sand
dunes 180,000,000 years
ago. Now called "Navajo
sandstone", it holds the best water.

0     5     10     15
Miles

Vertical scale exaggerated

4,000

Source: U.S.G.S.

If you cut the earth exactly down the middle of Black Mesa, the edge would look something like the drawing above. The rocks of the mesa are stacked up like layers of a cake.

Oceans moving back and forth across the land made the layers over millions of years, but at some time the layers bent, as the drawing shows. Then the seas left lakes where Black Mesa is now. Plant life in the lakes became the coal mined there now. From the road through Marsh Pass west of Kayenta you can see red rock to the north sloping down under gray mesa rock.

Black Mesa is still a lake. The rock under it holds some of the best water in Navajo Country, and this water may be worth as much as the coal.

Most Navajos depend on water from underground — from wells and springs. Without it no one could live on the land at all.

However, in 1968 the Navajos and Hopis allowed the Black Mesa Pipeline Company to mine water for moving coal. Daily, 43,000 tons of coal are ground to powder, mixed with water, and sent through a pipe to a power plant by Davis Dam in southern Nevada. This water comes from the same rocks that give water to communities around Black Mesa, such as Rough Rock, Kayenta, and Keams Canyon. Nature won't replace it for many hundreds of years.

The pipeline company sucks up over 10 acre-feet of water a day — enough to nearly cover 10

football fields a foot deep. They pay $7.50 an acre-foot.

A little arithmetic shows how much this water is really worth. A family in Tucson pays $400 an acre-foot for household water. Irrigation water in Arizona sells for over $200. Navajos who haul water may pay $7,710.

Figure it out: *An average family hauls six barrels a week (330 gallons). They drive 30 miles (24c a mile). An acre-foot is 353,388 gal. Of course a family may take over 20 years to use one acre-foot. The pipe gobbles that much in 2 hrs. and 24 min. — a 200-year supply every day. Even so, after 35 years the pipe will have used up less than 1% of the water stored under the mesa.*

# STRIP MINING

High wall shooters like Ned Yazzie blast the earth above the coal; draglines strip it off and pile it in spoil banks; coal shooters blast the coal, and trucks haul it away.

Spoil piles are too steep for plants. They erode badly, and poisonous minerals washed out of broken rock may get into streams.

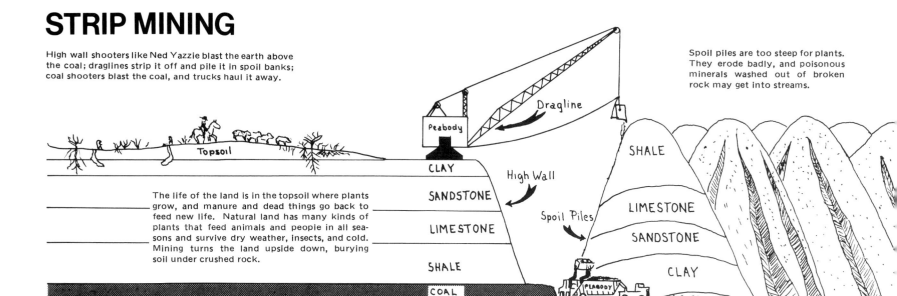

The life of the land is in the topsoil where plants grow, and manure and dead things go back to feed new life. Natural land has many kinds of plants that feed animals and people in all seasons and survive dry weather, insects, and cold. Mining turns the land upside down, burying soil under crushed rock.

# PEABODY'S RECORD

Peabody is the nation's largest coal producer, and in 1980 its Black Mesa mines were the third largest coal operation in the U.S. However, one man who had to enforce the federal strip mine law felt Peabody used its wealth for the wrong goals. "The money and time they spent on lawyers and politicians to weaken the law could have made a difference on Black Mesa," said Tom Tippeconnic of the U.S. Office of Surface Mining.

Before the law Peabody saved no topsoil, left spoil areas too steep, and planted few wild seeds. By 1980 they obeyed the law but were doing little extra. Plant life was worse than on other Navajo mines, although rainfall is better on Black Mesa than elsewhere. Tumbleweed was still the main plant. The numbers and graph show the work by February 1980.

| Total land to be mined | 15,000 acres |
|---|---|
| Land mined by February 1980 | 4,707 acres |

Of those 4,707 acres, nearly half had seen no reclamation work.

Ungraded spoil piles, pits, etc. 2,008 acres = 43% of mined land.

Graded spoil piles without topsoil or planting: 540 acres – 11%

Graded and planted spoil piles without topsoil: 1725 acres = 37%

Graded and planted spoil piles with topsoil: 431 acres = 9%

Where 100 kinds of plants grew before, 12 were seeded, and only six had grown there before. Two others, alfalfa and clover, had never grown in that climate. Four wing saltbush was the only bush. Much seeding was done by plane which gives poor results.

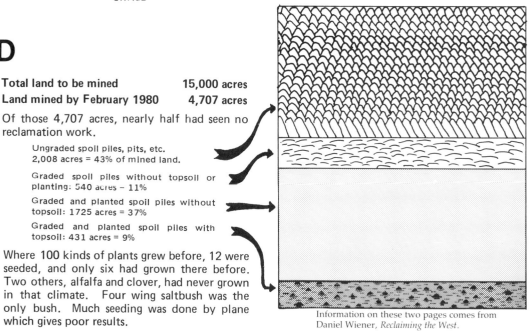

Information on these two pages comes from Daniel Wiener, *Reclaiming the West.*

# RECLAMATION

Life may never return to the land if the spoil piles are left. The federal strip mining law of 1977 required mines to level them.

Topsoil must be scraped off and saved before mining — and put back after leveling spoil piles.

The land should be plowed and planted with seeds that grow wild in the mine area. Plowing and planting must be done around the hills so the plowing will catch water and stop erosion. Many kinds of seeds should be planted so the land again will have plants for all seasons.

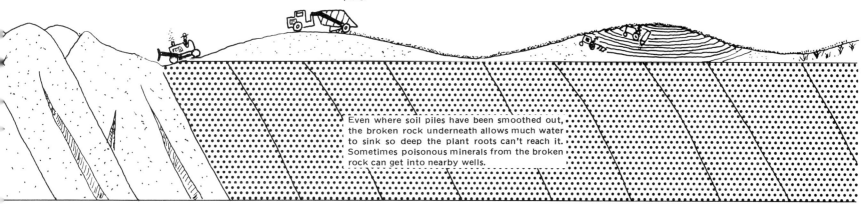

Even where soil piles have been smoothed out, the broken rock underneath allows much water to sink so deep the plant roots can't reach it. Sometimes poisonous minerals from the broken rock can get into nearby wells.

# SEE IT YOURSELF

Anyone can visit coal mines in Navajo Country by calling mine headquarters. Mine tours show all steps of mining and often end at grassy areas of "reclaimed" land. However, a green patch doesn't prove that the company seriously tries to make the land as rich as it was. You can find the true story by looking for the right things and asking the right questions. Here is a check list:

Grading spoil piles is important. Notice:
How many rows of piles are by each pit? More than two means more time spent tearing up land than putting it back. Erosion and topsoil loss may be serious.

How steep are hills on graded land? NONE should be steeper than unmined slopes nearby. Steep slopes mean more care for saving money than growing plants.

Topsoil is important. Ask:
Is it saved and put back after mining?
How soon is it put back after mining?
On how much land was it not put back?
Can you see some of this land?

Plowing and planting must be done carefully.
Do machines work around hills? (good) OR
Do they go up and down hills? (bad)
Is planting by hand or tractor? (good) OR
By airplane? (cheap but works poorly).

What is planted? Ask for a list of plants.
How many kinds? (some mines plant 25-30.)
Did any grow wild before? (They are best.)
Are grasses, bushes and other plants included? (All are necessary.)

Experimenting is necessary. Do they test:
Irrigation? How much? When? How long?
Fertilizer? How much? For how long?

Soil protection? Does straw, ash or other soil treatment help seed and stop erosion?

Time is the true test. Ask to see:
Land mined 2, 4, 6, & 8 years ago. If no improvement shows four years after planting, irrigation, and fertilizing have stopped, something is going wrong.

Many green areas may be only tumbleweed (also called Russian Thistle). There should be at least a dozen kinds of plants including *young* grasses, bushes, and others that started naturally *without extra help*.

Look at all areas you pass. If the planted area you are shown is better than other "reclaimed" areas, ask "why?" Ask why bare spots exist where nothing grows. If no one can find answers for you, it is a sign that the company doesn't really care about the land.

# TOWN AND COUNTRY

Through most of their history, Navajos have not been townspeople. Town life and country life have mixed often, however.

In Anasazi times, the *Kin Yaa'áanii* Clan took its name from the Towering House, a town where they stopped. Later, Pueblo people, forced from their towns by hunger or war, joined the Navajos.

Now because of the crowding of the land and the loss of land to the Hopis and to mines, thousands of Navajos like the Lunas are being forced into towns.

Towns grow for many reasons. They may be government towns, market towns, stopping places along highways and railroads, mining towns, factory towns, religious centers, or forts. The map here shows towns around Navajo Country where Navajos are settling and the reasons why these towns grew.

People move to towns because they hope to find homes, work, and friends, but every town is different. Reservation towns like Kayenta have special problems because they are so new and few laws or traditions guide what happens there.

## The Land

Not everyone wanted a town to grow at Kayenta. The land itself belonged to people who had farmed and herded on it for years. But land was taken from them for schools, roads, airports, houses. And it is still being taken.

In many places on the reservation where towns have grown, meetings have been held to decide what land should be used. No one, however, wants to stand up and say, "I give my land." In the end the tribal government has power to take land, so they take it. Sometimes the people are paid, but not always what they think the land is worth. Many reservation communities will face this problem in years to come.

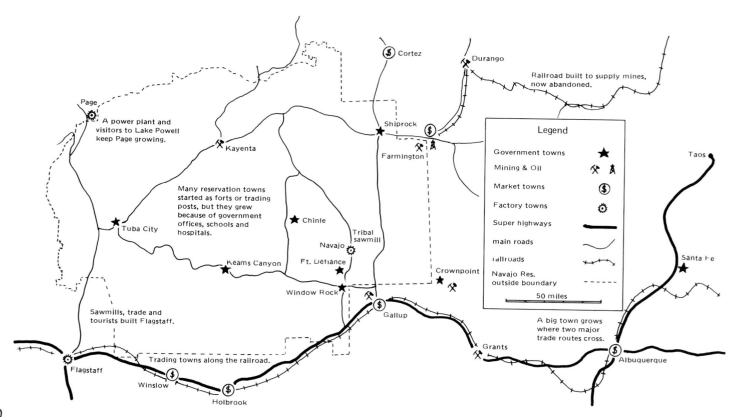

Railroad built to supply mines, now abandoned.

A power plant and visitors to Lake Powell keep Page growing.

Many reservation towns started as forts or trading posts, but they grew because of government offices, schools and hospitals.

Sawmills, trade and tourists built Flagstaff.

Trading towns along the railroad.

A big town grows where two major trade routes cross.

### Legend

| | |
|---|---|
| Government towns | ★ |
| Mining & Oil | ⚒ ⚓ |
| Market towns | $ |
| Factory towns | ⚙ |
| Super highways | ▬ |
| main roads | ～ |
| railroads | ╫ |
| Navajo Res. outside boundary | - - - |

50 miles

## Living Anaashii

Towns grow whether or not the tribal government takes land for them. When Florence Luna found work in Kayenta, she built a hogan on land belonging to her relatives. She was lucky they let her live there at all. She could not have livestock or even be sure her son could live with her.

Around most reservation towns, hundreds of people like Florence have put trailer homes and hogans on land that is not really theirs. Most can find no other way to live, so they live *anaashii*.

In English they are "squatters", and they anger people who do own land. New houses scattered around without any plan make it hard to use the land for anything else. Water, power, sewers, and roads are difficult to put in.

The tribe does have laws that say no house can be built without a "home site lease", but getting one may be difficult. The people on the land and the chapter officials must agree. At the time Florence built her hogan, the paperwork alone took months or even years, and tribal officials had no way to enforce the laws anyway. Until land is found where people can live legally, they cannot be blamed for living *anaashii*.

## Housing

In many communities, legal residents are in fact not much better off than squatters. Many "legal" houses are built and owned by the U.S. government, the Navajo Tribe, or some other organization. The people in them pay rent.

Some houses go with jobs. Only school employees may live in school housing. Only hospital workers may live in Public Health Service housing. Losing a job or not paying rent may mean losing a house.

## Friends

In the story Eugene says, *"Down here you never know who your child's friends are."* In all new towns people have come from different places and don't know each other. Towns can be lonely for that reason. Neighbors don't always help each other. Thieves and gangs do their dirty work and nobody stops to look. Nobody knows who they are.

## Government

When reservation towns like Kayenta started growing, they had no government to deal with town problems. Few people wanted a town at all. They didn't like squatters moving in on them, but nobody wanted to give up grazing land so newcomers could build homes legally. The problems therefore became worse.

The new people moving in from other places could not change things because they were not welcome at local chapter meetings and could not vote. Only the tribal government could take land for houses, build roads, and enforce laws in reservation towns, but tribal headquarters was too far away to handle many problems.

Without leadership, towns grew out in all directions without any plan, without recreation areas for young people, without thought for traffic and health dangers, without thought for the grazing land nearby.

## Money

Most people living in reservation towns have jobs of some kind. Some, like Eugene, earn good pay. The towns themselves, however, are often poor. Muddy streets, no street lights, garbage piled everywhere, wild dogs, and poor fire and police protection can make town life rough.

Most towns elsewhere pay for these things by taxing the people who live in them. The first reservation towns had no way to collect any taxes. In the case of Kayenta, the coal company that caused the town to grow also paid no taxes.

## Work

Housing projects with lights and running water were planned in scattered isolated places for people forced off the Hopi side of the JUA. Butane, light, and power bills must be paid, and there is no work anywhere nearby. Living there means living on welfare and doing nothing. Many would rather live *anaashii* somewhere else and work. A town is not just people living together. It is people working together as well.

\* \* \*

In spite of the problems, towns can be exciting places where people learn new ways of life, make new friends, and hear new ideas. If people escaping from towns once lent their strength to Navajo life, perhaps Navajos now will pass that strength on to the towns where they go.

# REMEMBER THE LAND

Clan: *Kin Yaa'áanii*
Born for: *Áshįįhí*

# REMEMBER THE LAND

There was never a time in the history of the *Diné* when one generation followed another without change. New ideas, new discoveries, new people, wars, invasions, and slow changes in the land itself have forced every age to add something to the experience of the past.

In every age the elders have said to young people, "Go, learn, help your land and your people." They said it because they too learned and did new things in their time. Today's grandparents are no different. They say to take responsibility for the land. They do not say how, but they remember themselves in the strength of their own youth facing problems and opportunities that long ago were also new.

Today Navajo Country faces the questions of the modern world. Will jobs and town life replace livestock and hogans? How will we use our mineral wealth? Can we live a "modern" life and still be Navajo? Should we try? And there are questions of the land itself. Where will growing numbers of people live? How will we all live? How do we protect our land—against outside forces . . . against misuse by our own people?

This chapter is about young people who all went, learned, and came back to the land. They do not live the lives their grandparents led, and their ideas come not only from Navajo tradition, but from all the modern world as well. They do what they do because of the land itself—*Diné Bikéyah*—and that ties together past and present. Their story must begin with a grandfather speaking to his children, because that is how the love of the land and the wisdom to care for it passes from generation to generation.

Charles Yazzie Morgan of Dalton Pass near Crownpoint spoke to his children in 1978. The land where he had grown up was dry and full of snakeweed. Uranium had been discovered, and a mining company had dynamited springs, torn up family graves, and planned enough mines and mills to change the place forever. He might have said the land was lost. He might have despaired that the life he knew had lost its power and only waited to be bulldozed like the bones of his ancestors. However, giving up easily was never the tradition of his family.

Morgan's grandfather came back to Dalton Pass from Fort Sumner and was known until the end of his life as *Hastiin Náhodeeshgiizh*, which is the Navajo name for Dalton Pass. The leaders and medicine men among his nine children were well known across most of Navajo Country. Charles Morgan is the son of Stephen Morgan, a medicine man and singer who lived to the age of 93 and who remembered well the history of his land.

Morgan himself is an owner of cattle and sheep and father of 16 children, several of whom have also held important jobs around Crownpoint. He speaks slowly to give each word its full power:

*"I grew up knowing the beauty of the land. We used to look at the earth and see it dressed in flowers of all kinds and colors. All the gifts of the earth were thought of as blessings and were kept holy. A long time ago, if rains came at night, mothers and fathers would waken their children and tell them, 'You should not be lying down. Sit up!' And fathers would keep the fire going until the rain passed. It was a holy moment. When the rains passed, parents would say, 'We are blessed. New plants will grow now. Our water has been replaced.'*

*"We think of the Earth as Our Mother. The Sky is Our Father. From the time the sun rises, to the time the sun sets and all through the night, not a day comes out too short. Not a day comes out too long. All is balanced, and this, I think, is what is meant when we say in the Blessingway Ceremony, 'Są'ąh Naagháíí Bik'eh Hózhóón.' All is balanced. Without balance there is no life.*

*"We people think of ourselves as something very important. Mother Earth is the same way. She is made of the same things as we are. The way we hurt, that is the way she hurts too. The way we live, that's the way she lives too. Those things that are within us, those things are inside her too.*

*"From her, plants grow. We eat of those plants. Because of her we are able to eat and drink. We are like children who still suck at the mother's breast. Water is like the milk from Mother Earth. We still suckle Our Mother.*

*"Those who live on this earth, the insects, the plants, the animals, and ourselves, should have a place to live. But we bring starvation and thirst to all of these things. To all of them we bring great sorrow and grief. We have not thought about any of them.*

*"What we do to the land can destroy what gives us life. Even now there are springs that no longer run. I am talking not only for myself, but for those who may be born tonight. We have to think of them. How will they drink? How will they live? What kind of life are we giving them?*

*"My father always told us that from the time of the Long Walk our ancestors' strongest advice was never to leave this land again, trade it, or sell it, because they suffered grief, tears, and death for their land.*

*"I say to you, my children: Study! Prepare for a job! Plan for the future! But don't forget the land and the people who went before you. They will be your blessing and will make you strong."*

# TAKING ACTION

It isn't always easy for young people to follow the advice of their elders. Elsie Peshlakai, Charles Morgan's niece, grew up in two worlds. At age 14 she left Dalton Pass and lived among Mormons in Utah for ten years.

As she tells it, "The old people used to say, 'Go! Get an education so you can help us.' I could go away only because I knew my home would always be here, and no matter what happened, this land and these people would always take care of me if I needed them. I've known many people who move here and there all their lives, but they really have nowhere to go home. They have no roots that give them strength.

"I loved my Mormon family. I learned a great deal about the world. I got used to the conveniences there, and I began to be proud of how I handled that life. I was flying high. Coming home really brought me down with a crash. The life here was so hard, but I realized what my home meant to me and how much my parents really cared.

"But terrible things were going on. Drill crews were everywhere looking for uranium. Their voices and trucks and engines were with us day and night. They cut fences, bulldozed roads, and listened to no one. They drilled almost at our front door, and my mother once threatened them with a gun. They moved then, but not very far. My parents and their friends could not understand what had happened."

Elsie had to find out and explain.

From sacred Mount Taylor west beneath the roots of Lobo Mesa where legend says the Mirage Stone Children live, below the fallen stones of the Towering House, *Kin Yaa'á*, and the cities of Chaco where the Great Gambler walked, and north along the Chuska and Carrizo Mountains, uranium had been found. Uranium is a rare and powerful mineral. Atom bombs and electric power are made from it, and the radiation it leaves behind can kill for a hundred thousand years.

The tribal government had leased land at Dalton Pass to several uranium mining companies. On nearby land off the reservation, other leases had been signed by Navajo landowners or by BIA officials who had the power to sign leases without the owners' permission. Like coal mines, the uranium mines would bring jobs and money, but they would bring problems too.

According to government reports that few people saw or could read,[1] the mining companies planned to pump so much water out of the ground to keep their mines from flooding that wells would be sucked dry for hundreds of square miles. The town of Crownpoint would lose its water supply. The San Juan River, 60 miles to the north, could be affected for over 200 years. Water pumped from the mine shafts would not be drinkable without expensive treatment, and no company planned to do that. They hoped to sell the dirty water at a profit to cool power plants planned for coal lands further north.

That was not all. The mining companies also planned to build mills to grind up the ore and separate the pure uranium from the rock. These mills might leave behind more than 300 million tons of radioactive sand that would be dangerous for thousands of years.

"That's how things were when I came back from Utah," says Elsie. "I saw at once that I had to educate people to see those things that they can't see now. They must understand how the modern world booms and races, how by a single telephone call across the country, a mining company can move thousands of dollars, set bulldozers going, rip something down overnight, and build great works in its place. The world of my parents

---

[1]Working papers and reports by the San Juan Basin Regional Uranium Study.

moves slowly according to nature. They cannot believe that anything can change their world so fast."

So Elsie stayed home for the sake of the land. She pulled on her boots and set out across the muddy roads of Eastern Navajo Agency, talking to people, teaching, getting testimony to use in courts of law, and calling meetings to protect the land as best she could.

"I did what I could," she says, "but at the same time I was trying to get used to living at home again without electricity or running water or paved roads. I had forgotten what it is like to care for livestock day in and day out in mud and snow and boiling heat. It was hard for me, but slowly I realized that up in Utah I had forgotten what life really is. My parents and the older people I talked to did not understand uranium mining, but they knew the truth about life. They had lived close to Mother Earth all their lives, and they had learned the truth.

"For them the truth has nothing to do with pickup trucks, money, or good clothes. They may have those things, but what really matters is nature and the land and the life that is in it."

Elsie gets in her pickup. The ruts of an old road snap her small body back and forth at the steering wheel. She has legal papers for an old lady to sign at Mariano Lake. Snow and darkness are falling together, and mud is starting to freeze behind the tires. She smiles. "I am not really like my parents," she says. "I need the modern world, but there must be a way we can have it in our own style. We can protect the land, and the old people can teach us and not see everything they gave us destroyed. That's how I dream it should be."

Elsie's work did help. The story of Dalton Pass was told nationwide in magazines and on television. It became part of an international fight to control the nuclear power that depends on uranium, and many of the mines planned had not been built by 1982. But the ore is still in the ground, and the old plans may be pulled off the shelf again one day. By that time, however, the Navajo Tribe and the people of Dalton Pass should have plans of their own to see that work is done their way.

Clan: *Áshįįhí*
Born for: *Tó Baazhní'ázhí*

# PLANS

Clan: *Áshįįhí*
Born for: *Hooghan Łání*

Al Henderson works in a world of ideas, trying to make them real. In 1981 he was put in charge of the Navajo Tribe's Department of Economic Development. His job: to plan how the tribe should spend its money and use its resources to make the best future for the Navajo people.

Al was 33 when he took the job, but he had prepared himself for it since starting college. He is a college student still, working for a higher degree. Books line the walls of his office, and he sorts papers like a cowboy cuts steers. His white shirt and fine slacks are the clothes of someone who works more with his head than his hands, but his thoughts touch every side of Navajo life.

"I come from Twin Lakes Chapter north of Gallup," says Al, "but I left the reservation in sixth grade to go to school in Gallup. I lived in the BIA dorm and learned about TV and how to be a regular American teenager. That's all I thought about. I saw college as just a new adventure. I couldn't think of anything else to do.

"For a year or so I just enjoyed myself and got by any old way. Then a professor of economics took an interest in me, and I got the habit of chatting with him after class. Soon I was spending hours at his place, talking over everything under the sun. He made me think of what's wrong with the world and of ways different groups of people look at each other.

"I began to think about Navajo Country in a new way. I remember him telling me, 'It's a mean world, and if Navajos have problems, then Navajos will have to solve them.' That's when I became a serious student. If we were tough enough to survive Fort Sumner, I couldn't sit by and watch us go downhill in my generation.

"Back home I found the tribe split three ways—the old traditional people on one

side, and the young space-age Navajos on the other. I belonged to another group in between. The land itself is all that keeps us together, but that is a lot.

"The old people say, '*Nihikéyah nihąąh niníyá*, "Our land is tired," ' and it's true. We need all our space-age knowledge to make it rich again."

## SELF SUFFICIENCY

According to Al Henderson, the Navajo Nation must think again about how it survived in the first place: by livestock, farming, forest, and water resources.

Minerals—coal, oil, gas, and uranium—are *non-renewable* resources. They run out. Ranches, farms, forests, and water, however, are *renewable*. If protected and cared for, they last forever.

When Al spoke, Navajo renewable resources had been going down for 50 years. The reservation grew less food and timber, and owned less water in 1980 than in 1930. People lived better because of welfare, government jobs, mines, and off-reservation work, but the land itself was poorer. To change this, Al plans to:

1. *Get more from non-renewable resources.* For years all mines and oil wells on Navajo land were owned by companies that paid the tribe too little because of badly written agreements. More money could be raised by: a) Making companies sign new agreements with higher rates, b) Taxing companies to cover extra costs their operations bring, and c) Having the tribe share ownership of future mines, power plants, etc., so it can also share profits. Some day the tribe may supply its own needs from its own mines and power plants.

2. *Use money from non-renewable resources to improve renewable ones.* With extra money from mines and wells already working, the tribe could improve irrigation, turn tired rangeland into money-making ranches, and build towns and Navajo-owned businesses where people can work and shop without leaving home. Such things can continue long after minerals are gone.

3. *Use non-renewable resources slowly.* Sell only enough to pay for improvements in the land and to help people who really need it. Many nations have spent mineral wealth quickly and ended up poor. Mining Navajo minerals at top speed would give people more money—now. Future generations would have nothing. Improving the land takes time, and mineral wealth should be saved for that purpose.

The tribe should become *self-sufficient*, which means filling our needs with our own hands on our own land without help.

# THE LAW

Clan: *Tsé Níjíkiní*
Born for: *Táchii'nii*

"Decide what you want to do. Then do it."
Claudeen Arthur's father always gave her
that straightforward advice, and in 1974
she became the Navajo Nation's first
woman lawyer.

It wasn't always easy, but whenever she
had trouble with studies or anything else,
she thought about the times her father got
truckloads of stamping horses stuck in
mud up to the axles.

"Sure he got angry," she remembers. "But
he didn't stop to complain. 'All right,' he'd
say. 'Get out! Get the shovel! Find a rope!
Let's get busy!' So we'd get busy. If you're
stuck in the mud, you do what must be
done to get out."

That's how Claudeen faces problems now.

Her father was a maintenance man in
reservation schools. Her mother was a
dorm aide. They worked at Tuba City,
Toadlena, and Shiprock, but also kept
cattle on family land near Crownpoint.

Claudeen met her future husband, Harris
Arthur, in second grade. They went
through school together, graduated from
Navajo Methodist Mission School in
Farmington, New Mexico, and married
sophomore year at New Mexico State University.

Soon Claudeen had a daughter, then a
son, but she didn't stop studying. She
graduated in 1965, found a teaching job,
had a second son, and worked several
years as a teacher and mother.

Then one day she decided she didn't want
to teach all her life. She would be a lawyer.
That meant three more years of school,
and she now had three active children. A
dean of students at one school said,
"Forget the idea. The work is too hard. No
one can be both law student and mother of
three children."

But she had decided what she wanted, so
she went ahead. She finished University
of Arizona Law School in 1974 and became
the first Navajo woman licensed as a
lawyer in Arizona and New Mexico. Since
then she has worked for DNA Legal Services in Shiprock, and as legal advisor to
the secretary of the interior, both in Washington and in Window Rock.

## SELF-DETERMINATION

Claudeen thinks the tribe could use her
father's advice. "We must decide what we
want to do, then do it!" she says. "Our
goal should be *self-determination*, which
means controlling our future ourselves.
That is legally possible *ONLY* if we show
we can do it."

1. *We must USE powers we have over our own
land.* By law, powers Congress hasn't
taken from us are still ours. But if we don't
USE those powers, and if state governments DO, we may lose them.

For example, we can tax companies taking
minerals from the reservation. The Supreme Court recently said we could, but

we must USE that power soon. State governments already tax those companies. Our chance to do it may pass.

We can also make companies obey strict rules to protect our air, land, and water. If we don't make and enforce such rules, however, the states will—and they may not do it as we would like.

2. *We must defend our water by USING it.* The water law of the West says that whoever uses water first keeps the right to use it. The states are already trying to claim power over the water in rivers on the reservation and underground. Whatever we use is less likely to be taken from us. We use it or lose it.

3. *We must make the laws of business work for us.* Past agreements between the tribe and non-Navajos usually gave up control of land and resources in return for money. By law, however, we can do many other things. The tribe can go into business itself, as it did with the tribal sawmill. It can share ownership of a mine or factory. Instead of accepting money, the tribe could be paid in ownership shares, so it will own the business after a period of time. That is all legally possible, if we know the laws.

4. *We must become experts in everything concerning our land.* That means finding out ourselves what coal under our land is worth *before* someone asks to lease it. It means understanding everything said in Washington and state capitals affecting our land.

Now the secretary of interior holds our land "in trust," and we must trust him to protect it. We complain of his power over us, but recently he saved us millions of dollars by changing a coal lease our tribal leaders had approved. They agreed to 8½% royalty payments. He knew more about the high value of coal elsewhere and raised payments to 12½%.

We must develop our own experts if we want "self-determination" instead of "self-extermination!"

*In 1983, Claudeen Arthur was appointed by newly-elected Tribal Chairman Peterson Zah to be Attorney General of the Navajo Nation.*

# FARMS

Clan: *Tsé Deeshgiizhnii*
Born for: *Kin Yaa'áanii*

Byron Huskon was in Germany when Navajo Country called him home. "From the time I went to school at Tuba City, I did everything I could to escape from the reservation," he says now. "When I left for college in California I had no idea I would ever come back.

"In the service I traveled all over, but one day I realized that wherever I went I felt a bit out of place. In 1974 I returned. Home was nice, but there was nothing to do in Cameron chapter. I lived on the silver-

smithing I knew from my grandfather and went to chapter meetings."

The chapter elected Byron to the Community Action Committee. "I had no idea what to do," he says, "but there we were by the Little Colorado River, and people kept saying, 'All this water goes by. How can we grow something with it?'

"The idea grew on me. My family had farmed for generations at Willow Springs below the Echo Cliffs. My grandfather used to say hunger drove others to Fort Sumner, but our family had the farm and escaped. It was our best defense.

"Other chapter officers and our councilman liked the idea, and some people let us use land by the river. BIA officials gave us no help, but our councilman told them, 'Look, Navajos, Hopis, and all kinds of Indians have farmed here. Anasazi were here. We dig up pottery everywhere.'

"We went ahead on our own, but just then United Nuclear Corporation and some others came around looking for uranium. They wanted to lease 80% of the chapter, and everyone began talking about mine work.

"I took it personally. My dad drilled uranium around here 25 years ago from Black Point down to Shadow Mountain. He has cancer now, and people still lose stock in the old pits. We had a meeting. We all said, 'Let's stay out of that. The mines came once and left us nothing. What we make of our own land we keep always.' The farm went ahead."

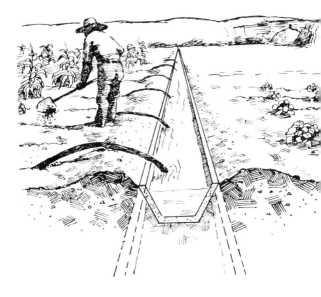

The Little Colorado floods in spring and dries up in summer. Past irrigation dams always washed out, and only traditional crops survived the dry months. However, the people found that shallow wells on the river bank would supply clean water all year from a river under the sand. They drilled wells and planted.

## GETTING THE MOST FROM LAND AND WATER

The Cameron farms were tiny compared to the tribe's huge farm south of Farmington, New Mexico. The tribe hopes

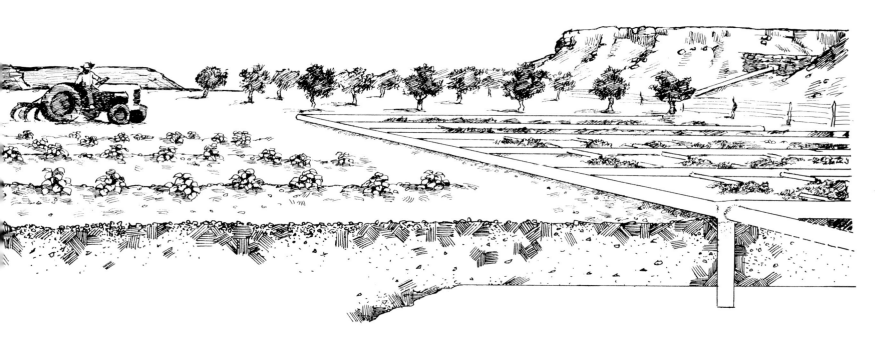

to irrigate 110,000 acres there, making Navajo Agricultural Products Industries one of America's biggest farm businesses. But Cameron caused many to believe that small farms could also become big business.

Before welfare and paying jobs were known in Navajo Country, farms like the Cameron farm existed everywhere. Now as the land becomes more crowded, Byron believes they are needed again. "Land, water, and people are our most important resources," he says, "and most communities have all three. It's up to us to put them together and use them."

1. *Communities should organize and plan the best use of their land and water.* Why should we drive hundreds of miles to town to buy hay and vegetables trucked from Phoenix, if we can grow it all here?

2. *The tribe should use mineral money to help small family farms*—with irrigation, machinery, and advice. Where farming does well the tribe could help people sell what they don't use to local schools, restaurants, and stores.

3. *New ways to farm with less water in harsh conditions should be tried.* Traditional crops and ways of planting work well in Navajo Country. Other countries with dry climates, especially Israel, have also discovered methods that might give Navajo farmers an even bigger choice of crops.

4. *Small farms will help the Navajo Nation protect its water rights.* State governments are already talking of limiting the amount of water the tribe can use each year. The right to use water may depend on what the tribe actually uses at the time limits are set.

The Navajo Irrigation Project south of Farmington will use water, but new canals can't be built without government help. Small farms can start up faster because people already have much of the necessary skill and equipment.

"Now, as in the past, small farms may be our best defense," says Byron, "not only against poverty and hunger, but against attempts to take our land and water."

# RANGELAND

Clan: *Tł'ízí Łání*
Born for: *Táchii'nii*

Leo Beno says it hurts to look at Navajo rangelands when he drives. "These lands are in such bad shape I can't stand it."

But as director of the tribe's department of range conservation, he drives a lot to help communities do something about their tired land.

At chapter and grazing committee meetings, he talks to gray-haired leaders and tough-handed herders, listening to their problems and giving the best advice he can. It is a double life. Back at his office he must handle all the paper work and politics of tribe and BIA. Bringing these two lives together is his goal.

"I finished high school at Intermountain and had no idea what I wanted to do," says Leo. "I could wait to be drafted, hide out at home doing nothing, or go to college. College was the easy way out.

"At Northern Arizona University (NAU), the only thing I could tell my advisor was that I wanted to do something out of doors, so he started me in forestry. I liked it and wanted to become a forester until I took a required course in range management. I was amazed. Here were college professors teaching about things I already knew from my experience as a kid. I transferred from NAU to University of Arizona so I could major in range, and I went straight through the program without any trouble.

"Coming home, however, was a real shock. I got a job doing community work at Chinle, and it took me a while to see that I couldn't just walk up to people and say, 'Hi! You want to try some new range management ideas?' They would probably look at me like a crazy man.

"My father had to tell me how things were. I had to learn who my clan relatives were, and who I was, and how to talk to people. I saw a lot happening around me. Sometimes it was fair and sometimes not, but I learned to be realistic about how things work.

"I have no land myself. My dad's land is very crowded now, and since I went to college, it is understood that I can support myself somehow. But I want to help the land, even though I won't be the one raising stock. As a tribe we can do so much better. I see myself as a developer of people."

## SERIOUS RANCHING

As Leo Beno sees it, stock reduction and the grazing regulations that it brought killed the old way of managing livestock, but put nothing better in its place. Now he sees neighbors fighting over land, herds

**1,000 High Quality Sheep on a "Serious" Ranch**

| | |
|---|---:|
| 1,120 100-pound lambs sold @ 45¢/lb. | $50,400 |
| 10,000 pounds of wool sold @ 45¢/lb. | 4,500 |
| 280 mature sheep sold @ $35 each | 9,800 |
| TOTAL INCOME | $64,700 |
| *Expenses* | |
| 1,000 sheep × 365 days × 4¢/day | 14,600 |
| 1,400 lambs × 180 days × 4¢/day | 10,080 |
| TOTAL EXPENSE | $24,680 |
| PROFIT | $40,020 |

**300 Low Quality Sheep and Goats in 1981**

| | |
|---|---:|
| 5 85-pound lambs sold @ 45¢/lb. | 191 |
| 2,200 pounds wool and mohair | 1,080 |
| 60 mature sheep eaten: value $30 | 1,800 |
| TOTAL INCOME | $ 3,071 |
| *Expenses* | |
| 300 sheep × 365 days × 2¢/day | 2,190 |
| 65 lambs × 180 days × 2¢/day | 234 |
| TOTAL EXPENSE | $ 2,424 |
| PROFIT | $ 647 |

too small to be worth caring for, and no way to handle the needs of a growing nation.

"Many things have caused our grasses to disappear," he says. "We are just drifting along now, waiting for something to happen. As a tribe we held onto our land because we used it. If we can't use it well now, it will be taken from us. Not everyone can be a rancher, but those who are will have to do it *seriously*."

1. *We must bring back the grass.* I believe this can be done without reducing stock. One key is more skillful herding. If families bring small herds together into bigger herds, then keep them moving from one grazing area to another, plants will have a better chance to grow back.

2. *We can have bigger herds and better management by changing the old grazing system.* Now, many family members may each have a permit for a few sheep. Instead, a piece of land could be licensed for one big herd. Family members could own shares in the herd, decide together how to manage it, and share meat, wool, and profit according to their shares.

Members of these "livestock associations" might not even live on the land. They might hire herders to run the ranch. The associations could be any size, but the herd would be managed as one.

3. *Grazing committees in each chapter could keep track of all herd areas.* They could allow another association to rent any unused area. That way the land would be used well, and people who couldn't handle the work could still get an income from their land without giving up the right to use it in the future. When grasslands improve, the grazing committees could allow herds to be increased.

"There are many details to work out," says Leo, "but some communities are already discussing changes. They say, 'We have had enough fights among ourselves over land. Let's change things so it won't be worse for our children.' We can do so much if we start now!"

# FORESTS

Clan: *Táchii'nii*
Born for: *Ta'neeszahnii*

The danger and excitement of the work made Robert W. Billie want to earn his living in the woods. He used to hear his father and brother talk of big trees, high mountains, and bulldozers that often rolled over on the steep slopes.

For 44 years his father worked as a logger for the tribal sawmill, first at Sawmill, Arizona, then at the new mill in Navajo, New Mexico. His brother followed. The two rose at 3:30 to be on the mountain before dawn. As a boy Robert roamed the woods north of Sawmill, hunting small animals with a sling-shot, or often with only his eyes and ears. "I loved nature," he says now.

The woods gave his family everything: firewood, houses, food, herbs and medicines for his grandfather's ceremonies, and of course pay checks from the sawmill. The sawmill was the first successful business owned by the tribe. It gives work to over 400 people, and the tribe uses money from timber for scholarships and other projects.

Robert won a tribal scholarship to Northern Arizona University. "I never studied too hard at Window Rock High," he says. "I wanted to run around the woods and learn from my grandfather. I didn't need school for that. But two sisters went to college, and my dad kept saying the world is changing, and I needed an education to help my people.

"I kept the habit of not studying hard, though, and sophomore year I failed to get into forestry school. I had to decide to give up or start over. I knuckled down and tried again. It took me five years to get a degree that should have taken four."

Forestry school taught Robert how to care for the health of the woods, to decide what can be cut, to help young trees grow, and to direct hunters, herders, and woodcutters so each fills his needs without harming the future of the forest.

He learned all that in school, but he says his grandfather first helped him see how the plants, animals, and people of the forest depend on each other. "He taught that trees are there to use, not to waste," says Robert. "He says that the fir, the

Shimá Nahasdzáán,
*My Mother Earth,*
*I offer you fine pollen.*
*That which grows from you,*
*Trees unharmed in any way,*
*I ask you to mark for me.*
*That which grew from you*
*And now stands strong,*
*I will use for a long time,*
*    my Mother,*
*Strongly as it grew.*

*And now, you, the tree,*
*From your limbs to your bark*
*    to your roots,*
*You were made to be used,*
*And thus I shall use you.*
*You grew well,*
*But you will be chopped.*
*You will not think badly of me,*
*Because I will use you.*
*I will give you pollen,*
*And you will make a home for me.*
*Be happy, standing on all sides*
*Of the home I build.*

pine, the spruce are all living things. They hold water that is necessary for life. He prays before he cuts a tree, and I myself pray when I cut a fir tree at Christmas.

"Respecting living things means using them carefully, taking care of them. My grandfather and father taught that respect. That's what my job is now."

## CARING FOR THE FOREST

The mountain forests of Navajo Country are perhaps the tribe's most important *renewable resource.*

Please accept this prayer,
    all that is Holy.
You, my Mother, please accept this.
I did not abuse what grew from you.
And you that grows, I will use you.
I will not use you carelessly.
As you have grown,
You will grow with me.
Thus I pray for you, my home to be,
From the time you are marked
Until the future.
You will be marked in all ceremonies
I bring to my home.
From this home my prayers
    will be accepted.

—Frank Harvey
Lukachukai

They feed the tribal sawmill that supports the families of workers. The mill in turn makes payments to the tribal government that benefit the whole tribe. But those benefits are small compared to the value of firewood, hogan logs, corral poles, livestock food, wild game, fish, herbs, and other things taken from the mountains. The water held in forest soil supplies streams that irrigate fields below.

All of that depends on the health of trees, but as Robert Billie will say, the Navajo forest is in real danger of disappearing forever. If trees go, soil goes, and a million years may not be time enough to bring it back.

Robert and other members of the tribe's Forestry Department have studied and measured all parts of the forest and found three problems that need answers.

1. *Too few young trees are growing.* In 1980 they found that half the forest could be growing more trees. More trees can be planted, but until that happens, foresters will mark fewer for cutting.

2. *Too much wood is cut wastefully*, especially corral and hogan poles. The foresters can mark enough for all, but when people illegally cut everything in one place, nothing remains for the future.

3. *The forest is over-grazed.* Livestock in summer leave nothing for deer in winter. Hungry animals bite off young pines, which kills them or makes them grow crooked and useless.

"We have written up rules and started planting trees," Robert says. "Our first job is to see that the mill cuts wisely and not too much, but we must also find ways to keep stock away from young trees without making life hard on people who depend on that stock. I have hope. At meetings I say, 'If you want your children and grandchildren to have what you have, we must do something now.' When people understand that, they agree."

257

# RECLAMATION

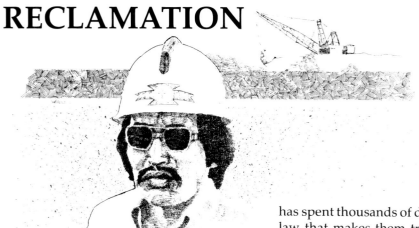

Clan: *Honágháahnii*
Born for: *Kin Yaa'áanii*

In July and August the great summer rain clouds begin boiling up over Navajo Country. Bill Skeet remembers how he waited for them as a boy out herding near Bread Springs south of Gallup. June skies were blue, flat, and empty, but July brought full rich thunderheads, shifting, changing, bringing promise of cool rain— cool rain for plants.

Now in 1981 Bill waits for those clouds at the coal mine near Shiprock, where few plants grow at all except tumbleweed. Once many grew: grasses, bushes, and flowers. That was before the mine. Then the shovels ripped up the ground for coal. Bulldozers covered the pits. Bill was hired to bring back the plants.

Many people still believe it can't be done. The mining company, Utah International, has spent thousands of dollars fighting the law that makes them try, and as little as possible really trying. At first they let the shovels bury good topsoil under tons of blasted rock. Only the law forced them to level the land enough to give plants a chance at all.

Bill studied agriculture in college. "I planned to work on the big Navajo Irrigation Project," he says. "Then I heard about this job, and I thought, 'Here's a chance to do something that's never been done.' "

Other men with degrees in agriculture had planted the mined land before him. They had tried plants from other places: alfalfa and Kentucky bluegrass. Both survived under irrigation but died quickly without it. Wild plants that grew nearby often failed to sprout, or weeds choked them. It looked like the Plant People might stay away forever.

But Bill's family had lived on land like that since the world began. He had a special feeling for that land where others saw only worthless desert. Others had not under-

stood the plant life of Navajo Country. "This is a hard land. You have to be tough to survive," Bill's grandfather used to say.

Bill decided to forget alfalfa and bluegrass and to trust tough Navajo plants. And since Navajo plants were used to waiting for those July storms, he wouldn't irrigate unless the July rain didn't come.

His ideas worked. Most of the weeds came from seeds in the straw used to protect bare ground from the wind. Without irrigation they did not survive long enough to choke the wild plants.

His scientific training told him to doubt everything, to test everything, and to look at

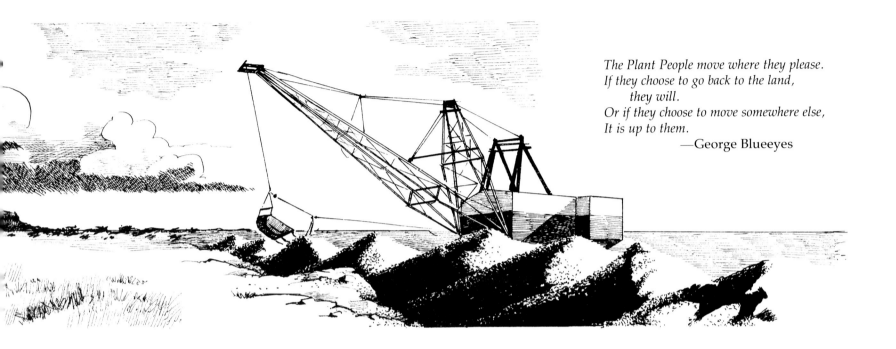

*The Plant People move where they please.*
*If they choose to go back to the land,*
*   they will.*
*Or if they choose to move somewhere else,*
*It is up to them.*
                              —George Blueeyes

all possibilities. After changing the irrigation, he began to peel away other ideas that experts before him had tried. He thought more and more about things he had heard from his elders or seen himself when he was out on his horse with the stock. It made him ask questions others had missed.

*Is fertilizer necessary?* He knew that in nature wild plants are part of the Circle of Life and are fertilized by animal manure and other living things that go back to the soil. Chemical fertilizer without irrigation water can be too strong for young plants. Could he get this Circle of Life started on bare ground without fertilizer?

*How do plants help each other?* He saw that four-wing saltbush grew well on the salty soil. His grandfather had said it belongs with the sheep, and he knew sheep ate it and that grass often sprouted under it, protected from wind and sun. From college he knew about plant communities, "succession," and "interdependence." Could he fit these ideas together and see clearly what to do? Could he explain why sacaton grass started faster than Indian rice grass? Would snakeweed move in?

*How does livestock fit in?* Regulations said he could not put stock on the land because "experts" believed that sheep would kill plants. Bill doubted that. "Sheep belong with the saltbush," his grandfather had said. What about the animal manure? What would sheep do to the weeds?

On his own he let a small herd graze a few days on land taken over by seed from the straw and tumbleweed. At the end of the summer that land looked better than areas that had seen no sheep. Why? What other advice from his elders could be useful?

With these questions in his head, he looks for answers everywhere in the land around him and among the people who live on the land. And he dreams of a time when the small tough plant people may win back the land that miners once destroyed.

259

## MY LAND

*I am sitting outside my hogan.*
*I am thinking,*
*Looking at the red rocks,*
        *the ridges, the sheep,*
        *the plants,*
        *and all in my world.*
*I look at my parents.*
*They are getting old,*
        *weak, and limping.*

*There aren't any of my*
        *sisters and brothers*
        *around.*
*I am thinking*
*What it will be like here*
*In the Future.*

—Thomas Littleben
Grandson of *Hashk'aan Ts'ósí*
10th Grade, Rock Point School

# READING NAVAJO WORDS

Reading Navajo words can be easier than reading English words. Most of the letters sound the same as they do in English. Here are the most important things you need to know to read the Navajo words in this book.

- Navajo VOWELS sound like the vowels in these English words:

Navajo word:

| | | |
|---|---|---|
| a . . . . art | *Gad* | (Juniper) |
| e . . . . met | *Tsé* | (rock) |
| i . . . . it | *Chidí* | (car) |
| o . . . . note | *Hóla* | (I don't know) |

- These double vowels sound the same but are held for a longer time:
aa   ee   oo

| | | |
|---|---|---|
| In English say "beat." | *tó* | (water) |
| Then say "bead." | *atoo'* | (stew) |
| You hang onto the vowel of "bead" longer. | *Hózhóójí* | (Blessing Way Ceremony) |
| | *ná* | (take it) |
| | *anáá'* | (one's eye) |
| | *Iináájí* | (Life Way Ceremony) |

- These double vowels sound different:

| | | |
|---|---|---|
| ii . . . . machine | *Hastiin* | (Mister) |
| ai . . . . kite | *Hai* | (Winter) |
| ei . . . . day | *ajéí* | (Heart) |

- When there is a TONE MARK or ACCENT on a letter, raise your voice on that syllable.

| | |
|---|---|
| *Hóla* | (I don't know) |

- Vowels with HOOKS under them are NASALIZED. That means that breath goes through your nose when you say them.

| | | |
|---|---|---|
| In English, the word *dean* is nasalized; | *ma'ii* | (coyote) |
| The word *deed* is not. | *díí'* | (four) |

- The GLOTTAL STOP (') tells you your voice should STOP before you say the next syllable—just like your voice stops before the second "oh" when you say in English, "Oh Oh!"

| | |
|---|---|
| *só'* | (star) |
| *Biye'* | (his son) |
| *Yá'át'ééh* | (Hello! Good) |

- The letter ł is like the English L, only it is silent. Fix your mouth to say "L," but don't say it. Blow through it.

| | |
|---|---|
| *łíí'* | (horse) |
| *dził* | (mountain) |

- To make the sound "Tł," try to put a t with the silent Ł sound you made above.

| | |
|---|---|
| *tł'ízí* | (goat) |

- *Ni* at the beginning of a Navajo word is read as if there were no "i," like the "nnn" sound in "Ham-(a)n(d)-eggs," or "up-(a)n(d)-down."

| | |
|---|---|
| *nidi* | (but) |
| *nitł'aaí* | (left-handed) |

# BIBLIOGRAPHY

This bibliography is organized by chapter. It includes books, articles, maps, films, and other materials for further study.

Listed first are the most useful and readable materials for students and teachers. Some of these may be difficult to find except in specialized collections. Several excellent libraries in Navajo Country itself do have such collections, however. The Navajo Community College Library in Tsaile, Arizona, the Window Rock Public Library in the Navajo Nation capital, the Gallup Public Library, the University of New Mexico Library in Albuquerque, and the Museum of Northern Arizona in Flagstaff all take professional interest in helping teachers, scholars, and students.

Other materials, including many incidental and technical sources used in preparing each chapter, are listed together following the more general items.

## LAND

*Many interesting types of maps of Navajo Country are available, including the following:*

Automobile Club of Southern California. "Indian Country in Arizona, New Mexico, Utah and Colorado." Los Angeles, 1977.
*This excellent road map of Navajo Country may be ordered by writing the Automobile Club of Southern California, 2601 South Figueroa Street, Los Angeles, California 90007.*

Cooley, M. E.; Harshbarger, J. W.; Akers, J. P.; and Hardt, W. F. "Regional Hydrogeology of the Navajo and Hopi Indian Reservations, Arizona, New Mexico, and Utah." U.S. Geological Survey Professional Paper 521-A. Washington, D.C.: Government Printing Office, 1969.
*Includes a set of eight full-color geologic wall maps of the Navajo Reservation, along with maps showing information on geography, climate, vegetation, and water.*

Goodman, James M. *Navajo Atlas: Environments, Resources, People, and History of the Diné Bikéyah.* Norman: University of Oklahoma Press. (In press.)
*A comprehensive collection of maps of Navajo Country, showing plants, soils, population, mineral resources, renewable resources, political boundaries, and more.*

Holliday, Babette; Diné, Inc.; and Rough Rock Demonstration School. "Navajo Reservation Map and Index." Rough Rock, Arizona: Navajo Curriculum Center, Rough Rock Demonstration School, n.d.
*A map of the Navajo Reservation, with place names in Navajo and English.*

*Photos taken by satellite, U-2 high-altitude planes, and even more detailed photos used for map making are available from:*

User Services
EROS DATA CENTER
U.S. Geological Survey
Sioux Falls, South Dakota 57198
Phone: 605/594-6511
*The many kinds, sizes, and prices of these photos is confusing, but a phone call will get you expert advice. Generally, the satellite pictures cover 75-mile squares in rough detail. The mapping photos cover small areas and show fences, foot paths, and even people. Before calling EROS for satellite pictures, know the boundaries of the area by latitude and longitude, and the time of year you want (think of snow, plant life, farming, etc.). For mapping photos, know the latitude and longitude of the point you wish.*

*Names in Navajo and English of many places and land forms in Navajo Country may be found in:*

Austin, Martha A., ed. *Saad Ahgąh Sinil: Dual Language Dictionary.* Rough Rock, Arizona: Navajo Curriculum Center, Rough Rock Demonstration School, 1972.

Franciscan Fathers. *An Ethnologic Dictionary of the Navajo Language.* St. Michaels, Arizona: The Franciscan Fathers, 1910.

Van Valkenburgh, Richard F. *Diné Bikéyah.* Window Rock, Arizona: U.S. Dept. of Interior, Bureau of Indian Affairs, 1941.

*Photographs and comments on many Navajo sacred places, along with their names in Navajo and English, may be found in:*

Van Valkenburgh, Richard F. *Navajo Sacred Places.* Navajo Indians, 3, Garland American Indian Ethnohistory Series. New York: Garland Publishing Inc., 1974.

*A beautifully illustrated edition of the Navajo origin stories for young people is:*

Yazzie, Ethelou, ed. *Navajo History,* vol. 1. Rough Rock, Arizona: Rough Rock Demonstration School, 1971.

*Navajo medicine men and elders tell traditional stories of the sacred mountains and the boundaries of Navajo Country in:*

Tsosie, Tony, with Robert W. Young and William Morgan. *Diné Bikéyah #39; Diné Bikéyah. (Navajo Land Series #39: Old Stories of Navajo Land.)* Albuquerque: Navajo Reading Study, University of New Mexico, 1975. *(In Navajo only.)*

Young, Robert W. and Morgan, William. *Navajo Historical Selections.* Phoenix: U.S. Dept. of Interior Bureau of Indian Affairs, 1954. *English:* pp. 10–17; *Navajo:* pp. 86–92.

*A Navajo explains the traditional relationship between Navajos and the land in:*

Begay, Jimmie C. "The Relationship between People and the Land." Paper prepared for the Institute for Indian Studies Spring Conference, April 19–21, 1979, University of South Dakota. Reprinted in the *Rough Rock News,* May 15, 1979.

*A Navajo story of how high desert was formed, as well as Hopi, Ute, Paiute, and Hualapai stories of the land, may be found in:*

Trimble, Stephen, ed. "Stories from the Land." *Plateau* 53 no. 2 (1981).

*An excellent geology text which uses aerial photographs to illustrate clear explanations of common land forms, including many in Navajo Country, is:*

Shelton, John S. *Geology Illustrated.* San Francisco: W. H. Freeman & Co., 1966.

*Other sources used in preparing this chapter are:*

Brugge, David M. "Navajo and Western Pueblo History." *The Smoke Signal,* no. 25 (1972), pp. 90–112.

Carter, George F. *Man and the Land: A Cultural Geography.* 2nd edition. New York: Holt, Rinehart & Winston, 1968.

Gregory, Herbert E. "The Navajo Country: A Geographic and Hydrographic Reconnaissance of Parts of Arizona, New Mexico and Utah." U.S. Geological Survey, Water Supply Paper 380. Washington, D.C.: Government Printing Office, 1916.

Mitchell, Frank. "Version II." In *Blessingway,* edited by Leland C. Wyman. Tucson: University of Arizona Press, 1975, p. 397.

## PLANT WATCHERS

*Lists of Navajo Country plants in Navajo and English may be found in:*

Austin, Martha A. *Saad Ahąąh Sinil: Dual Language Dictionary.* Rough Rock, Arizona; Navajo Curriculum Center, Rough Rock Demonstration School, 1972.

Bryan, Nonabah G. *Navajo Native Dyes: Their Preparation and Use.* Palmer Lake, Colorado: The Filter Press, 1978.
    *Lists plants used in the making of Navajo rug dyes.*

Elmore, Francis H. *Ethnobotany of the Navajo.* University of New Mexico Bulletin no. 392. Albuquerque: University of New Mexico Press, 1943.
    *By far the most comprehensive list of Navajo Country plants, with names in Navajo and English, scientific names, and a summary of some of their traditional uses. Non-standard spelling system is used for Navajo words.*

Parrill, Frank, and Blacksheep, Allan H. *Navajo Nation Range Management Handbook.* Tucson: University of Arizona Cooperative Extension Service, 1981.
    *Lists common range plants, with Navajo, English, and scientific names.*

*Several illustrated guides useful for identifying plants in Navajo Country are available from the Southwest Parks and Monuments Association, P. O. Box 1562, Globe, Arizona 85501:*

Dodge, Natt N. *100 Roadside Wildflowers of the Southwest Uplands,* 1967.

Elmore, Francis H. *Shrubs and Trees of the Southwest Uplands,* 1976.

Patraw, Pauline M. *Flowers of the Southwest Mesas,* 1953.

*Stories of how wild plants were traditionally gathered and prepared are told by Mrs. Bob Martin and Tom Ration in:*

Johnson, Broderick H., ed. *Stories of Traditional Navajo Life and Culture.* Tsaile, Arizona: Navajo Community College Press, 1977. pp. 120–29; 299–302.

*For two simple and nicely illustrated booklets on ecology, write:*

National Audubon Society, 950 Third Avenue, New York, N.Y. 10022. Ask for *Ecosystems* and *The Story of Ecology* (with Leader's Guide).

*Some scholarly sources used in preparing this chapter are:*

Bohrer, Vorsila L. "A Non-Palynological Method of Reconstructing Vegetation on the Heavily Overgrazed Puerco Valley." Paper presented at the 43rd annual Society of American Archeology Meeting, Tucson, Arizona, May 4–6, 1978. Mimeographed.

———. "Plants that have become Locally Extinct in the Southwest." *New Mexico Journal of Science* 18, no. 2 (December 1978): 10–18.

———. "The Prehistoric and Historic Role of the Cool-Season Grasses in the Southwest." *Economic Botany* 29 (July–Sept. 1975): 199–207.

Dawes, Maggie, Navajo plant specialist from Fort Defiance–Mexican Springs. Interview at Rock Point and Lukachukai, August 14, 1979.

Harlan, Annita S. and Dennis, Arthur E. "The Wild Plant Remains." *Kiva* 41, no. 1 (1975): 7–14.

Mayes, Vernon, range management instructor, College of Ganado. Interview at Rock Point and Lukachukai, August 14, 1979.

Savory, Allan, consultant ecologist, S.G.M. Range Consultants, Albuquerque, New Mexico. Interview at Rock Point, July 14, 1981.

Schmutz, Ervin M.; Dennis, Arthur E.; Harlan, Annita; Hendricks, David; and Zauderer, Jeffrey. "An Ecological Survey of Wide Rock Butte in Canyon de Chelly National Monument, Arizona." *Arizona Academy of Science* 2, no. 3 (October 1976): 114–25.

Struever, Mary B. "Relation of Pollen and Flotation Analyses to Archeological Excavations, Chaco Canyon." Thesis, University of New Mexico, 1977.

Turk, Amos; Wittes, Janet T.; Turk, Jonathan; and Wittes, Robert E. *Environmental Science.* Philadelphia: W. B. Saunders Co., 1978. pp. 35–67, 77, 78, 88, 93.

## HUNTERS

*A colorful time line showing mammoths, bison, ground sloths, western horses, and other animals that have lived and then become extinct during the last 38,000 years is:*

George C. Page Museum. "The La Brea Story and the History of Man." Los Angeles: Los Angeles County Museum of Natural History, 1977.

*A clear, well-illustrated article on early man in the Americas from the point of view of modern non-Indian archaeologists is:*

Canby, Thomas Y. "The Search for the First Americans." *National Geographic* 156, no. 3 (September 1979): 330–63.

*Drawings and descriptions of the animals living today in and around Navajo Country may be found in:*

Olin, George. *Mammals of the Southwest Mountains and Mesas.* Popular Series no. 9. Globe, Arizona: Southwest Parks and Monuments Association, 1961.

*Son of Old Man Hat describes a hunting trip in:*

Dyk, Walter, and Dyk, Ruth, eds. *Left Handed: A Navajo Autobiography.* New York: Columbia University Press, 1980. pp. 19–42.

*Some scholarly sources used in preparing this chapter are:*

Agenbroad, Larry D. "The Distribution of Fluted Points in Arizona." *Kiva* 32, no. 4 (April 1967): 113–20.

Alexander, George. "On the Trail of Man in the Americas: How Far Back Does He Go?" *Los Angeles Times,* November 29, 1976.

Ayres, James E. "A Clovis Fluted Point from the Kayenta, Arizona Area." *Plateau* 38, no. 4 (Spring, 1966): 76–78.

Bartlett, Katharine. "A Primitive Stone Industry of the Little Colorado Valley, Arizona." *American Antiquity* 8, no. 3 (1943): 266–68.

Campbell, John Martin, chief curator of collections and research, Maxwell Museum of Anthropology; and professor of Anthropology, University of New Mexico, Albuquerque. Interview in Albuquerque on the prehistoric range of bighorn sheep, February, 1979.

Danson, Edward B. "Early Man Points from the Vicinity of Sanders, Arizona." *Plateau* 34, no. 2 (October 1961): 67–68.

Goodman, Jeffrey. *American Genesis: The American Indian and the Origins of Modern Man.* New York: Summit Books, 1981.

Gumerman, George J. "A Folsom Point from the Area of Mishongnovi, Arizona." *Plateau* 38, no. 4 (Spring 1966): 79–80.

Jennings, Jesse D. *Ancient Native Americans.* San Francisco: W. H. Freeman & Co., 1978. pp. 23–27.

Kelley, James E. "Zooarchaeological Analysis at Antelope House: Behavioral Inferences from Distribution Data." *Kiva* 41, no. 1 (1975): 81–83.

Luckert, Karl W. *A Navajo Bringing Home Ceremony: The Claus Chee Sonny Version of Deerway Ajiłee.* Flagstaff: Museum of Northern Arizona Press, 1978.

———. *The Navajo Hunter Tradition.* Tucson: University of Arizona Press, 1975.

Martin, Paul S. and Plog, Fred. *The Archaeology of Arizona: A Study of the Southwest Region.* Garden City, N.Y.: Doubleday/Natural History Press, 1973.

McNitt, Frank. *Navajo Wars: Military Campaigns, Slave Raids, and Reprisals.* Albuquerque: University of New Mexico Press, 1972. p. 412, n. 2.

Reichard, Gladys A. *Navaho Religion: A Study of Symbolism.* Bollingen Series no. 18. Princeton: Princeton University Press, 1963. pp. 443–45.

Walker, Michael Thomas. "Ecological Similarities Between Feral Burros and Desert Bighorn Sheep, Black Mountains, Northwestern Arizona." Masters Thesis, Arizona State University, 1978.

Willey, Gordon R. *An Introduction to American Archaeology, Volume I: North and Middle America.* Englewood Cliffs, N.J.: Prentice-Hall, Inc., 1966. pp. 29–33; 37–43; 72–74.

## ANASAZI

*For another version of the story of the Great Gambler, read Tom Ration's account on pages 316–18 in:*

Johnson, Broderick H., ed. *Stories of Traditional Navajo Life and Culture.* Tsaile, Arizona: Navajo Community College Press, 1977.

*Four books with clear text and large color photographs of Anasazi ruins, pottery, jewelry, and other artifacts are:*

Ambler, Richard J. *The Anasazi: Prehistoric People of the Four Corners Region.* Photos by Marc Gaede. Flagstaff: Museum of Northern Arizona, 1977.

Anderson, Douglas and Barbara. *Chaco Canyon.* Globe, Arizona: Southwest Parks and Monuments Association, 1976.

Jacka, Jerry D. and Hammack, Nancy S. *Indian Jewelry of the Prehistoric Southwest.* Tucson: University of Arizona Press, 1975.

Pike, Donald G. *Anasazi: Ancient People of the Rock.* Photos by David Muench. Palo Alto, California: American West Publishing Co., 1974.

*A clear, easy-to-read summary of recent archaeological findings in Chaco Canyon is:*

Earley, Frank Lee. *Chaco Canyon.* Museum Study Series no. 2. Chaco Canyon National Monument, n.d.

*The following films on the Anasazi are available from the Audio-visual Department, Library, Navajo Community College, Tsaile, Arizona 86556. Phone 602/724-6132.*

*Chaco Legacy, The* (1980), 16mm Film Optical Sound, Color, 60 min., Public Broadcasting Associates (PR), Dist.: Documentary Educational Resources, Cambridge, Mass.
*The story of Chaco Canyon, as it is being pieced together by archaeologists; covers recent discoveries of irrigation systems, roads, and evidence of an extensive trading network.*

*In Search of a City* (1964), 16mm Film Optical Sound, Color, 9 min., National Educational Television (PR), Dist.: Indiana University.
*Archaeologists excavate, map, and record their discoveries in ancient cliff dwellings at Mesa Verde, Colorado.*

*Mystery of the Anasazi, The* (1974), Nova Series, ¾-inch Video Cassette, Color, 59 min., WGBH-TV, Boston (PR), Dist.: Public Television Library.
*Story of the search for clues to the mystery of the Anasazi.*

*Southwest Indians of Early America* (1973), 16mm Film Optical Sound, Color, 14 min., Coronet Films (PR), Dist.: Coronet Films.
*Dramatization of how the early Anasazi might have lived.*

*Sticks and Stones Will Build a House* (1971), 16mm Film Optical Sound, Color, 30 min., KEUD-TV (PR), Dist.: Indiana University.
*Traces the development of early Southwestern Indian architecture, from pit-house through apartment complex housing.*

*Stone Age Americans* (1970), 16mm Film Optical Sound, Color, 21 min., ABC-TV (PR), Dist.: International Film Bureau.
*Story of the farmers and cliff dwellers of Mesa Verde, as it is being pieced together by archaeologists.*

*Some scholarly sources used in preparing this chapter are:*

Bennett, Edna Mae. *Turquoise and the Indian.* Denver: Sage Books, 1966. pp. 41; 107.

Brugge, David M. *A History of the Chaco Navajos.* Albuquerque: U.S. Dept. of the Interior, National Park Service, 1980.

DiPeso, Charles C. *Casas Grandes: A Fallen Trading Center of the Gran Chichimeca.* 8 vols. Flagstaff: Northland Press, 1974.

Franciscan Fathers. *An Ethnologic Dictionary of the Navaho Language.* Saint Michaels, Arizona: Saint Michaels Press, 1910.

Gillespie, Bill, staff archeologist, Chaco Center, National Park Service, Albuquerque, New Mexico. On-site interviews at Chaco Canyon National Monument, September 16–17, 1979.

Grebinger, Paul. "Prehistoric Social Organization in Chaco Canyon, New Mexico: An Alternative Reconstruction." *Kiva* 39, no. 1 (1973): 3–23.

Jett, Stephen C. "Pueblo Indian Migrations: An Evaluation of the Possible Physical and Cultural Determinants." *American Antiquity* 29, no. 3 (January 1964): 281–300.

Judd, Neil M. *The Material Culture of Pueblo Bonito.* Smithsonian Miscellaneous Collections, vol. 124. Washington, D.C., 1954.

Judge, James W. "The Development of a Complex Cultural Ecosystem in the Chaco Basin, New Mexico." Paper submitted to the First Conference on Scientific Research in the National Parks, New Orleans, Louisiana, November 9–13, 1976. Xeroxed.

———. "The Emergence of Complexity in Chaco Canyon, New Mexico." Symposium Paper, 76th annual meeting of the American Anthropological Association, Houston, Texas, December 1, 1977. Xeroxed.

O'Bryan, Aileen. "The Story of Noqoilpi, the Great Gambler." In *The Dine: Origin Myths of the Navajo Indians,* pp. 48–62. Smithsonian Institution, Bureau of American Ethnography Bulletin no. 163. Washington, D.C., 1956.

Powers, Robert P. et al. *The Outlier: A Regional View of Settlement in the San Juan Basin.* Albuquerque: National Parks Service Chaco Center, n.d. Unpublished.

Schumm, S. A. and Chorley, R. J. *The Fall of Threatening Rock.* Denver: U.S. Dept. of Interior Geological Survey, 1964.

Vivian, R. Gwinn; Dodgen, Dulce N.; and Hartmann, Gayle H. *Wooden Ritual Artifacts from Chaco Canyon, New Mexico: The Chetro Ketl Collection.* Tucson: University of Arizona Press, 1978.

## ANCESTORS

*A beautifully illustrated edition of the Navajo origin stories for young people, including an account of the first four clans, is:*

Yazzie, Ethelou, ed. *Navajo History, vol. 1.* Rough Rock, Arizona: Rough Rock Demonstration School, 1971.

*Some stories on the origin of various Navajo clans may be found in:*

Aronilth, Wilson Jr., "The Clan System." In *Diné Culture Instruction Handbook.* Rock Point, Arizona: Rock Point Community School. Xerox.

Brugge, David M. "Events in Navajo History No. 14: Origin of the *Ma'iidesgizhnii* Clan." *Navajo Times,* June 9, 1966.

———. "Events in Navajo History No. 16: Origin of the *Nakaidine'e* and *Toyahedliin* Clans." *Navajo Times,* September 8, 1966.

Mitchell, Frank. *Navajo Blessingway Singer: The Autobiography of Frank Mitchell, 1881–1967.* Edited by Charlotte J. Frisbie and David P. McAllester. Tucson: University of Arizona Press, 1978. pp. 17; 168–91.
*How some of the first clans originated and were named.*

———. "Version II." In *Blessingway.* Edited by Leland C. Wyman. Tucson: University of Arizona Press, 1975. pp. 458–59.
*Naming of first clans.*

Preston, Scott. "The Clans." In *Navajo Historical Selections.* Edited by Robert W. Young and William Morgan. Phoenix: U.S. Dept. of Interior Bureau of Indian Affairs, 1954. *English:* pp. 23–27. *Navajo:* pp. 98–101.

Sandoval, Albert Sr. "The Different Navajo Clans." In *Navajo Historical Selections. English:* pp. 20–22. *Navajo:* pp. 95–97.

Sapir, Edward. *Navajo Texts.* Edited by Harry Hoijer. William Dwight Whitney Linguistic Series. Iowa City: Linguistic Society of America, 1942.
*Includes a story of the original Navajo clans, and origin stories of the Honágháahnii, Tó'aheedlíinii, and Salt Clans. In Navajo and English. Difficult to read due to non-standard Navajo spelling and literal English translation.*

Slim Curly. "About the Origin of Other People." In *Blessingway.* Edited by Leland C. Wyman. Tucson: University of Arizona Press, 1975. pp. 327–34.

*Clan stories by Scott Preston and Albert Sandoval Sr. have been published in Navajo only:*

Preston, Scott. *Diné Bikéyah #17—Ał'ąą Dadine'é.* (Navajo Land Series #17–The Clans.) Albuquerque: Navajo Reading Study, University of New Mexico, 1973.

Sandoval, Chic. *Diné Bikéyah #16—Naabeehó Ał'ąą Dadine'íi.* (Navajo Land Series #16—The Different Navajo Clans.) Albuquerque: Navajo Reading Study, University of New Mexico, 1973.

*A large wall map of North American Indian languages is:*

Voegelin, C. F. and F. M., compilers. "Map of North American Indian Languages." American Ethnological Society, 1966.

*Other sources used in preparing this chapter are:*

Brugge, David M. "Navajo and Western Pueblo History." *The Smoke Signal,* no. 25 (1972), pp. 90–112.

Jett, Stephen C. "Pueblo Indian Migrations: An Evaluation of the Possible Physical and Cultural Determinants." *American Antiquity* 29, no. 3 (January 1964): 281–300.

Matthews, Washington. *The Mountain Chant.* Fifth Annual Report of the Bureau of American Ethnology (1883–84) of the Smithsonian Institution (1887). Reprint. Glorieta, New Mexico: Rio Grande Press, 1970.

Mitchell, Barney. "Children of the Gods." Shiprock, New Mexico. Xerox.

Valkenburgh, Richard F. *Diné Bikéyah.* Window Rock: U.S. Dept. of Interior Office of Indian Affairs, 1941.

Young, Robert W. and Morgan, William. *The Navajo Language: A Grammar and Colloquial Dictionary.* Albuquerque: University of New Mexico Press, 1980.

## SPANIARDS

*The story of the 1680 Pueblo Indian Revolt may be found in:*

Sando, Joe. *The Pueblo Indians.* San Francisco: The Indian Historian Press, 1976.

———. "The Story of the Pueblo Revolt." In *Tricentennial Commemoration of the Pueblo Indian Revolt, 1680–1980.* San Juan Pueblo, New Mexico: All Indian Pueblo Council Tricentennial Commission, 1980.

*For an account of the August, 1980 run celebrating the tricentennial of the Pueblo Indian Revolt, see:*

Nabokov, Peter. *Indian Running.* Santa Barbara: Capra Press, 1981.

*A richly illustrated history of Spanish New Mexico from the perspective of Pecos Pueblo is:*

Kessell, John L. *Kiva, Cross, and Crown: The Pecos Indians and New Mexico, 1540–1840.* U.S. Dept. of Interior, National Park Service. Washington, D.C.: Government Printing Office, 1979.
*In ordering, mention the stock number: #024-005-00737-7.*

*Some books which tell the history of early contact between Spaniards and Indians in the Southwest are:*

Forbes, Jack. *Apache, Navajo and Spaniard.* Norman: University of Oklahoma Press, 1960.

Horgan, Paul. *Centuries of Santa Fe.* New York: Dutton, 1956.

———. *Great River: The Rio Grande and North American History.* Vol. 1. Rivers of America Series. New York: Rinehart, 1954.

Jenkins, Myra Ellen, and Schroeder, Albert H. *A Brief History of New Mexico.* Albuquerque: University of New Mexico Press, 1974.

Simmons, Marc. *New Mexico: A Bicentennial History.* New York: Norton, 1977.

Spicer, Edward H. *Cycles of Conquest: The Impact of Spain, Mexico, and the United States on the Indians of the Southwest, 1533–1960.* Tucson: University of Arizona Press, 1962.

The main story in this chapter is based on facts documented in:

Correll, J. Lee. *Through White Men's Eyes: A Contribution to Navajo History. A Chronological Record of the Navajo People from Earliest Times to the Treaty of June 1, 1868.* 6 vols. Window Rock, Arizona: Navajo Heritage Center, 1979. 1:34–40.

de Vargas, Diego. Report to Viceroy Conde de Galve, Santa Fe, Sept. 1, 1694. Archivo General de la Nación. *Historia*, 37, 249–52. Photocopy in the Coronado Library of the University of New Mexico, Albuquerque, New Mexico. Translated by John L. Kessell.

Espinosa, J. Manuel. *Crusaders of the Rio Grande: The Story of Don Diego de Vargas and the Reconquest and Refounding of New Mexico.* Chicago: Institute of Jesuit History, 1942. pp. 199–205.

Hackett, Charles W., ed. *Historical Documents Relating to New Mexico, Nueva Vizcaya, and Approaches Thereto, to 1773.* vol. 3. Washington, D.C.: Carnegie Institute, 1937. pp. 131–35, 156, 162, 186–93, 216, 282.

Scholes, France V. "Civil Government and Society in New Mexico in the 17th Century." *New Mexico Historical Review* 10, no. 2 (April, 1935): 81, 85.

———. "The Supply Service of the New Mexican Missions in the Seventeenth Century Part II: 1631–1664." *New Mexico Historical Review* 5 (1930): 186–210.

———. "Troublous Times in New Mexico, 1659–1670: The Holy Office Tries Don Bernardo López de Mendizábal and Dona Teresa de Aguilera y Roche." *New Mexico Historical Review* 15 (October 1940): 369–417.

Other sources used in preparing this chapter are:

Aronilth, Wilson Jr. "The Origin of Livestock." Taped speech given at Grazing Seminar, Rock Point Community School, Rock Point, Arizona, July 14, 1981.

Bakewell, Peter John, visiting assistant professor of history, University of New Mexico, Albuquerque. Interview on the economics of 17th-century Spanish silver-mining, Albuquerque, February, 1979.

Brugge, David M. "Events in Navajo History No. 14: Origin of the *Ma'iidesgizhnii* Clan." *Navajo Times*, June 9, 1966.

Findley, James S; Harris, Arthur H.; Wilson, Don E.; and Jones, Clyde. *Mammals of New Mexico.* Al-

buquerque: University of New Mexico Press, 1975. p. 337.

George C. Page Museum. "The La Brea Story and the History of Man." Los Angeles: Los Angeles County Museum of Natural History, 1977.

Hallenbeck, Cleve. *Land of the Conquistadores.* Caldwell, Idaho: Caxton Printers, 1950.

Heyerdahl, Thor. *Early Man and the Ocean: A Search for the Beginnings of Navigation and Seaborne Civilizations.* New York: Vintage Books, 1978. pp. 76–78.

Kemp, Capt. Donald C. *Quicksilver to Bar Silver: Tales of Mexico's Silver Bonanzas.* Pasadena, California: Socio Technical Publications, 1972. pp. 151, 152.

Kessell, John L., research historian on the Spanish Southwest, and editor of *The Journals of Diego de Vargas.* Interviews in Albuquerque, New Mexico, February, 1979.

Robinson, T. W. "Introduction, Spread and Areal Extent of Saltcedar (Tamarix) in the Western States." Geological Survey Professional Paper 491-A. Washington, D.C.: Government Printing Office, 1965.

West, Robert C. "The Mining Community in Northern New Spain: The Parral Mining District." *Ibero Americana,* no. 30. Berkeley and Los Angeles: University of California Press, 1949.

Young, Otis E. Jr. *Western Mining: An Informal Account of Precious-Metals Prospecting, Placering, Lode Mining, and Milling on the American Frontier from Spanish Times to 1893.* Norman: University of Oklahoma Press, 1970.

## WAR AND RESERVATION

Two books with numerous large black-and-white photographs of Navajos during the Fort Sumner years are:

Link, Martin A. *Navajo: A Century of Progress—1868–1968.* Window Rock, Arizona: The Navajo Tribe, 1968.

Roessel, Robert A. Jr. *Pictorial History of the Navajo.* Rough Rock, Arizona: Navajo Curriculum Center, Rough Rock Demonstration School, 1980.

Tales by Navajo elders of raiding and warfare between Navajos, Utes, Hopis, Apaches, Mexicans, Americans, and others may be found in:

Roessel, Ruth, ed. *Navajo Stories of the Long Walk Period.* Tsaile, Arizona: Navajo Community College Press, 1973.

Tales by Zuni elders of raids, gambling, and trade between Navajos and Zunis may be found in:

Zuni People. *The Zunis: Self-Portrayals.* Translated by Alvina Quam. Albuquerque: University of New Mexico Press, 1972.

A tale of a Navajo raid on the Hopis, written in Navajo and English, is:

Preston, Scott. "The Oraibi Massacre." In *Navajo Historical Selections,* edited by Robert W. Young and William Morgan. Navajo Historical Series no. 3. Phoenix: U.S. Department of Interior, Bureau of Indian Affairs, 1954.
The same story is available in Navajo only. See below.

Tales of raiding and warfare between Navajos and Mexicans from a Mexican point of view are told in:

Simmons, Marc. *The Fighting Settlers of Seboyeta.* New Mexico: San Marcos Press, 1971.

———. *The Little Lion of the Southwest.* Chicago: Sage Books, 1973.

———. *Taos to Tomé: True Tales of Hispanic New Mexico.* Albuquerque: Adobe Press, 1978.

Compare the story "Capture by Mexicans" with two other stories of Navajo heroines who were captured by Mexicans in the 1860s:

The story by Ch'ahádiniini' Binálí, pp. 57–74 in *Navajo Stories of the Long Walk Period.*

The story of Raggedy Lady, told by Ruth Roessel, pp. 137–47 in her book, *Women in Navajo Society.* Rough Rock, Arizona: Navajo Resource Center, Rough Rock Demonstration School, 1981.

The story "Capture by Mexicans" is available in Navajo:

Jim, Emma Lee. *Naakaitahgoo Tazhdiiya: Asdzą́ą́ Atsidí Baa Hane'.* (*Capture by the Mexicans: The Story of Asdzą́ą́ Atsidí.*) Edited by Rex Lee Jim. Rock Point, Arizona: Rock Point Community School, 1981.

Some other stories written in Navajo about the Long Walk period are:

Mitchell, Charlie and Benny Hale. *Ałk'idą́ą́' Ádahóót'įįdii Bééhániihígíí Baa Hane'.* (*Memories of Old Stories.*) Albuquerque: Navajo Reading Study, University of New Mexico, 1974.

Preston, Scott. *Diné Bikéyah #18—Ałk'idą́ą́' Oozéí Ásdįįd Jiní.* (*Navajo Land Series #18—The Oraibi Massacre.*) Albuquerque: Navajo Reading Study, University of New Mexico, 1973.

Rock Point Bilingual Education Project Title VII. *Diné Nóóda'í Yił Anada'ahijishchįįgi. (War Between the Navajos and the Utes.)* Rock Point, Arizona, 1977.

*Biographies of eight early Navajo leaders, Narbona, Antonio Cebolla Sandoval, Zarcillos Largos, Manuelito, Barboncito, Ganado Mucho, Jesus Arviso, and Henry Chee Dodge, may be found in:*

Hoffman, Virginia. *Navajo Biographies, Vol. 1.* Rough Rock, Arizona: Rough Rock Demonstration School, 1974.

*For the complete text of the 1868 Treaty, see:*

*Treaty Between the United States of America and the Navajo Tribe of Indians, with a record of the discussions that led to its signing.* Las Vegas, Nevada: KC Publications, 1968.

*A sequence of maps detailing the growth of the Navajo Reservation may be found in:*

Correll, J. Lee and Alfred Dehiya. *Anatomy of the Navajo Indian Reservation: How It Grew.* Revised edition. Window Rock, Arizona: The Navajo Times Publishing Co., 1978. *Written in English.*

Native American Materials Development Center. *Diné Bikéyah (Navajo Land).* Albuquerque, 1976. *Written in Navajo.*

*Several books contain detailed historical accounts of the Long Walk era, including:*

Bailey, L. R. *Bosque Redondo—An American Concentration Camp.* Pasadena: Socio-Technical Books, 1970.

———. *The Long Walk—A History of the Navajo Wars, 1846–68.* Pasadena: Socio-Technical Books, 1970.

Brown, Dee. "The Long Walk of the Navahos." In *Bury My Heart at Wounded Knee,* pp. 13–36. New York: Holt, Rinehart & Winston, 1970.

McNitt, Frank. *Navajo Wars: Military Campaigns, Slave Raids, and Reprisals.* Albuquerque: University of New Mexico Press, 1972.

Thompson, Gerald. *The Army and the Navajo: The Bosque Redondo Reservation Experiment, 1863–1868.* Tucson: University of Arizona Press, 1976.

Trafzer, Clifford Earl. *Anglo Expansionists and Navajo Raiders; A Conflict of Interests.* Historical Monograph no. 3. Tsaile, Arizona: Navajo Community College Press, 1978.

———. *Diné and Bilagáana: The Navajos and the First Anglos.* Historical Monograph no. 2. Tsaile, Arizona: Navajo Community College Press, 1978.

———. *Navajos and Spaniards.* Historical monograph no. 3. Tsaile, Arizona: Navajo Community College Press, 1978.

Underhill, Ruth M. *The Navajos.* Norman: University of Oklahoma Press, 1956.

Young, Robert W. *The Role of the Navajo in the Southwestern Drama.* Gallup, New Mexico: The Gallup Independent, 1968.

*For more information on Gen. James Carleton's plans to clear Navajo Country of Navajos so Americans could mine gold, and for other interesting commentary, see:*

Roessel, Robert A. Jr. *Pictorial History of the Navajo.* Rough Rock, Arizona: Navajo Curriculum Center, Rough Rock Demonstration School, 1980.

U.S. Congress, Joint Special Committee appointed under Joint Resolution of March 3, 1865. *Condition of the Indian Tribes.* Washington, D.C.: Government Printing Office, 1867. pp. 98, 110, 114, 116, 122, 333.

Young, Robert W. *A Political History of the Navajo Tribe.* Tsaile, Arizona: Navajo Community College Press, 1978, pp. 33–36.

*For historical documentation of the presence of U.S. Army troops near Rock Point, Arizona in 1860, see:*

Brugge, David M. "Events in Navajo History No. 6: Inscriptions Near Rock Point." *Navajo Times,* March 31, 1966.

*Documents, letters, and other accounts relating to Navajo history from Spanish contact through the Fort Sumner period are presented chronologically in:*

Correll, J. Lee. *Through White Men's Eyes: A Contribution to Navajo History. A Chronological Record of the Navajo People from Earliest Times to the Treaty of June 1, 1868.* 6 vols. Window Rock, Arizona: Navajo Heritage Center, 1979.

*The story of Chee Dodge's purchase of the land at Tanner Springs was told by his son Tom Dodge in an interview at his home in Scottsdale, Arizona, March 12, 1976. Other background on the episode comes from:*

Valkenburgh, Richard F. *Diné Bikéyah. (The Navajo Country.)* Window Rock, Arizona: U.S. Department of Interior, Office of Indian Affairs, 1941. p. 154.

*Two maps used in the preparation of this chapter are:*

U.S. Dept. of Interior, Bureau of Land Management. "Surface Minerals Management Color Quadran-

gles; Pueblo Pintado NW-13." Revised April 1977. Santa Fe, New Mexico.

U.S. Dept. of Interior, Geological Survey. "Federal Lands: Principal Lands Administered or Held in Trust by Federal Agencies: January 1, 1968." Washington, D.C.: Government Printing Office, 1970.

## PEACE AND LIVESTOCK

*Son of Old Man Hat tells about the first twenty years of his life growing up on the Navajo Reservation over one hundred years ago in:*

Dyk, Walter, recorder. *Son of Old Man Hat.* 1938. Reprint. Lincoln: University of Nebraska Press, 1966.

*In a sequel to the first book, Son of Old Man Hat gives a detailed account of three years in his life as a young man in the late 1880s in:*

Dyk, Walter, and Dyk, Ruth, eds. *Left Handed: A Navajo Autobiography.* New York: Columbia University Press, 1980.

*Some scholarly research on traditional Navajo herding methods has been done by:*

Fanale, Rosalie, cultural anthropologist, San Juan Basin Ethnographic Project. Interview at her offices, Remote Sensing Division, National Park Service, Albuquerque, New Mexico, February 1979.

Schoepfle, Mark; Nabahe, Kenneth; Johnson, Angela; and Upshaw, Lucie. "First Draft Report: Navajo Perceptions of Land Use and Conservation in Modern Ecological and Economic Contexts." Xerox. Shiprock, New Mexico: Navajo Community College, 1980.

## STOCK AND PEOPLE

*Fictionalized humorous stories of Navajo community problems, many involving land use, may be found in:*

Bingham, Sam and Janet. *Slippery Rock Stories.* Rock Point, Arizona: Rock Point Community School, 1976.

*The impact of Stock Reduction on the people and history of Navajo land is shown well in:*

Aberle, David F. *The Peyote Religion Among the Navajo.* Chicago: Aldine, 1966.
  *Gives an overall history of Stock Reduction and the national and tribal politics behind it. Not easy reading but full of facts.*

Roessel, Ruth, and Johnson, Broderick, eds. *Navajo Livestock Reduction: A National Disgrace.* Tsaile, Arizona: Navajo Community College Press, 1974. *Easy-to-read and vivid first hand accounts of Stock Reduction told by the people who lived through it.*


*Short, clear descriptions of the range management principles that evolved out of the range science practiced in America at the time of Stock Reduction can be found in:*

New Mexico State University Cooperative Extension Service. *Managing Semidesert Ranges of the Southwest.* Circular 456. Las Cruces, New Mexico, 1974.

Parrill, Frank, and Blacksheep, Allan H. Jr. *Navajo Nation Range Management Handbook.* Tucson: University of Arizona Cooperative Extension Service, 1981.

University of Arizona Cooperative Extension Service. *Guide to Improvement of Arizona Rangeland.* Bulletin A-58. Tucson, 1973.


*Information about the Savory Grazing Method is available from trained personnel at the Navajo Tribe's Department of Agricultural Resources, and training courses have been held by the BIA and the Navajo Tribe. Clear descriptions of the methods and principles are available from: SGM Range Consultants, P. O. Box 7128, Albuquerque, N.M. 87194. They include:*

Savory, Allan. "Ranch and Range Management Using the Short Duration Grazing Method." Savory & Parsons Agricultural Consultants, n.d. Mimeographed.

———. "Range Reclamation and Principles." Savory & Parsons Agricultural Consultants, n.d. Mimeographed.

———. "Short Duration Grazing Related to Primitive Societies and Communal Tenure of Land." Savory & Parsons Agricultural Consultants, n.d. Mimeographed.

Savory, Allan, and Parsons, Stanley D. "The Savory Grazing Method." *Rangelands* 2, no. 6 (December 1980): 234–37.


*Other sources used in preparing this chapter are:*

Brown, Lester R. "The Worldwide Loss of Cropland." Worldwatch Paper 24, October 1978. Washington, D.C.: Worldwatch Institute, 1978.

Collier, John. *On the Gleaming Way.* Chicago: Sage Books, 1949, 1962.

Eckholm, Erick, and Brown, Lester R. "Spreading Deserts—the Hand of Man." Worldwatch Paper 13, August 1977. Washington, D.C.: Worldwatch Institute, 1977.

New Mexico State University, Range Improvement Task Force. *Proceedings: Grazing Management Systems for Southwest Rangelands Symposium.* Albuquerque, New Mexico, April 1–2, 1980. Las Cruces: New Mexico State University.

Seltzer, Jack A. Utah State University Extension Agent, Indian Programs. Telephone interview, Blanding, Utah, 1979.

Spurlock, Ted and Pat, owners of Spurlock Ranches. Interview at Navajo, Arizona, July 1980.

## NAVAJOS AND HOPIS

*Many books are available for those who would like to learn more about Hopi history and life. A few of them are:*

James, Harry C. *Pages from Hopi History.* Tucson: University of Arizona Press, 1976.

Nequatewa, Edmund. *Truth of a Hopi: Stories Relating to the Origin, Myths, and Clan Histories of the Hopi.* Flagstaff, Arizona: Northland Press, 1967.

Simmons, Leo W., ed. *Sun Chief: The Autobiography of a Hopi Indian.* New Haven: Yale University Press, 1942.

Yava, Albert. *Big Falling Snow: A Tewa-Hopi Indian's Life and Times and the History and Traditions of his People.* Edited by Harold Courlander. New York: Crown Publishers, Inc., 1978.


*An excellent book on the Navajo-Hopi Land Dispute is:*

Kammer, Jerry. *The Second Long Walk: The Navajo-Hopi Land Dispute.* Albuquerque: University of New Mexico Press, 1980.


*Black-and-white photographs of Navajos who face relocation because of the Land Dispute, along with their comments about what this will mean to their lives, may be found in:*

People of Big Mountain. *Endangered Diné: The Big Mountain Peoples and other Land-Dispute Navajos.* Photos by Dan Budnick and John Running. Window Rock, Arizona: Navajo Land Dispute Commission, 1980.


*A short objective article which summarizes the Land Dispute, is:*

Shaw, Gaylord, "Hopi-Navajo Dispute Over Tribal Lands Ending in Heartbreak." *Los Angeles Times,* September 16, 1979.


*Dramatic color photographs of the Land Dispute area and mines, and an article which argues for a connection between the Land Dispute and mineral development, may be found in:*

Matthiessen, Peter. "Battle for Big Mountain." *GEO* 2 (March 1980): 12–30.


*An article which documents how government and mining officials leased coal from the Hopis on Black Mesa without open hearings or community discussion is:*

Clemmer, Richard O. "Black Mesa and the Hopi." In *Native Americans and Energy Development,* pp. 17–34. Cambridge, Mass: Anthropology Resource Center, 1978.


*Two reports on the negative effects of forced relocation on traditional Navajos are:*

Schoepfle, Mark; Begishe, Kenneth; Morgan, Rose T.; and Johnson, Angela. "The Human Impact of the Navajo-Hopi Dispute: The Navajo View." Shiprock, New Mexico: Navajo Community College, 1980.

Topper, Martin D. "Mental Health Effects of Navajo Relocation in the Former Joint Use Area: A Report." Window Rock, Arizona: Mental Health Branch, Navajo Area Office, Indian Health Service, 1979.


*Detailed relocation plans and statistics, including a list of the names of 9525 Navajos and 109 Hopis who may be forced to leave lands in the divided JUA, may be found in:*

Navajo and Hopi Indian Relocation Commission. *Report and Plan.* Flagstaff, Arizona: April 1981.


*The following films and video tapes might be used to supplement this chapter. Films only are available from the Audio-Visual Department, Library, Navajo Community College, Tsaile, Arizona 86556. Phone: 602/724-6132.*

*Diné: The People.* (1978), 16mm Film Optical Sound, Color, Part I: 40 min., Part II: 40 min. Dist.: Tiresias Films, Berkeley, California. Narrated by Peterson Zah.

*Story of the Navajo-Hopi Land Dispute, told from the Navajo point of view. Part I: Introduction to the Navajo. Part II: The Land Dispute. Part II may be shown independently of Part I.*

*Hopi Way, The* (1972), 16mm Film Optical Sound, Color, 23 min., Shoshoni Productions Inc. (PR), Dist.: Films Inc.

*Tells about the traditional Hopi way of life, and how coal mines will affect traditional lands. Both young and old Hopis interviewed have a negative reaction to the mines.*

*Navajo-Hopi Land Dispute, The* (1981), ¾-inch Video Cassette, Color, KOOL-TV, Phoenix (PR).

*Relocation and the Navajo-Hopi Land Dispute* (1981), 16mm Film Optical Sound, or ¾-inch Video Cassette, Color, 27 min. Earthworks, Santa Monica, California (PR and Dist.).

*Tells the tragic effects of relocation on traditional Navajos forced to move by the Navajo-Hopi Land Dispute.*

*The following sources were used in preparing the relocation map and statistics:*

Benally, Chester, Consolidation Coal Co., Burnham Mine. Telephone interview at his office, October 30, 1980.

Chee, Sally, community relations, Peabody Coal Co. Telephone interview at her office, Black Mesa, Arizona, October 30, 1980.

*Gallup Independent.* "Residents Face Possible Relocation." October 22, 1980.

Goodman, James M. "Mineral Resources Map: Potential Areas of Production and Lease Holdings." In *The Navajo Atlas. Environments, Resources, People, and History of the Diné Bikéyah.* Norman: University of Oklahoma Press. (In press.)

Hamilton, Kent, economist, Bureau of Land Management, Albuquerque, New Mexico. Telephone interview at his office, November 3, 1980.

Keller, Al, project engineer, Bureau of Indian Affairs, Navajo Indian Irrigation Project. Telephone interview at his office, Farmington, New Mexico, October 30, 1980.

Kelly, John, and Hughes, Richard, attorneys for the Burnham residents. Telephone interview at their offices in Albuquerque, New Mexico, October 29, 1980.

McKinney, Chuck, community relations, McKinley Mine. Telephone interview at his office, October 30, 1980.

Navajo and Hopi Relocation Commission. *Report and Plan.* Flagstaff, Arizona, April 1981. p. 31.

Peabody Coal Co. *Mining Coal on Black Mesa.* 1970.

Raymond, Ed, community relations, Utah International Navajo Mine. Telephone interview at his offices near Fruitland, New Mexico, October 30, 1980.

San Juan Basin Regional Uranium Study. *Uranium Development in the San Juan Basin Region: A Report on Environmental Issues.* Final Edition. Albuquerque: U.S. Dept. of Interior Office of Trust Responsibilities, Bureau of Indian Affairs, 1980. pp. VII-31-2.

U.S. Department of the Interior, Bureau of Land Management. *Draft: Environmental Statement Star Lake–Bisti Regional Coal. Appendix A: Maps.* New Mexico State Office, 1978.

*Other sources used in preparing this chapter are:*

Anderson, Jack. Articles on Wayne Aspinall. *Washington Post,* July 22, 1974; March 21, 1976.

———. Articles on Harrison Loesch. *Washington Post,* December 13, 19, 24, 1972.

Associated Press. "Aspinall Sellout to Mining, Oil Charged." *Gallup Independent,* June 1, 1972.

Bingham, Sam, and Riddell, Janet. "An Unknown Future Awaits 6000 Navajos." *Boston Globe,* July 16, 1972.

Kalectaca, Milo. *Lessons in Hopi.* Edited by Ronald Langacker. Tucson: University of Arizona Press, 1978.

Littell, Norman M. "Affidavit in Support of Answer to Supplemental Brief of Amicus Curiae." Littell v. Morton, U.S. Court of Appeals for the Fourth Circuit, No. 74-1709, 1974.

———. "Statement on Conflicting Claims of Navajo and Hopi Tribes." Letter to the *Navajo Times,* January 6, 1966.

Miller, Mark; Miller, Judith; and Moreno, Jonathan. "The Navajo Mineral Swindle: Wheeling and Dealing on the Reservation." *Akwesasne Notes* (Summer 1981), 24–28.

*National Journal.* Article on Harrison Loesch. February 3, 1979.

*Navajo Times.* Articles on 1981 protests by JUA residents. April 23, 30, 1981; May 7, 14, 1981.

Navajo Tribal Council. Minutes relating to discussion on HR 3789, May 7, 1957.

*New York Times.* Articles on Wayne Aspinall. September 27, 1972; November 9, 1972; July 18, 1974.

Peabody Coal Co. *Mining Coal on Black Mesa.* St. Louis, Missouri, 1970.

Reno, Philip. *Mother Earth, Father Sky, and Economic Development: Navajo Resources and their Use.* Albuquerque: University of New Mexico Press, 1981.

Sekakuku, Gloria. Census office, Bureau of Indian Affairs, Hopi Agency, Keams Canyon. Telephone interview on population of Hopi Tribe, October 1, 1981.

*Washington Post.* Article on Wayne Aspinall. November 10, 1976.

———. Article on Harrison Loesch. November 22, 1972.

Young, Robert G. "Cretaceous Stratigraphy of the Four Corners Area." In *Guidebook of Monument Valley and Vicinity, Arizona and Utah,* ed. by H. L. James, p. 90. New Mexico Geological Society 24th Field Conference, October 4–6, 1973.

Young, Robert W., ed. Text of the Navajo-Hopi Long Range Rehabilitation Act (PL 474—81st Congress). In *The Navajo Yearbook: 1951–1961—A Decade of Progress,* p. 1. Window Rock, Arizona: U.S. Dept. of Interior, Bureau of Indian Affairs, Navajo Agency, 1961.

———. *A Political History of the Navajo Tribe.* Tsaile, Arizona: Navajo Community College Press, 1978.

———. Telephone interview at his home in Albuquerque, New Mexico, November 24, 1981.

## MODERN TIMES

*Some of the largest strip mines and power plants in the United States are located on the Navajo Reservation. Tours and free information are available from:*

Peabody Coal Company
(Black Mesa and Kayenta mines)
P. O. Box 606, Kayenta, Arizona 86033

Pittsburg & Midway Coal Company
(McKinley Mine)
P. O. Box M, Gallup, New Mexico 87301

Utah International, Inc. (Navajo Mine)
P. O. Box 155, Fruitland, New Mexico 87416

Four Corners Power Plant
Fruitland, New Mexico 87416

Navajo Generating Station
Page, Arizona 86040

*A comprehensive book on Navajo resources, both renewable and non-renewable, is:*

Reno, Philip. *Mother Earth, Father Sky, and Economic Development: Navajo Resources and Their Use.* Albuquerque: University of New Mexico Press, 1981.

*Two easy-to-read booklets on Navajo resources and Navajo coal are:*

Bingham, Sam and Janet. *Navajo Coal.* Rock Point, Arizona: Rock Point Community School, 1976.

————. *Navajo Resources.* Rock Point, Arizona: Rock Point Community School, 1974.

*Some material on the Black Mesa mines from the point of view of the coal company is:*

Peabody Coal Company, Arizona Division. "Media Information." Flagstaff, Arizona, 1980.

————. *Mining Coal on Black Mesa.* St. Louis, Missouri, 1970.

*Some material on reservation mines from the point of view of environmentalists is:*

Budnik, Dan. "Black Mesa: Progress Report on an Ecological Rape." *Art in America.* Special Issue: The American Indian (July-August 1972): 98–109.

Gordon, Suzanne. *Black Mesa: The Angel of Death.* New York: The John Day Co., 1973.

Josephy, Alvin, Jr. "The Murder of the Southwest." *Audubon Magazine.* July 1971, pp. 54–67. *With color pictures.*

Matthiessen, Peter. "Battle for Big Mountain." *GEO* 2 (March 1980): 12–30.

*A simply written book, illustrated with photos, on the life of a Navajo woman living near the Utah International mine is:*

New Mexico People & Energy Collective. *Red Ribbons for Emma.* Stanford, California: New Seed Press, 1981.

*An illustrated chapter on the day-to-day life of a Black Mesa coal miner may be found in:*

Witt, Matt. *In Our Blood: Four Coal Mining Families.* Washington, D.C.: Highlander Research and Education Center, 1979.

*An informative reference on reclamation, with chapters on all of the Navajo Reservation strip mines, is:*

Wiener, Daniel Philip. *Reclaiming the West: The Coal Industry and Surface-Mined Lands.* New York City:

INFORM, Inc., 1980.
*To order, write INFORM, Inc., 381 Park Ave. South, New York City, N.Y. 10016.*

*The impact of energy development on Navajos and other Native Americans is discussed in:*

Jorgensen, Joseph G.; Clemmer, Richard O.; Little, Ronald L.; Owens, Nancy J.; and Robbins, Lynn A. *Native Americans and Energy Development.* Cambridge, Mass.: Anthropology Resource Center, 1978.

Lamphere, Louise. "The Internal Colonization of the Navajo People." *Southwest Economy & Society* 1, no. 1 (Spring 1976): 6–14.

Native American Studies, University of New Mexico. *Economic Development in American Indian Reservations.* Development Series no. 1. Albuquerque: Native American Studies, U.N.M., 1979.

Ruffing, Lorraine Turner. *A Mineral Development Policy for the Navajo Nation.* Window Rock, Arizona: Navajo Tribe Minerals Department, 1979.

Schoepfle, Mark; Begishe, Kenneth; Reno, Philip; Morgan, Rose; John, Johnny; Thomas, Henry; and Davis, Joanne. *A Study of Navajo Perceptions of the Impact of Environmental Changes Relating to Energy Resource Development.* Shiprock, New Mexico: Navajo Community College, 1979.

*The relationship between mineral development and the founding of the Navajo and Hopi Tribal Councils is documented in:*

Clemmer, Richard O. "Black Mesa and the Hopi." In *Native Americans and Energy Development,* pp. 17–34. Cambridge, Mass.: Anthropology Resource Center, 1978.

Young, Robert W. *A Political History of the Navajo Tribe.* Tsaile, Arizona: Navajo Community College Press, 1978.

*The following films and slide shows might be used to supplement this chapter. Films only are available from the Audio-Visual Department, Library, Navajo Community College, Tsaile, Arizona 86556. Phone 602/734-6132.*

*Black Coal, Red Power* (1969), 16mm Film Optical Sound, Color, short version, 58 min.; long version, 100 min. National Educational Television (PR), Dist.: Indiana University.
*Survey of the issues surrounding the strip mining of coal by Peabody Coal Company on Black Mesa. Traditional Navajo residents, industry spokesmen, miners, tribal officials, and scientists all give their views on how*

*the mines will affect the land itself and the lives of the people who live on it.*

*Last Chance for the Navajo* (1977), 16mm Film Optical Sound, Color, 28 min., ABC News (PR), Dist.: ABC News.
*Pros and cons of the strip mining of coal near Burnham, New Mexico, with input from both Navajo residents and spokesmen for Consolidated Coal Company.*

*Look What We've Done to This Land* (1973), 16mm Film Optical Sound, Color, 20 min., Central Clearing House (PR and Dist.).
*How strip mines on Black Mesa and power plants in the Four Corners area are destroying the land and the traditional way of life of both Navajos and Hopis.*

*People and Energy in the Southwest* (1978.) Slide/Tape show, 130 slides, Color, 27 min., New Mexico People and Energy (PR and Dist.).
*Shows effect on the land of rapid, uncontrolled development of gas, uranium, and coal. Slides and tape available for rent or sale in Spanish, English, or Navajo from New Mexico People and Energy, Box 4726, Albuquerque, New Mexico 87196.*

*Some sources of information on Black Mesa groundwater are:*

Eychaner, James H. "Geohydrology and Effects of Water Use in the Black Mesa Area, Navajo and Hopi Indian Reservations, Arizona." Open File Report 81-911. Tucson: U.S. Department of Interior Geological Survey, July 1981.

McGavock, E. H., and Levings, Gary W. "Groundwater in the Navajo Sandstone in the Black Mesa Area, Arizona." In *Guidebook of Monument Valley and Vicinity Arizona and Utah,* ed. by H. L. James, pp. 150–55. New Mexico Geological Society 24th Field Conference, October 4–6, 1973.

Njaa, Bev. "Hauling Water to Survive." *Rough Rock News,* October 10, 1978.

————. "What's Under the Windmill? Where Our Water Comes From." *Rough Rock News,* November 8, 1978.

Turk, Jonathan, "Case History: Water and Coal in the Southwest United States." In *Introduction to Environmental Studies,* pp. 139–42. Philadelphia: W. B. Saunders, 1980.

*Some sources on Indian water rights, most of them legal or scholarly, are:*

*Arizona v. California,* 373 U.S. 546 (1963) (opinion); 376 U.S. 340 (1964) (decree).

Lichtenstein, Grace. "The Battle Over the Mighty Colorado." *The New York Times Magazine,* July 31, 1977.

MacMeekin, Daniel H. "The Navajo Tribe's Water Rights in the Colorado River Basin." Memorandum. Window Rock: DNA-People's Legal Services, Inc., 1971.
*Available at the American Indian Culture and Research Center, University of California, Los Angeles.*

Martone, Rosalie. "The United States and the Betrayal of Indian Water Rights." *The Indian Historian* 7, no. 3 (Summer 1974): 3–11.

Navajo Tribal Council. Resolution No. CD-108-68, December 11, 1968.
*Tribe appears to limit its claim to Colorado River water and give two-thirds of it to Navajo Power Plant at Page.*

Reno, Philip. "Water: The Navajo Lifeline." In *Mother Earth, Father Sky, and Economic Development: Navajo Resources and Their Use,* pp. 46–64. Albuquerque: University of New Mexico Press, 1981.

Veeder, William H. "Indian Prior and Paramount Rights to the Use of Water." *Rocky Mountain Mineral Law Institute* 16 (1971): 631–93.

*Winters* v. *The United States,* 207 U.S. 564 (1908).


*Some maps showing Navajo area mineral resources are:*

Goodman, James M. "Mineral Resources Map: Potential Areas of Production and Lease Holdings." In *The Navajo Atlas: Environments, Resources, People, and History of the Diné Bikéyah.* Norman: University of Oklahoma Press. (In press.)

U.S. Department of the Interior, Bureau of Land Management. *Draft: Environmental Statement, Star Lake–Bisti Regional Coal. Appendix A: Maps.* New Mexico State Office, 1978.


*Other sources used in preparing this chapter are:*

Armstrong, W.D. "Navajo Minerals Development, 1966–1985." Window Rock, Arizona: The Navajo Tribe, Office of Minerals Development, 1976.

Barry, Tom. *Coal: The Stripping of Northwestern New Mexico.* NMPE Power Structure Report #25. Albuquerque; New Mexico People and Energy, 1980.

———. "Kerr-McGee is Most Active Energy Company." First in a series. *Navajo Times,* August 3, 1978.

———. "The Navajo Lung Cancer Widows." Second in a series. *Navajo Times,* August 24, 1978.

———. "How Agencies Ignored Uranium Dangers: The Deaths Still Go On." Third in a series. *Navajo Times,* August 31, 1978.

———. "Red Rock Widows Seek Compensaton." Fourth in a Series." *Navajo Times,* September 7, 1978.

*Business Week.* "Corporate Scoreboard." November 16, 1981, pp. 93–134.

Cannon, James S. *Mine Control: Western Coal Leasing and Development.* New York: Council on Economic Priorities, 1978.

Chenoweth, William L. and Malan, Roger C. "The Uranium Deposits of Northeastern Arizona." In *Guidebook of Monument Valley and Vicinity, Arizona and Utah,* ed. by H. L. James, pp. 139–49. New Mexico Geological Society Twenty-fourth Field Conference, October 4–6, 1973.

Cooley, M. E.; Harshbarger, J. W.; Akers, J. P.; and Hardt, W. F. "Regional Hydrogeology of the Navajo and Hopi Indian Reservations, Arizona, New Mexico, and Utah." U.S. Geological Survey Professional Paper 521-A. Washington, D.C.: Government Printing Office, 1969.

Council on Economic Priorities. "Southern California Edison and the Four Corners Project." In *The Price of Power. Electric Utilities and the Environment,* pp. M-31–M-40. Cambridge, Mass.: The MIT Press, 1974.

Eychaner, James H., head of Black Mesa Monitoring for the U.S. Geological Survey, Tucson, Arizona. Interviews in Tucson and Rock Point, September and October 1981, on the effects of groundwater pumping on Black Mesa by the Peabody Coal Co.

Ford, Bacon and Davis Utah Inc. "Phase II—Title I Engineering Assessment of Inactive Uranium Mill Tailings, Monument Valley Site, Monument Valley, Arizona." GJT-4. Prepared for the U.S. Energy Research and Development Administration, Grand Junction, Colorado, under Contract No. E(05-1)-1658. Salt Lake City, March 31, 1977.

———. "Phase II—Title I Engineering Assessment of Inactive Uranium Mill Tailings, Shiprock Site, Shiprock, New Mexico." GJT-2. Prepared for the U.S. Energy Research and Development Administration, Grand Junction, Colorado, under Contract No. E(05-1)-1658. Salt Lake City, March 31, 1977.

*Gallup Independent.* Articles on Aneth Oilfield Takeover. March 31, 1978; April 1, 3, 5, 6, 7, 8, 11, 14, 17, 25, 1978.

———. Articles on Church Rock Tailings Spill. July 17, 18, 26, 1979; August 10, 21, 1979; September 8, 24, 1979.

———. Articles on Peabody coal mines near Kayenta. May 4, 6, 1972; June 1, 1972; October 16, 17, 18, 22, 25, 1974; December 12, 1974; December 6, 1975; March 29, 1976; April 24, 1976; May 27, 1976; June 22, 1976; October 2, 1976; June 1, 1977; November 29, 1977; December 5, 6, 7, 8, 14, 21, 23, 1977; May 1, 1978; February 10, 13, 15, 1979; April 9, 11, 1979; August 31, 1979; October 18, 1979; November 17, 1979; December 24, 1979; February 28, 1980; March 7, 1980; April 30, 1980; May 27, 1980; April 5, 12, 1982.

Henderson, Al. "The Navajo Nation Energy Policy: A Means to Economic Prosperity for the Navajo Nation." Master's thesis, University of New Mexico, 1982.

Melvin, Gary, manager of environmental quality, Black Mesa and Kayenta mines, Peabody Coal Co. Arizona Division. Interview on Black Mesa, February 20, 1980.

Moskowitz, Milton; Katz, Michael; and Levering, Robert. "Princes of Petroleum: the Ten Highest Paid Oil Company Executives in 1979." In *The Irreverent Guide to Corporate America. An Almanac,* p. 505. San Francisco: Harper & Row, 1980.

Natwig, Eric. *Economic Development Options Available to the Navajo Tribe: Projections of Employment Effects of Major Economic Developments in the Navajo Nation, 1975–1990.* Window Rock, Arizona: Navajo Tribe Office of Program Development, 1976.

*Navajo Times.* Articles on Aneth Oilfield Take-over. April 13, 20, 1978.

———. Articles on Peabody coal mines near Kayenta. January 6, 1966; February 15, 1979; March 24, 1982.

Navajo Tribe, Division of Economic Development. *The Navajo Nation Overall Economic Development Program: 1980 Annual Progress Report.* Window Rock, Arizona, 1980.

Wagoner, Joseph. "Uranium Mining and Milling: The Human Costs." written text of a presentation at the University of New Mexico Medical School, Albuquerque, New Mexico, March 10, 1980.

Webbe, Stephen. "In His Sky-Blue Waters: Radioactivity." *Christian Science Monitor.* January 9, 1980.

# REMEMBER THE LAND

*For information about agricultural and range resources, including local farm projects and experimental projects in new techniques such as drip irrigation, water harvesting, Savory grazing, and livestock improvement, contact the Agricultural Resources Department, Division of Natural Resources, Navajo Tribe, Window Rock, Arizona 86515. Guided visits and help with your own projects are possible.*

*For guided tours, illustrated annual progress reports, and other free information on the Navajo sawmill and the 110,000-acre Navajo Indian Irrigation Project, contact:*

> Navajo Agricultural Products Industries (NAPI)
> Box 86, Farmington, New Mexico 87401

> Navajo Forest Products Industries (NFPI)
> Navajo, New Mexico 87328

*An easy-to-read series of books on Navajo renewable resources is:*

Bingham, Sam and Janet. *Navajo Farming.* Rock Point, Arizona: Rock Point Community School, 1979.

———. *The Navajo Forest.* Rock Point, Arizona: Rock Point Community School, 1976.

———. *The Navajo Sawmill: The Story of Navajo Forest Products Industries.* Rock Point, Arizona: Rock Point Community School, 1976.

*Various possibilities for reservation economic development are described in:*

Benson, Michael. *Sovereignty: The Navajo Nation and Taxation.* Window Rock, Arizona: DNA–People's Legal Services, Inc., 1976.

Native American Studies, University of New Mexico. *Economic Development in American Indian Reservations.* Development Series no. 1. Albuquerque: Native American Studies, U.N.M., 1979.
*Includes a chapter written by Al Henderson.*

Reno, Philip. *Mother Earth, Father Sky, and Economic Development: Navajo Resources and Their Use.* Albuquerque: University of New Mexico Press, 1981.

Ruffing, Lorraine Turner. *A Mineral Development Policy for the Navajo Nation.* Window Rock, Arizona: Navajo Tribe Minerals Department, 1979.

*For up-to-date information on the tribe's economic development plans, contact the Division of Economic Development, Navajo Tribe, Window Rock, Arizona 86515. The division has a library, and has access to many fact-filled and informative reports, including:*

Natwig, Eric. *Economic Development Options Available to the Navajo Tribe: Projections of Employment Effects of Major Economic Developments in the Navajo Nation, 1975–1990.* Window Rock, Arizona: Navajo Tribe Office of Program Development, 1976.

Navajo Tribe, Division of Economic Development. *The Navajo Nation Overall Economic Development Program: Annual Progress Report.* Window Rock, Arizona.
*Issued Annually.*

*The following films and video tapes might be used to supplement this chapter. Films only are available from the Audio-Visual Department, Library, Navajo Community College, Tsaile, Arizona 86556. Phone 602/724-6132.*

*Indian Rights, Indian Law* (1978), 16mm Film Optical Sound, Color, 56 min., Dist.: Films Inc.
*Discusses legal issues facing tribes in different parts of the country, including water rights, land claims, and strip mining. All are typical of cases being handled by the Native American Rights Fund.*

*Navajo Nation: Meeting the Challenge to Develop.* (1980), 16mm Film Optical Sound, Color, 20 min., K. M. Productions (PR).
*Traces the recent economic development of the Navajo Tribe. Produced for the Navajo Tribe to show to outside businesses interested in coming to the reservation.*

*Uranium Factor, The* (1980), ¾-inch Video Cassette, Color, 58 min., ABC-TV (PR).
*Documentary on effects of uranium mining in New Mexico, including the tailings spill near Church rock, unprotected tailings piles on the Navajo Reservation, and health problems of uranium miners.*

*Uranium, Its Aftermath* (1980), ¾-inch Video Cassette, Color, 58 min., KOAT-TV, Albuquerque (PR).
*Includes more industry input than in The Uranium Factor.*

*Wealth from the Navajo Forest* (1978). 16mm Film Optical Sound, Color, 40 min. Produced for Navajo Forest Products Industries (NFPI).
*Tells about the Navajo forest and the tribally owned sawmill and lumber business. Contact NFPI in Navajo, New Mexico (505/777-2211).*

*Working papers and reports on the possible effects of uranium development in the San Juan basin include:*

George, Helen. "Navajo Perceptions and Attitudes towards Uranium Development." Working Paper no. 36. Albuquerque: U.S. Department of Interior, San Juan Basin Regional Uranium Study, 1979.

Lyford, Forest. "Modeled Effects of Uranium Mine Dewatering on Water Resources in Northwestern New Mexico." Working Paper no. 37. Albuquerque: U.S. Department of Interior, San Juan Basin Regional Uranium Study, 1979.

San Juan Basin Regional Uranium Study. *Uranium Development in the San Juan Basin Region: A Report on Environmental Issues.* Albuquerque: U.S. Department of Interior, Bureau of Indian Affairs. Draft, 1979. Final, 1980.

Sorenson, J. B. "Radiation Issues, Government Decision-Making, and Uranium Expansion in Northwestern New Mexico." Working Paper no. 14. Albuquerque: U.S. Department of Interior, San Juan Basin Regional Uranium Study, 1978.

*Two scientific reports on the health effects of uranium mining and milling are:*

Wagoner, Joseph. "Uranium Mining and Milling: The Human Costs." Written text of a presentation at the University of New Mexico Medical School, Albuquerque, New Mexico, March 10, 1980.

———. "Uranium: The United States Experience—A Lesson in History." Xerox. Washington, D.C.: Environmental Defense Fund, 1980.

*Other sources used in preparing this chapter are:*

Arthur, Harris. "Preface." In *Native Americans and Energy Development*, pp. 1–2. Cambridge, Mass.: Anthropology Resource Center, 1978.

Associated Press. "Tribes May Levy Tax on Resources." *Gallup Independent*, January 25, 1982.

Barry, Tom. Series on Uranium Development in the Four Corners area. *Navajo Times*, August 3, 24, 31, 1978; September 7, 1978; October 12, 1978; November 2, 16, 1978; December 28, 1978; January 4, 1979.

*Gallup Independent.* Articles on Dalton Pass anti-uranium resolution and protests. April 19, 1980; April 23, 26, 28, 29, 1980.

———. "Tribe OKs $4.6 Million Water Plan." February 13, 1982.

Saltzstein, Kathie. "Israeli Farming Method Comes to Reservation." *Gallup Independent*, April 8, 1982.

Schwartz, Loretta. "Uranium Deaths at Crownpoint." *MS Magazine*, October 1979.

Wiener, Daniel Philip. *Reclaiming the West: The Coal Industry and Surface-Mined Lands.* New York City: INFORM, Inc., 1980.

# INDEX

285

## PHOTOGRAPHS:

Front Cover: *Monument Valley.*—Dick Arentz.

LAND: *Steppe country, southern Utah.*—Dick Arentz.
    High Country Forests: *Lake in the Lukachukai Mountains.*—J. Bingham.
    Canyons: *Eagle's view of Canyon de Chelly and Canyon del Muerto.*—S. Bingham.
    Pinon and Juniper: *Defiance Plateau.*—William Rada.
    Steppe: *View south from Rock Point toward Tsé Biná'ookahí.*—J. Bingham.
    Desert: *Thomas Littleben, Jr., jumping off a dune.*—R. L. Jim.
    Earth, Air, Fire, and Water: *1. Wind-deposited sandstone. View north from Tséłchíít'aa near Rock Point.*—J. Bingham. *2. Tsé Bit'a'í, Shiprock, showing volcanic dike.*—John Shelton.

PLANTS: *1. Sunflowers.*—J. Bingham. *2. George Blueeyes with the Plant People (alkali sacaton).*—S. Bingham.

HUNTERS: *1. Bighorn sheep.*—Jeremy Schmidt. *2. Antlers in Chuska Mountains.*—S. Bingham.

ANASAZI: *1. Pueblo del Arroyo in Chaco Canyon.*—J. Bingham. *2. Pueblo Bonito in Chaco Canyon.*—S. Bingham.

ANCESTORS: *1. Lewis Tsosie rides past petroglyphs in Wepo Wash on Black Mesa.*—S. Bingham. *2. George Blueeyes with Rock Point students, LaVerne Gene and Lorraine Coggeshall.*—S. Bingham.

SPANIARDS: *1. Taos runner Bruce Gomez leaves Taos Pueblo on Pueblo Revolt Tricentennial.*—S. Bingham. *2. Tricentennial runners enter Jemez Pueblo.*—S. Bingham.

WAR AND RESERVATION: *1. One of Lt. Guilfoyle's Navajo Scouts. ca. 1883.*—Ben Wittick. School of American Research Collections in the Museum of New Mexico. *2. Riders at Dalton Pass.*—S. Bingham.

PEACE AND LIVESTOCK: *1. Woman and Cattle.*—John Running. *Navajo Camp. ca. 1935.*—T. Harmon Parkhurst. Museum of New Mexico.

STOCK AND PEOPLE: *1. Horse at water.*—John Running. *2. Horse skeleton.*—S. Bingham. *3. Sheep corral at twilight.*—S. Bingham.

NAVAJOS AND HOPIS: *1. Michelle Judy (Navajo).*—S. Bingham. *2. Johanna Day (Hopi).*—Sam Minkler. *3. Katherine Smith with the rifle she fired at fence crew near Big Mountain in the JUA.*—S. Bingham.

MODERN TIMES: *1. Hogan and jet trails.*—John Running. *2. McKinley Mine Dragline near Window Rock.*—S. Bingham. *3. Mariano Lake uranium mine.*—Mark Lennihan, Gallup Independent.

REMEMBER THE LAND: *Boy and Four-Corners Power Plant.*—Mark Lennihan.

THE FUTURE: *1. Thomas Littleben, Jr. on dune.*—R. L. Jim. *2. Thomas Littleben, Jr. at home in Halgai Tó, southeast of Rock Point.*—S. Bingham.

Back Cover: *Power line near Kayenta.*—Dick Arentz.